The Business Communication Casebook

A Notre Dame Collection

James S. O'Rourke

SOUTH-WESTERN

THOMSON LEARNING

Australia · Canada · Mexico · Singapore · Spain · United Kingdom · United States

The Business Communication Casebook: A Notre Dame Collection
by James S. O'Rourke, IV

Acquisitions Editor: Pamela Person
Developmental Editor: Taney Wilkins
Marketing Manager: Marc Callahan
Production Editor: Heather Mann
Manufacturing Coordinator: Diane Lohman
Cover Design: Christy Carr
Printer: Webcom Limited

Printed in Canada
1 2 3 4 5   04 03 02 01

For more information contact South-Western, 5101 Madison Road, Cincinnati, Ohio, 45227 or
find us on the Internet at http://www.swcollege.com

For permission to use material from this text or product, contact us by
• **telephone: 1-800-730-2214**
• **fax: 1-800-730-2215**
• **web: http://www.thomsonrights.com**

Library of Congress Cataloging-in-Publication Data

O'Rourke, James S.
      The business communication casebook : a Notre Dame collection / James S. O'Rourke.
          p. cm.
      Title on copyright p.: Casebook for business communication.
       Includes bibliographical references.
         ISBN 0-324-14795-3 (pbk.)
        1. Issues management—Case studies. 2. Corporations—Public relations—Case studies. 3.
Business communication— Case studies. I. Title: Casebook for business communication. II.
Title.

HD59.5 .O76 2001
659.2—dc21

                                                    2001042688

INTRODUCTION

The value of case studies – particularly in the education of young managers and executives-in-training – is well known. Cases provide both the instructor and the learner with an opportunity to examine authentic, real-world problems in a careful and detailed way. The facts of each case are laid out in methodical, if sometimes incomplete, fashion for the student of management to examine.

"What should the manager do?" you ask. "What's the best strategy in this case?" More to the point, good problem-solvers always ask: "What do I *not* know about this situation that would be helpful to know?" And, "Is there any way I can gather missing information that seems important?" What about assumptions? "What do I believe to be true that I can't actually prove? How do I know that my view of the facts in this instance is accurate, fair, or complete?"

Good questions. And, for the most part, that's what case study is about: asking good questions and seeking the answers on behalf of the stakeholders. Case studies are never about identifying heros and villains, nor are they written for the purpose of highlighting the inept or skillful handling of an administrative situation. They are always written for the purpose of gathering information that will help a student of management make better decisions.

Good case studies provide as much accurate, current, and relevant information as possible about an incident, a problem, an event, or an opportunity. No two such problems, events, or opportunities are ever *precisely* the same, so knowing what happened in one will only be partially helpful in deciding what to do in the next. Times change, circumstances differ, stakeholder interests shift. Knowing how to summarize the central events of a case, identify and rank order the critical issues, identify and analyze the interests of various stakeholders, and then outline options for managerial action are skills that will be essential to a successful career in business. This collection of case studies can help.

While this book is not unique, it is different in an important way. Each of the cases in this collection is about communication. Each explores some aspect of the communication process that is so vital to the success of a business. Some cases involves more than one aspect of that process: multiple issues involving separate messages for more than one audience. These cases will require communication skill from the reader – skill in organizing, supporting, and expressing those messages. They will require that students begin to apply theories of communication and integrate them with the management strategies they are learning as students of business.

Each of these cases was written by second-year graduate students in the Mendoza College of Business at the University of Notre Dame. Most were pursuing a Master of Business Administration degree. Others were enrolled in Master of Science in Administration (the not-for-profit sector) or Master of Science in Accountancy programs. All were members of small teams of two or three who chose to pursue a case topic in great detail for at least fifteen weeks.

The details contained in the 36 cases you're about to read have come, in part, from public sources such as *The Wall Street Journal*, *The New York Times*, *The Financial Times*, *The Economist*, or similar publications. Other bits of information come from corporate websites and Internet press rooms. Still others come from professional news-gathering organizations such as the Associated Press, Reuters, Bloomberg, or networks such as MSNBC or CNN. Many of these cases, however, contain information which came from sources inside the organizations being examined – from personal interviews with employees, managers, executives, and shareholders. In some instances, the views of government regulators or civic officials have been sought out and included in the text. In all instances, every effort was made to verify, confirm, and identify the source of each fact, each quote, and each piece of information. Where disagreement exists, the case authors identify that. Where uncertainty exists, that, too, is flagged for the reader's attention.

In each instance, case authors have given competing factions, including companies in crisis, an opportunity to read a preliminary draft of the case study and to either comment or respond. Many firms, such as Accenture, Advantica, Bayer Corporation, Ford Motor Company, Sears-Roebuck and Company, McDonald's Corporation, Navistar, United Airlines, Quality Dining, AM General Corporation, and The Coca-Cola Company, responded in a thoughtful and cooperative fashion. Others, perhaps fearful of saying the wrong thing or uncertain of what to say, simply did not respond.

In a few instances – each clearly noted – the authors promised anonymity to sources in exchange for their views of the events they were researching. In a few instances, we have chosen to identify them only as "employees close to the situation." For a few others, we have selected a pseudonym to disguise the identity of the manager or executive involved. In every instance, case authors and their editor had at least two independent sources for every fact, assertion, or assumption included in the case.

Keep in mind as you examine each case that your own knowledge of the events involved may color your response to the questions your instructor will ask. Even though you may know what actually happened in a particular instance, please remember that particular outcome was just one of many that could have occurred had the executives or managers chosen a different path. What actually happened may not have been the best of all possible outcomes. Think carefully about what you might do differently if faced with similar circumstances.

Finally, a few acknowledgments. First, to the men and women of Notre Dame who wrote these cases: congratulations on a job well done. These are interesting, current, well-crafted stories of organizations facing crisis or change. Second, to the hundreds of managers and executives who cooperated in the interviews which were indispensable to the completion of each of these cases, thank you. The stories wouldn't have been as rich, accurate, or complete without your help.

To Pamela Person, Taney Wilkins, and Heather Mann of South-Western, my thanks for your belief in the project, your patience with me, and your help in getting it done. To my own research assistants, Elizabeth Clark and Beth Davis, thanks a thousand times for flagging a sentence that made no sense, chasing down a footnote that seemed incomplete, or grappling with a phalanx of balky paragraphs and format-resistant pages. To my colleagues, Carolyn Boulger, Sandra Collins, Cynthia Maciejczyk, and Renee Tynan: thank you for your inspiration, assistance, and ideas. And thanks for your friendship. No man could ask to work with better friends.

And to my family: Pam, Colleen, Molly, and Kathleen. Thanks is insufficient for the inspiration, patience, and encouragement. As ever, you are the reason I do this.

James S. O'Rourke, IV
Notre Dame, Indiana
Summer 2001

TABLE OF CONTENTS

Part IV: Protecting the Environment

Part V: Crisis Management

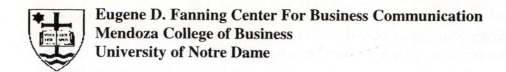
Analyzing a Case Study

Among the many tools available to business educators, the case study has become increasingly popular. Professors use it to teach the complexities of many different, modern business problems. That's not a surprising development. Beyond the fundamentals, memorization and description will take you just so far. The real test of whether you are ready to manage a business will come when you are asked to assume the role of a manager, step into an authentic business situation, make sense of the circumstances you see, draft a plan, and take action.

Why Study Cases?

Schools of law have studied cases for many years as a means of exploring legal concepts and understanding the practices of the courts. Harvard Business School began inviting executives and managers into their classrooms after the First World War, hoping to provide students with some insight into the thinking of successful businessmen. Not long afterward, professors of business began writing down the narratives of these business managers in an effort to capture the ambiguities and complexities involved in the day-to-day practice of commerce and administration.

The idea spread to other schools of business and migrated from graduate to undergraduate programs. Today, many business educators use case studies because their narratives are so valuable in developing analytic and critical thinking abilities, as well as organizational and communication skills. You can memorize lists, procedures, and attributes. You can occasionally guess successfully at the answer to a multiple-choice question. But you cannot memorize the answer to a problem you have never encountered, nor can you guess at the options available to a manager who must resolve a complex, difficult, often ambiguous situation.

Types of Cases

Although each case is different, you are likely to encounter three basic types of case studies, depending on the subject you are studying: field cases, library cases (sometimes referred to as public record cases), and armchair cases.

Field cases. Field cases are written by professors and students of business with the cooperation of managers and executives who experienced the events and problems described in the case. They involve extensive interviews with people who are often identified by name as the narrative unfolds. Information contained in these cases is known best – and sometimes only – to insiders in a business. Newspaper accounts and descriptions of events contained in the business press may play a role in establishing key facts, but the sequence of events, what was said to whom, what each manager knew at the time, and which managerial options were open to the principals of the case are often a mystery to the public-at-large.

Extensive interviews with employees, managers, and executives will often reveal more. Careful examination of business records and data bases can provide background and context for the events. And, frequently, the active cooperation of a company is the only way a case author will ever know exactly what happened with any measure of certainty.

Field cases are often more extensive and thorough than other case types, but present a dilemma for the case writer: what does the company have to gain by granting access to its premises, its records, and its employees? Is this merely an attempt to make executives look good after the fact? Are such cases an attempt at public relations when things go wrong in a business? Often, to gain access to a business, a case writer must have some special relationship with those who own or manage it, and must have a reputation for reporting on events in an accurate and fair manner. One disadvantage of such cases is that, once they are published, they are difficult to modify and may quickly become dated.

Library cases. Unlike a field case, library or public record cases do not involve special access to the businesses being studied. They do not involve interview material or direct quotes which are unavailable elsewhere. And they most often do not include figures, data, or information which are not somehow a part of the public record, available to anyone with a library card and basic research skills.

Companies that have failed somehow – blown a great opportunity, overlooked the obvious, chosen the wrong path, or failed to act when they should – are understandably reluctant to permit case writers to speak with their employees or look at the evidence. If they've done something terribly wrong – committed a crime or imperiled the public welfare – a company may do all it can to withhold, obscure, or cover up what has happened. That is precisely the challenge facing most business reporters as they gather information for publication each day. Journalist David Brinkley once said, "News is what you don't want to tell me. Everything else is public relations."

Writers who produce library cases, however, have a wealth of information available to them. In addition to stories produced for broadcast, print, and online news organizations, business case writers can look to numerous government documents and other sources, particularly for publicly-held firms. Annual filings with the Securities and Exchange Commission, such as forms 10-Q and 10-K, can be very helpful.

When one company declares its intention to acquire another, or is sued in Federal Court, numerous documents relevant to the issues at hand may become a part of the public record. When a company prepares to launch an IPO or float a bond offering, numerous public disclosures are required. Case writers have a high degree of confidence in the accuracy of such records, since the penalty for falsifying them may involve heavy fines or jail time.

Armchair cases. These are fictional documents about companies that don't really exist and events that have never really occurred. While they bear some resemblance to authentic cases, they are often lacking in the richness of detail and complexity that accompany real events. They may be useful, however, in introducing basic concepts to students or in provoking a discussion about key issues confronting businesses.

Business educators produce armchair cases when they are denied access to the people and data of real businesses, or when they wish to reduce very complex events to a series of simple decision opportunities. Armchair cases are often useful to begin a discussion about change management, the introduction of technology, or a rapidly-unfolding set of events in other cultures. A principal advantage of these cases is that they can be modified and updated at will without securing the permission of the fictional companies and managers they describe.

Producing a Case Solution

To produce a case solution that demonstrates you are ready for management-level responsibility will involve the following steps:

Read the case. The first step to a successful case solution is to read the case, carefully and with an eye for detail – more than once. Personality theorists tell us that some people are eager to get to the end of a story quickly. "Don't bother me with details," they say. "Just tell me what happened." Such people, often dependent on *Cliff's Notes* and executive summaries will bypass the details of a case in order to reach a conclusion about what happened in the story. They are often reluctant to read the case attachments and will frequently avoid tables of numbers altogether. Many arrive at conclusions quickly and begin formulating responses before they have all the facts. The less clever in this crowd see the details of a case as a nuisance; reading the facts will only interfere with their preparation of a response.

After you have read and thought about the issues in a case, if you are uncertain about what to do, read it again. As you mature in the experiences of business school, you will get better at this, but at first, your best defense against being surprised or frustrated by a case is to read it thoroughly.

Take notes. College students typically want to either underline or highlight much of what is contained in a book chapter, reprint, or essay. Case studies, however, are constructed a bit differently. Textbook chapters are typically organized in a hierarchical fashion, with key points and sub-points listed in order of importance, carefully illustrated and summarized. Not so with case studies, which are often simply arranged in chronological order. Textbooks usually proceed in logical fashion, with one concept building on others that came before it. Case studies, on the other hand, are seemingly chaotic: many events happen at once, order and discipline are sometimes missing, and key issues are not always self-evident.

Case studies may also contain substantial amounts of information in tabular form: annual revenues, product shipment rates, tons of raw materials processed, or cost data organized by business units. To know what such data mean, you will have to read the tables and apply what you have learned about reading a balance sheet, or about activity-based costing. You may find crucial information contained in a sequence of events or a direct quote from a unit manager. Sometimes you will discover that the most important issues are never mentioned by the principals in the case – they are simply ideas or tools that they weren't clever enough to think of, or didn't think were important at the time.

Your notes should focus on the details you will need to identify the business problems involved the case, the issues critical to solving those problems, as well as the resources available to the managers in the case. Those notes will be helpful in producing a case solution.

Identify the business problem. In each case, at least one fundamental business problem is present. It may be a small, tactical issue, such as how this company will collect money from a delinquent customer. But the issue may be broader in nature: "How can they reduce accounts receivable ageing to 30 days or less?" Larger, more strategic problems might involve the company's chronic, critical cash-flow difficulties. "If this company were no longer cash-starved, what longer-term opportunities might open up?"

You may identify more than one problem in a case. Complex cases often involve several such problems simultaneously. They may be technical in nature and involve accounting or cost control systems. They may involve the use of technology. You might see supply-chain problems in the business you are studying. You may identify marketing deficiencies. Or, you might see human problems that involve supervision, communication, motivation, or training.

Specify an objective for the managers involved. Once you have identified one or more business problems present in the case, think about the outcome(s) you would most hope to see for the company and people you have read about. If you were asked to consult on this company's problems – and that is the role most business students are playing as they read a case study – what results would you hope for? Don't limit your thinking to what the company should *do*, but what the most *successful outcome* would look like. Be specific about how the company will know if they have succeeded. Quantify the desired results whenever you can.

Identify and rank order the critical issues. These issues are at the heart of the case. If you miss a critical issue, you may not be able to solve the case to the satisfaction of your professor.

- *Some issues are interdependent.* That is, a solution to one issue might necessarily precede or depend on another. In a product-contamination case, for example, a media relations team can't draft a press release until the production or packaging team knows what's wrong with the product. The team responsible for a new product launch can't make final advertising and promotion decisions until issues related to packaging, transportation, and distribution have been solved.

- *Some issues are more important than others.* A company may have a great opportunity to launch a product line extension, but not have sufficient market research data to support the idea. More to the point, they may not have the talent on staff to understand and properly use such data. Thus, hiring a market research chief might be more important than simply contracting with an outside firm to find the data.

- *Each issue has a time dimension.* While two problems may be equally important to the success of a company, one may be near-term in nature while the other is long-term. Setting up a corporate web site may be important, but it won't solve the longer-term issue of marketing strategy: should we sell direct over the web or use retail partners to market our products? Specify which problems must be addressed first, but think, as well, about the duration of the solutions – how long will it take to fix this?

- *Some issues are merely symptoms of larger or deeper problems.* Two managers in open warfare with each other about budget or resource issues may be symptomatic of more serious, long-term budget problems, inadequate communication among the management team, or perhaps a corporate culture that encourages confrontation over minor issues. When Sears-Roebuck & Co. discovered that auto service managers in California were charging customers to replace parts that were not yet worn out, the problem was deeper than a few overzealous managers. After analyzing the complaints brought by the California Attorney General, Sears realized that their compensation system rewarded managers for selling more parts, and not for simply servicing customers' vehicles.

Consider relevant information and underlying assumptions. Accept the fact that much of the information contained in the case will not be useful to your analysis. You should also accept the fact that you will never know all that you would like in order to produce a solution. Life is like that. So are case studies. Identify the relevant facts contained in case and think carefully about them. Identify additional information you might like to have – that might be part of your solution – but don't dwell on it.

Separate facts from assumptions. Recognize that there are some things you will know for sure and others that you will not. Recognize further that you may be required to subjectively interpret some evidence and to assume other evidence not directly stated in the case. The more suppositions you make, however, the weaker your analysis becomes.

List possible solutions to the problem. Every problem lends itself to more than one solution. Keep looking for good ideas, even when you have already thought of one that will solve the problem. Listing possible solutions is a form of brainstorming that will later permit you to assign values or weights to those ideas: is one solution less expensive than another? Will one be more effective than another? Will one idea work more quickly? Will one of these ideas have a more enduring effect?

Select a solution. After assigning weights and values to the various solutions you have thought about, select the one you like best and prepare to defend it. Show why the ideas you have thought about are superior and how they will work. If you have rejected other, more obvious ideas, you may want to explain why.

Decide how to implement the best solution. Having good ideas is insufficient. You must be able to put them to work. Graduate students of business are often praised by executives for being theoretically well-grounded, but criticized for lacking practical application. "A team of young MBAs told me that we needed to sell this division of my company," said an executive in the chemical industry. "But they couldn't tell me what to do or how to go about it. All they knew was that we should try to find a buyer. Interesting," he concluded, "but not very helpful."

Explain how to communicate the solution. In a management communication case study, you will be asked to identify key audiences for your message. That means identifying which groups you want to communicate with and the means you will use to reach them. Think carefully about the broad range of stakeholders in the case: employees, customers, shareholders, business partners, suppliers, regulators, and the marketplace-at-large. Identify exactly how you would plan to transmit your message, assure that it has been received and understood, and how you would analyze feedback from those audiences. You should think, as well, about timing and sequencing of messages. Who should you speak with first? Who should send the message? How should this particular audience hear about this particular message?

Write it up. Different professors will have different expectations about what they want from you in a written case solution. They will probably not provide you with specific, detailed instructions regarding their expectations, but they will certainly tell you if you've missed the boat or have produced a solid response. Some will ask for wide-ranging responses that cover many issues, while others will expect a more focused response. Just provide your professor with your best thinking and be as detailed as you think you can within the page limits you've been given.

What You Should Expect

If you have read the case thoroughly, identified the business problems, rank-ordered the critical issues, proposed various solutions, and then identified how you will implement and communicate them, you can expect to be more-or-less as well prepared for classroom case discussion as your classmates. Here's what else you should expect:

- *An occasional cold call.* Be prepared for your professor to ask you to provide key details from the case, sometimes referred to as a "shred." Simply explain what happened in the case, identifying the business and its principals, and give your best thinking on critical issues in two minutes or less. Don't worry about providing a solution just yet. Your professor is likely to want a more thorough discussion of the issues first. If you are feeling especially confident, you may wish to volunteer.

- *A logical, step-by-step approach.* If classmates offer information that is useful but not relevant or in line with the question the professor asks, expect the discussion to return to the issues the professor thinks are most important before you move on.

- *Different approaches from different professors.* No two professors are exactly the same in their approach or preferences. Virtually all of them, however, appreciate a bold, "do something" approach over hedging, caution, and a reluctance to act.

What You Should Not Expect

- *More information.* From time-to-time, your professor will present you with a "B" case that offers new or subsequent information. Such cases represent an extension of the facts in the "A" case and usually provide another managerial decision opportunity. For the most part, though, the information given in the "A" case is all you will have and you must make do with that.

- *A "right answer."* Because case studies are most often based on real events, no one can say for certain what would have happened if your ideas or other, "better" ideas had been implemented. Some solutions are clearly better than others, but many ideas will work. Some of the very best ideas may not yet have been thought of or spoken aloud.

- *An explanation of what "actually happened."* Many professors either don't know what happened to the managers and the businesses described in your case studies, or they don't think that your having that information will be useful or productive in the learning process. Your own thinking may be limited or skewed if you focus on actual outcomes.

- *A single discipline focus to each case.* While some cases are principally about accounting, they may contain issues related to finance, operations management, human resources, or communication. Authentic business problems are rarely, if ever, uni-dimensional. The more you are willing to think about other dimensions of business and their interdependency, the more you will learn about how real businesses work.

- *That your response will solve all of the problems in the case.* Focus on the most important, most urgent, and most relevant problems first. You may wish to identify issues for further thought or investigation by the management team described in the case, but you cannot and should not try to solve all the problems in the case.

In summary, your task is to read, identify and understand the business problems in the case. By identifying, rank-ordering, and exploring the critical issues it contains, you should be able to propose a workable solution, identifying how to implement and communicate it. From that point forward, you must explain your choices in writing be ready to defend them in the classroom.

For Further Reading

Barnes, L.B.; C.R. Christensen; and A.J. Hansen, *Teaching and the Case Method*, 3rd edition. Boston, MA: Harvard Business School Press, 1994.

Bouton, C. and R. Garth, eds., *Learning in Groups*. San Francisco, CA: Jossey-Bass, 1983.

Corey, R., "The Use of Cases in Management Education," Harvard Business School Case No. 376-240.

Erskine, J.; M.R. Leenders; and L.A. Mauffette-Leenders, *Teaching with Cases*. London, Ontario: School of Business, University of Western Ontario, 1981.

Gragg, C.J., "Because Wisdom Can't Be Told," *The Case Method at the Harvard Business School*. New York, NY: McGraw-Hill, 1954, p. 6.

McNair, M.P., "The Genesis of the Case Method in Business Administration," *The Case Method at the Harvard Business School*. New York, NY: McGraw-Hill, 1954, pp. 25-33.

Penrose, J. M.; R.W. Raspberry; and R. J. Myers, "Analyzing and Writing a Case Report," *Advanced Business Communication*, 3rd edition. Cincinnati, OH: South-Western College Publishing, 1997.

Wasserman, S., *Put Some Thinking in Your Classroom*. Chicago, IL: Benefic Press, 1978.

PART I

Brand Image and Identity

Bayer Corporation:
The Recall of Phenylpropanolamine (PPA)

For years, the consumer care division of Bayer Corporation has successfully marketed a number of well-known brands that have earned the trust of American consumers. These brands include Bayer aspirin, Aleve analgesic, Phillips' Milk of Magnesia, One-A-Day vitamins, and Alka-Seltzer medicines. Responding to concerns raised about an ingredient found in some of its products, Bayer and several other drug manufacturers co-sponsored a study to assess the safety of this ingredient. Not only was Bayer interested in the results, the Food and Drug Administration (FDA) was interested as well.

The results of the study concluded that the ingredient carried a risk. However, Bayer and the FDA did not agree on the severity of the risk. As a result, Bayer's supply chain was not prepared when the FDA requested a voluntary recall of all products containing the ingredient. Perhaps more importantly, Bayer management had not anticipated the media's interpretation of the FDA actions. The resulting headlines would likely tarnish the reputation of one of Bayer's key brands, Alka-Seltzer. If not addressed properly by the company, the headlines also had the potential to jeopardize the images of all the Bayer brands. Please see Exhibit 1 for a historical timeline of Alka-Seltzer from its introduction in 1931 through the FDA's actions in 2000.

Company Overview

Bayer Corporation is the wholly owned U.S. subsidiary of the German chemicals and pharmaceuticals giant, Bayer AG. Bayer AG's activities are divided into four business segments – Health Care, Agriculture, Polymers, and Chemicals – which comprise 15 business groups worldwide. The parent firm, based in Leverkusen, Germany, was formed in 1863 by chemical salesman Friedrich Bayer and Johann Friedrich Weskott. Bayer AG is made up of more than 350 companies in 150 countries. The majority of its sales come from Europe.

This case was prepared by Research Assistants Daniel Hwang, Michael Kolar, and Brendan Cox under the direction of James S. O'Rourke, Concurrent Associate Professor of Management, as the basis for class discussion rather than to illustrate either effective or ineffective handling of an administrative situation. Information was gathered from corporate as well as public sources.

In 1899, Bayer invented aspirin and changed the world forever. Western medicine finally had an inexpensive and reliable means for relieving pain and reducing fevers. Today, Bayer aspirin is a staple in most medicine chests and has been found to prevent blood clots, thereby reducing the risk of strokes and heart attacks.

Bayer Corporation invests 80 percent of its research and development dollars in health care and life sciences projects. It operates 50 sales offices and 50 manufacturing operations, while marketing some 10,000 products from nine divisions: agriculture; coatings and colorants; consumer care; diagnostics; fibers, additives, and rubber; industrial chemicals; pharmaceuticals; plastics; and polyurethanes. (Exhibit 2)[1] While Bayer's flagship product, aspirin, has been a strong sales performer throughout its existence, the company's robust research and development budget has enabled it to bring several other breakthrough over-the-counter (OTC) pharmaceutical products to the market.

Alka-Seltzer Medicines

Alka-Seltzer is an example of a breakthrough product introduced by Bayer. The original product was developed in the late 1920s when it was discovered that the main ingredients, acetylsalicylic acid and sodium bicarbonate, helped to combat flu symptoms. Today, products marketed under the brand are available in over 50 countries worldwide. The brand was first marketed in 1931 and gained mass popularity in the 1950s through advertisements about its effervescent nature, often featuring the product's mascot, "Speedy." However, Alka-Seltzer remedies are also currently available in liqui-gel and non-effervescent tablet forms. Though it was originally marketed to provide relief of headaches, stomach problems, and heartburn, many of today's Alka-Seltzer products are specifically formulated to provide relief of cold and flu symptoms. These products are known as Alka-Seltzer Plus cold medicines. Bayer had invested considerable resources in cultivating the Alka-Seltzer Plus brand. By 1998, annual advertising expenditures totaled over $44.8 million, of which 62 percent was spent on promoting the effervescent tablets.[2]

A Key Ingredient: PPA

Perhaps the most common symptom of cold and flu is sinus congestion. Many remedies contain phenylpropanolamine (PPA) because the chemical is highly effective in providing relief of sinus congestion. PPA is a stimulant similar to amphetamine and is also used in the manufacture of weight loss drugs because of its ability to act as an appetite suppressant. In addition to Alka-Seltzer Plus, PPA can be found in other popular cold medicine brands such as Comtrex, Dimetapp, and Robitussin.[3] The medication has been on the market for 50 years with annual usage surpassing one billion doses.[4] While

---

[1] http://www.bayerus.com/about/org.htm
[2] Competitive Media Reporting. Ad $ Summary: January-December 1998, Book I. New York: 1999, p. 98.
[3] http://healthwatch.medscape.com
[4] "Phenylpropanolamine & Risk of Hemorrhagic Stroke – Final Report of HSP." Yale University, May 2000.

Alka-Seltzer Plus cold medicines are available in both effervescent and liqui-gel forms, only the effervescent medicines contain PPA.

Federal Drug Administration Organizational Overview

As a unit of the U.S. Department of Health and Human Services, the FDA plays a critical role in the safety and security of the public health. Its mission statement is as follows:[5]

1. To promote the public health by promptly and efficiently reviewing clinical research and taking appropriate action on the marketing of regulated products in a timely manner;

2. With respect to such products, protect the public health by ensuring that foods are safe, wholesome, sanitary, and properly labeled; human and veterinary drugs are safe and effective; there is reasonable assurance of the safety and effectiveness of devices intended for human use; cosmetics are safe and properly labeled, and; public health and safety are protected from electronic product radiation;

3. Participate through appropriate processes with representatives of other countries to reduce the burden of regulation, harmonize regulatory requirements, and achieve appropriate reciprocal arrangements; and,

4. As determined to be appropriate by the Secretary (of Health and Human Services), carry out paragraphs (1) through (3) in consultation with experts in science, medicine, and public health, and in cooperation with consumers, users, manufacturers, importers, packers, distributors, and retailers of regulated products.

Of the several regulatory bodies within the FDA, the Center for Drug Evaluation and Research (CDER) focuses on both prescription and OTC drug markets. More specifically, all OTC initiatives are handled within CDER at the Office of Drug Evaluation V, Division of OTC Products.

FDA Drug Recall Policy and Process

As defined by the FDA, a recall is a "voluntary action that takes place because manufacturers and distributors carry out their responsibility to protect the public health and well-being from products that present a risk of injury or gross deception or are otherwise defective."[6] In the event that manufacturers or distributors refuse or fail to undertake an FDA requested recall, the FDA may pursue a court approved seizure. An ad hoc committee of FDA scientists evaluates all drugs being recalled or considered for recall. This committee may also elect to seek outside consultation and expertise as appropriate.

There are several main factors analyzed by the committee. First, it must determine whether the drug has already caused any disease or injury. Next, the

---

[5] http://www.fda.gov
[6] U.S. Code of Federal Regulations. 21 CFR 7.40

committee considers whether or not future exposure to the drug could cause health hazards such as illness or death. Finally, they assess the likelihood of the hazards occurring and the resulting consequences, short and long-term. Based upon these general guidelines, the FDA will decide whether or not a drug should be recalled.

If a recall is deemed necessary, the FDA assigns a classification to the recalled drug. The classifications are defined as follows:[7]

- Class I – reasonable probability that exposure to or use of the drug will cause serious adverse health consequences or death.

- Class II – remote probability that exposure to or use of the drug may cause temporary or medically reversible adverse health conditions.

- Class III – use of or exposure to the drug is not likely to cause adverse health consequences.

In the event of a recall, the FDA will immediately notify all affected companies by phone or by visitation from an authorized FDA representative, followed by a written confirmation by mail or telegram to a company official. The notification specifies the violation, the hazard classification, proposed recall strategy, and other instructions. Upon receiving the notification, the company may be asked to provide the FDA with additional information pertinent to the drug being recalled.

Following notification, a drug manufacturer develops a recall strategy in accordance with FDA guidelines. These guidelines govern the depth of the recall, public communication, and effectiveness checks. Depending upon how hazardous the drug is and the extent of its distribution, the recall depth can span from wholesale levels to retail/consumer levels. Each physical product recall is unique to the circumstances surrounding the situation. Ultimately, the FDA will specify to what level the recall should extend.

The FDA may also issue warnings to alert the public of the recall. This is reserved for "urgent situations where other means for preventing use of the recalled product appear inadequate."[8] Ordinarily, the FDA will issue public warnings through several channels including the general news media (national, regional, or local) or specialized news media such as the trade press to reach specific target segments (i.e., physicians, medical organizations, etc.). For a firm that decides to issue its own public warnings, the format, content, and extent of the communications must be submitted to the FDA for review and approval. All public communications must:[9]

- Display the product by name, size, lot number(s), code(s), serial number(s) and any other descriptive labeling to accurately identify the product.

- Explain the reason for the recall and the associated hazard.

- Provide instructions for product returns.

---

[7] 21 CFR 7.3m
[8] 21 CFR 7.45
[9] 21 CFR 7.49c

- Identify a means for recipients to communicate and contact the company.

The third and final component of a recall strategy is the effectiveness check. The purpose of an effectiveness check is to verify that affected parties have received the recall notifications and taken action. Normally, the drug manufacturer will be responsible for verifying the effectiveness of the recall notification, but the FDA can assist and perform audits when necessary. The FDA categorizes effectiveness checks into five levels:[10]

1. Level A – 100% effectiveness

2. Level B – Some of the recipients contacted, but not all

3. Level C – Less than 10% contacted

4. Level D – Less than 2% contacted

5. Level E – No effectiveness

The FDA will terminate a recall when it determines that "all reasonable efforts have been made to remove or correct the product in accordance with the recall strategy, and when it is reasonable to assume that the product subject to the recall has been removed and proper disposition or correction has been made commensurate with the degree of hazard of the recalled product."[11]

The PPA Controversy

PPA has been on the market for over fifty years, and the FDA had classified the chemical as "safe and effective." However, in the late 1970s, some concerns over its possible health hazards began to emerge. Several doctors theorized that PPA caused blood pressure to rise above normal levels, thus leading to stroke. In 1984, a research study concluded that any hemorrhagic risk related to PPA, if present at all, was very small (less than one percent likelihood).[12] By the late 1980s, lawsuits against drug manufacturers of medicines containing PPA were growing, especially the legal claims from patients and consumers of PPA alleging misconduct against the drug companies. Furthermore, case reports from medical organizations describing the occurrence of strokes after PPA ingestion were climbing.

In response to growing concerns, the FDA and several drug manufacturers jointly commissioned a research study called the Hemorrhagic Stroke Project (HSP) with the Yale University School of Medicine in late 1994. The study was comprised of 702 case subjects and 1,376 control subjects. The main purpose was to identify if there was an association between hemorrhagic stroke and the PPA found in cold remedies and appetite suppressants. By the end of the research study in May 2000, Yale University determined that "PPA increases the risk for hemorrhagic stroke. For both individuals considering use of PPA and for policy makers, the HSP provides important data for a contemporary assessment of risks associated with use of PPA."[13]

---

[10] 21 CFR 7.45b3

[11] 21 CFR 7.55a

[12] Jick, Aselton, Hunger, "PPA and Cerebral Hemorrhage." *Lancet*, 1984

[13] "Phenylpropanolamine & Risk of Hemorrhagic Stroke–Final Rept of the HSP."Yale Univ.,May 2000.

On October 19, 2000, the FDA's Nonprescription Drugs Advisory Committee (NDAC) discussed this report and other information on PPA. The NDAC determined that there is an association between PPA and hemorrhagic stroke. They recommended that PPA "not be considered generally recognized as safe for over-the-counter use as a nasal decongestant or for weight control."[14]

Media Interpretation of the FDA's Actions

On November 3, 2000, Janet Woodcock, M.D., Director at the Center for Drug Evaluation and Research, issued a written statement addressed to the senior management at Bayer Corporation, as well as to other OTC manufacturers (Exhibit 4). In the letter, Woodstock referred to the report that the FDA received from the researchers at the Yale University School of Medicine. The Yale report's research data suggested that PPA increases the risk for hemorrhagic stroke (bleeding into the brain or into tissue surrounding the brain) in women.[15] The report also determined that men who used PPA could be at risk. Woodcock's statement continued that, "as an interim measure to protect the public health, you (OTC manufacturers) should voluntarily discontinue marketing any drug products containing phenylpropanolamine. If applicable, you may reformulate such products to remove the phenylpropanolamine ingredient."[16]

As the news media became aware of this notice by the FDA, different interpretations of the warning began to surface in the headlines. The headline from the November 7, 2000, *Wall Street Journal* read "FDA Bans Use of Chemical Tied to Strokes." Similarly, the *USA Today* headline from the same day reported, "Drugmakers, stores move on FDA ban – Reformulated remedies on way for colds." The *New Jersey Star-Ledger* and *Pittsburgh Post-Gazette* also reported that the FDA would take steps to ban all use of PPA in cold remedies and appetite suppressants.

In reality, the FDA never issued a ban on the sale or use of PPA, but rather requested a voluntary recall of the product by the manufacturers whose products contained the chemical. Given the portrayals of the major newspapers, the public reaction had the potential to be much stronger than what was intended by the FDA or anticipated by companies like Bayer. Now, Bayer had to address the public perception that the FDA had banned the use of PPA, making cold remedies, such as Alka-Seltzer, dangerously unsafe.

Bayer's Dilemma

It is clearly ironic that Bayer was among several cold medicine manufacturers who funded the Yale University study that served as the basis for the FDA's decision. Despite the conclusions of the FDA, Bayer management still believed in the safety of all Bayer products, including those containing PPA.[17] However, management was also

---

[14] http://www.fda.gov/cder/drug/infopage/ppa/advisory.htm
[15] Ibid.
[16] FDA Letter to Manufacturers of Drug Products Containing Phenylpropanolamine, November 3, 2000.
[17] http://www.alka-seltzer.com/info_ppa.htm

intent on maintaining the trust and confidence of Bayer consumers.[18] These facts would undoubtedly influence the decision of whether or not to comply with the FDA's requested voluntary recall of all medicines containing PPA as an ingredient.

Several cost considerations would also impact Bayer's decision. At the time of the FDA's decision, management felt the costs of implementing the recall had the potential to reach $60 million.[19] Bayer would have to reimburse all retailers carrying its effervescent medicines for the costs of physically removing and returning the products to Bayer. Additionally, money spent on advertising campaigns, point-of-sale promotional displays, and slotting fees for the effervescent medicines would be lost. Finally, Bayer would have to make a decision about outstanding promotions that had been sent to consumers prior to the issuance of the FDA's decision. One such promotion was a coupon entitling customers who purchased an Alka-Seltzer Plus product to a free container of orange juice.

These outstanding consumer promotions were especially problematic considering the dynamics of supplying Alka-Seltzer Plus to retailers. Demand forecasts are prepared well ahead of anticipated deliveries because the production lead-time for Alka-Seltzer Plus products, both effervescent and liqui-gels, is approximately three months. The FDA's call for a voluntary withdrawal of PPA products took place in early November 2000, the beginning of what is considered the peak season for cold and flu medicines. Bayer had not anticipated the FDA's decision, and the production of liqui-gels was not adjusted during the months preceding the peak season. If a recall were implemented, the effervescent products would become unavailable and retailers would experience stock-outs of substitute Bayer products. Supply of Bayer substitutes would not be available to meet demand until after the conclusion of the peak cold and flu season. One thing was certain: if Bayer did not take action, the positive brand equity of Alka-Seltzer Plus, as well as the reputations of Bayer's other OTC brands, would suffer immensely.

---

[18] Ibid.

[19] "Phenylpropanolamine & Risk of Hemorrhagic Stroke – Final Rept of the HSP." Yale Univ., May 2000.

Questions

1.   How should Bayer respond to the media's portrayal of the voluntary recall as an FDA ban of PPA?

2.   Should Bayer continue to claim that its products containing PPA are safe? If so, should this message be consistent with a voluntary recall of products containing PPA?

3.   What is the most effective medium for communicating Bayer's message? Is there a danger of further misinterpretation by the media?

4.   What marketing strategy should Bayer implement given the outstanding Alka-Seltzer Plus coupons and the company's inability to supply the product or comparable substitutes?

Exhibit 1: History of Alka-Seltzer

1931: Alka-Seltzer is introduced on the market.

1950s: Alka-Seltzer gains mass popularity through national advertising.

1969: Alka-Seltzer Plus products are introduced on the market.

1970s: Health concerns about PPA begin to surface.

1980s: Lawsuits against OTC manufacturers are filed.

1984: The first study of the relationship between PPA and strokes is conducted. A minimal association is found.

1994: The FDA and OTC manufacturers jointly commission a research study at Yale University School of Medicine.

1995: Bayer introduces Alka-Seltzer Plus caplets.

1996: Bayer introduces Alka-Seltzer Plus liqui-gels.

May 2000: Yale University releases the results of the research study to the FDA's Nonprescription Drugs Advisory Committee (NDAC).

October 2000: NDAC reviews the results and recommends that PPA not be considered safe.

November 2000: The FDA requests a voluntary recall by the OTC manufacturers of all products containing PPA.

Exhibit 2: Bayer Group – Corporate Organization Chart

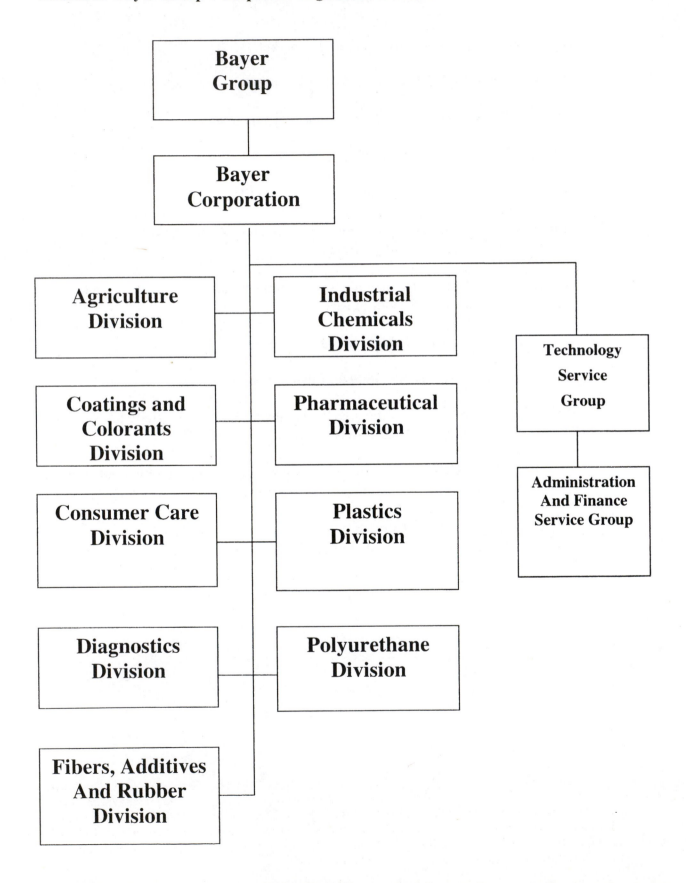

Exhibit 3: FDA Letter

DEPARTMENT OF HEALTH HUMAN SERVICES

Food and Drug Administration

Rockville MD 20857

November 3, 2000

Dear CEO or President:

This letter concerns drug products containing phenylpropanolamine and its salts marketed by prescription or over-the-counter (OTC), which are now or have previously been manufactured, relabeled, repacked, or distributed by your firm. Phenylpropanolamine is currently available by prescription and OTC as a nasal decongestant, and OTC for weight control. Your firm is receiving this letter based on information in the Food and Drug Administration's (FDA) Drug Listing System or because you have a new drug application (NDA) or abbreviated new drug application (ANDA) for a product containing phenylpropanolamine.

This letter is to inform you of recent developments relating to phenylpropanolarnine. Earlier this year, FDA received a report entitled "Phenylpropanolamine & Risk of Hemorrhagic Stroke: Final Report of the Hemorrhagic Stroke Project" from scientists at Yale University School of Medicine. This report, which is on display in Docket No. 8 1 N-0022 in the FDA Dockets Management Branch, states that the data suggest that phenylpropanolamine increases the risk for hemorrhagic stroke.

On October 19; 2000, the Agency's Nonprescription Drugs Advisory Committee (NDAC) discussed this report and other information on phenylpropanolamine. NDAC determined that there is.an association between phenylpropanolamine and hemorrhagic stroke and recommended that phenylpropanolamine not be considered generally recognized as safe for OTC use as a nasal decongestant or for weight control.[1]

Based on these recent developments, FDA intends to initiate rulemaking to classify phenylpropanolamine as nonmonograph (not generally recognized as safe and effective) for OTC use. Based on the recent research findings, FDA also has significant concerns about the continued use of phenylpropanolamine in prescription drug products. FDA also intends to take action to remove phenylpropanolamine from prescription drug products. FDA plans to issue a Public Health Advisory on phenylpropanolamine to alert consumers and health professionals about the report.

---

[1] In the mid- I 970s, phenylpropanolamine was classified as Category I (safe and effective) by two OTC drug advisory review panels. The Cough-Cold Panel's recommendations on phenylpropanolarnine as a nasal decongestant appeared in the FEDERAL REGISTER of September 9, 1976 (41 FR 38312) and the Miscellaneous Internal Panel's recommendations for weight control use appeared on February 26, 1982 (47 FR 8466). However, FDA deferred its classification of phenylpropanolamine because of subsequent safety issues that were raised, pending completion of additional studies.

Page 2

FDA also believes that, as an interim measure to protect the public health, you should voluntarily discontinue marketing any drug products containing phenylpropanolarnine. If applicable, you may reformulate such products to remove the phenylpropanolarnine ingredient.

Your cooperation and prompt attention to this matter will be appreciated.

Sincerely,

Janet Woodcock, M.D.
Director Center for Drug Evaluation and

Research

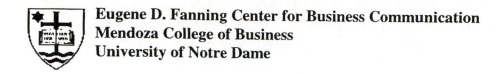
Lucent Technologies
Sustaining the Brand Identity of a Blue Chip Spinoff

As Lucent Technologies management formulated its new strategy that focused on becoming a smaller and leaner company with aggressive growth rates, it became clear that the company would need to shed divisions that were no longer an ideal fit. Having acquired 38 companies totaling $46 billion since its inception in 1996, Lucent was fated to develop business divisions that were not capable of sustaining the high growth rates to which the firm was committed. Over the course of its existence, Lucent evolved from a small American Telephone & Telegraph (AT&T) spin-off to a high-tech megalith.

AT&T Globalization and Lucent Technologies Spinoff

In 1989, AT&T Technologies branched into several business units, including AT&T Network Systems, AT&T Global Business Communications Systems, AT&T Microelectronics, and AT&T Consumer Products, which would all later combine with Bell Labs to become the original Lucent Technologies. During the 1990s, these business units continued to grow their market leadership in the U.S. and exhibited double-digit growth internationally. Complexities in the marketplace and within AT&T, however, led to a decision in 1995 to totally restructure the communications giant. In September 1995, AT&T proposed forming three separate, publicly traded companies to serve the increasingly divergent business needs of its customers.

By February of 1996, the soon-to-be-spun-off systems and technology unit of AT&T had renamed itself Lucent Technologies and launched its separation with an initial public offering of stock issued in April 1996. The spin-off was completed in September 1996 when AT&T distributed its shares of Lucent to AT&T shareholders. Since its launch, Lucent has become a major player in optical, data, and wireless networking; Web-based enterprise solutions that link public and private networks; communications software; professional network design and consulting services; and communications semiconductors and optoelectronics. The company has

This case was prepared by Research Assistants Chris Clark and Sam DiCicco under the direction of James S. O'Rourke, Concurrent Associate Professor of Management, as the basis for class discussion rather than to illustrate either effective or ineffective handling of an administrative situation. Information was gathered from corporate as well as public sources.

completed 38 acquisitions totaling more than $46 billion, including a $24 billion purchase of Ascend Communications, which made Lucent the leading provider of data networking equipment for service providers, facilitating the company's aggressive growth rate.

Lucent Technologies Background

Lucent Technologies is focused on being the leader in building a broadband and mobile Internet infrastructure that will change the way people communicate. Lucent provides the systems, software, silicon, and services for what is the largest network build-out in history. The company is focused on a triple play of optical, data, and wireless networking technologies with the software and services to support them.

With headquarters in Murray Hill, N.J., Lucent has about 125,000 employees worldwide — about one-quarter of them based outside the United States — and has offices or distributors in more than 90 countries and territories around the world. Bell Labs, Lucent's world-renowned research and development arm, has a presence in 32 countries, and has produced 11 Nobel laureates since 1937. Scientists and researchers at Bell Labs receive more than four patents every business day. In addition to acquisitions and its own internal developments, Lucent has made several moves to streamline its portfolio and sharpen its focus on the broadband and mobile Internet infrastructure.

Lucent Technologies Stock Performance

For the fiscal year ended Sept. 30, 2000, Lucent had approximately $34 billion in revenues from continuing operations.

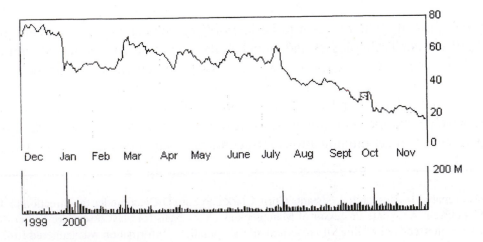

Period : Nov-29-1999 - Nov-28-2000

S = Spinoff

About the Enterprise Network Group

The Enterprise Networks Group (ENG) of Lucent Technologies is a leading provider of communications systems and software for enterprises, including businesses, government agencies, and other organizations. The Enterprise Networks Group is a worldwide leader in sales of messaging and structured cabling systems and a U.S. leader in sales of enterprise voice communications and call center systems. The broad customer base of the Enterprise Networks Group includes approximately 78 percent of the Fortune 500 companies. In fiscal 1999, Lucent's ENG recognized revenue of approximately $8 billion and net income of approximately $300 million.

The Enterprise Network Group offers solutions in these key areas:

- Customer Relationship Management (CRM) Software Applications;
- Unified Communications and Portal Software Applications;
- Lucent Hosted Solutions for Application Service Providers;
- Multiservice Infrastructure;
- Structured Cabling Solutions.

From system design to network management, ENG offers a full portfolio of services and support, including planning and consulting, integration and implementation, support and maintenance, operations and administration, and asset outsourcing. The global service organization provides customers around the world with end-to-end service, including remote monitoring, diagnostics, and trouble resolution.

Ultimate Divestiture

Lucent's management decided to identify the business units that were creating a drag on corporate growth. The Enterprise Networks Group (ENG) of Lucent Technologies, which provided communications systems and software to a broad range of enterprises, was a mature, slow-growth division that was an ideal target for divestiture.

On March 1, 2000, Lucent Technologies formally announced plans to spin-off its Enterprise Network Group. Lucent's board of directors, which approved the spin-off, planned to accomplish the divestiture through a tax-free distribution of new shares to Lucent's current shareholders. Company executives anticipated that the spin-off would be completed by the close of its fourth fiscal quarter of 2000, which would end on September 30, 2000.

Key Players in the Spin-Off

On June 27, 2000, Lucent Technologies Chairman and CEO Richard McGinn announced that Donald Peterson, then Lucent Executive Vice President and Chief Financial Officer, would become President and CEO of the new company. In addition, Henry Schacht, former Lucent Chairman and a member of the parent company's board of directors, would become Chairman of the new company.

In an announcement to the business press, McGinn said, "Lucent will concentrate greater resources on fast-growing areas like optical networking, Internet infrastructure, wireless, semiconductors, optoelectronics, Web-based enterprise solutions linking private to public networks, and professional design and consulting services for service providers and enterprises."

As a 22-year communications veteran for Bell Labs, AT&T, and Lucent, Steve Aaronson was appointed Vice President of Corporate Communications for the new company. Up to that point, Aaronson was vice president of Service Provider Networks Public Relations at Lucent Technologies. Prior to that assignment, he had been Vice President of Global Corporate Public Relations from Lucent's inception.

Aaronson has accepted the challenge of leading the company's branding and corporate image campaigns, investor relations, news media relations, employee communications, industry and financial analyst relations, and philanthropic activities. But as the spin off date quickly approaches, he realizes that he is now faced with the daunting task of leading the team that will create and implement the new company's multi million-dollar advertising and marketing campaigns.

Questions

1. Which facts in this case seem most important to you?

2. What are the critical issues for Aaronson and his team?

3. Which problem should they try to solve first?

4. What should the name of the new company be? How should Aaronson's team go about selecting it?

5. Should the new name directly reflect what the company would actually do? Or should the new name be more abstract and unique?

6. What are advantages and disadvantages of such an approach?

7. Should the identity of the new firm be linked in any tangible way to the identities of Lucent Technologies, AT&T, or Bell Laboratories?

8. Should the new corporate name evoke some specific meaning? If so, what should it be?

9.   For what audiences will the new name be most important? Who are those audiences and what are their interests?

10.   Does the name and public identity of this new company *really* matter? If so, to whom and why?

11.   How should Aaronson's team communicate the spin-off to key stakeholders?

12.   What media should they use for the new company's communication strategy?

13.   What are the potential risks that Lucent is likely to face resulting from the spin-off?

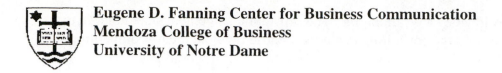
Accenture:
The Re-branding of Andersen Consulting

On January 1, 2001, Joe Forehand, Managing Partner and CEO of Accenture, sat in his office and contemplated the road ahead. The newly named company, formerly Andersen Consulting, had been launched on this historic New Year's Day, and Forehand was concerned with how it would fare. While they were an old company with a strong client base, they were being forced to relinquish their name and therefore a large part of their strategic image. At the same time, they had taken on a variety of new capabilities and restructured the company. Forehand hoped that the new name would become as valuable as the old one. He also hoped that they would be able to leverage this change to not only retain their former clients, but also to create added value for new ones.

History

In 1913, Arthur Andersen founded an innovative public accounting firm after leaving a professorship in accounting at Northwestern University. He hired some of his best students and trained them to be accountants who thought beyond the boundaries of the balance sheet. As early as 1919, the company began providing consulting services for the companies they served, identifying client strengths and weaknesses. Three employees were given the official responsibilities for the consulting division in 1954.

Concerns began to arise over a conflict of interest, and tensions between the two divisions grew as consulting was rising and accounting was falling. The two groups became separate business units in 1989, forming Arthur Andersen (AA) and Andersen Consulting (AC)

This case was prepared by Research Assistants Melissa Gaul and Laurie Cosenza under the direction of James S. O'Rourke, Concurrent Associate Professor of Management, as the basis for class discussion rather than to illustrate either effective or ineffective handling of an administrative situation. Information was gathered from corporate as well as public sources.

under the Andersen Worldwide (AW) umbrella. The separation agreement stated that Arthur Andersen could not enter into the consulting business because it would create competition for the other branch, and if either division sought to break from the other, it would pay a penalty of 150 percent of its annual revenue.

Conflict with Arthur Andersen

On December 17, 1997, Andersen Consulting filed suit in the International Chamber of Commerce to break with Arthur Andersen permanently. After the 1989 Florida separation agreement, this court had been designated as the arbitrator between the two groups if any conflict arose. Andersen Consulting managing partner and chief executive George Shaheen said, "a number of irreconcilable differences have come forth which we have just not been able to resolve."[1] The company cited a breach of contract, claiming Arthur Andersen had entered into the consulting business and was taking business away from its sister company. They accused their sister firm of a "dramatic expansion" in consulting areas such as business transformation and technology integration where Andersen Consulting was the market leader.[2] Additionally, Andersen Consulting partners still had to transfer money to the other company each year, although they created more revenue than their accounting counterparts. AC was essentially paying money to a company that was competing with them for business. Therefore, AA risked losing the 15 percent of AC profits it gained each year, causing the potential split to have a significant financial impact.

On January 19, 1998, Arthur Andersen responded to Andersen Consulting's accusations by demanding $14 billion, no further use of the Andersen name, and return of all technology to settle the dispute according to the Florida Accords. Nine days later, Andersen Consulting claimed Arthur Andersen owed them $400 million, plus interest, costs, legal fees, and other payments for the income sharing payments they had made since 1994. Jim Wadia, managing partner of Arthur Andersen warned that the split could take up to five years, stating, "We adhered to the contractual obligations. We will rebut the allegations. Even if AC prove the allegations, they have to show damage."[3]

To further complicate matters, Andersen Consulting also filed suit in a federal court in New York to prevent Andersen Worldwide from passing a resolution that would pre-empt the arbitration hearings and provide a "protection committee" to protect both AA and AW from AC, essentially removing AC from the business immediately. Judge John G. Koeltl in Manhattan denied AC's request, stating that the matter should be resolved with private arbitration.[4]

Arbitration continued for two and a half years until arbitrator Guillermo Gamba of the International Chamber of Commerce passed down a resolution. The delay was due in part to the

---

[1] "Andersen Consulting Seeks Split," *Chicago Sun-Times, Inc.,* December 17, 1997.
[2] Kelly, Jim. "Andersen split to go to arbitration: Consultants allege breach of contract by sister firm," *The Financial Times* (London), December 18, 1997.
[3] "Accountancy chief warns dispute may last five years," *The Daily Telegraph*, February 2, 1998.
[4] "Court Refuses to Intervene in Andersen Feud." *The New York Times.* March 17, 1998.

need to use Columbia for the arbitration site, as it was one of the few countries where neither company had a member firm.[5] The decision was final and did not allow either company the opportunity to appeal.

Through the decision, Arthur Andersen's request for $14 billion, the 150 percent of Andersen Consulting's annual revenue as stated in the Florida accords, was denied in favor of requiring a payment of approximately $1 billion for past payments to AA. Arthur Andersen did retain the rights to any jointly developed technology and the Andersen Consulting name.

Andersen Consulting would have to give up the name they had spent years building. Both sides claimed victory in the verdict: Andersen Consulting on the basis that it did not have to pay Arthur Andersen the proposed amount and Arthur Andersen on the basis that it was able to retain the valuable Andersen name. However, the financial consequences may have been more detrimental than Arthur Andersen admitted to the press, since the same day the announcement of the judge's decision was revealed, Jim Wadia retired from the company. Official word on this surprising announcement focused on Wadia's abilities as a negotiator and the fact that the negotiations were over. However, speculation existed that this move reflected the fact that AA had chosen to pass up a previous, more lucrative offer by AC.

In the decision, Arthur Andersen retained the rights to the Andersen name, forcing Andersen Consulting to give it up officially on January 1, 2001. AC would only be able to associate themselves with the former name of Andersen Consulting for three months, at which time they would have to completely terminate all use of the name. Arthur Andersen could begin to use the name as early as January of 2002.

Choosing a New Name

Under the direction of James E. Murphy, Managing Director for Marketing and Communications, the company set about finding a new name. After an extensive search that included the use of an outside consulting firm, Andersen Consulting was renamed Accenture. The new name is a coined word submitted by Andersen employee Kim Petersen, a senior manager working in the Oslo, Norway office. "Accenture" is a combination of "accent" and "future." It is intended to express an emphasis on the future, which is what the company wants to do for its clients. The new wordmark for the company is the word "accenture" in all lower-case letters, with a greater-than sign over the "t." The greater-than sign is intended to put an accent on the future, conveying the idea that the company offers its clients solutions that are "greater than" their expectations.

Selecting the new name was not an easy process. In addition to representing the new face of Andersen Consulting, the selected name needed to pass a URL search for availability, as well as tests of pronunciation in foreign languages and cultural sensitivities. Employees were encouraged to submit suggestions along with brief supporting explanations. In total 2,677 entries

---

[5] "Breaking up is hard to do." *Financial Times* (London), August 7, 2000.

were submitted, of which 230 employee suggestions passed to the second round. Forty-eight names went into the final selection round, eight of which were employee suggestions.[6]

Accenture, Formerly Known as Andersen Consulting

The new name was not the only thing changing at Accenture. Even prior to the decision to give up its name, Andersen Consulting was looking to change the way it was perceived by the business community. The firm wanted to extend its areas of expertise beyond the boundaries of traditional consulting firms. Accenture sees itself as "the market maker, architect and builder of the new economy, bringing innovations to improve the way the world works and lives."[7] To fulfill this strategy the firm has built, and will continue to build, a network of businesses and strategic alliances able to meet all of its clients needs. These include consulting, technology, outsourcing, alliances, and venture capital. This new position is believed to capture the synergies available to the old and the new Andersen Consulting. It combines the traditional consulting and outsourcing business, including its channel strength, relationships, and proven solutions, with the firm's venture capital business, operating companies, and alliances that emphasize new technologies and business models. The focus and basis of all of the activities of the new firm is knowledge and expertise in management and technology.

> *At the core of our activities is a global consulting organization with the deepest reservoirs of industry knowledge, technological expertise and strategic insight in the world. In addition, we have forged a series of landmark joint ventures to create a network of operating companies to develop and deliver the latest business solutions. And through our investments in emerging technologies and business approaches we are giving our clients immediate access to the nascent developments from the front lines of the new economy.*[8]

The Re-branding Campaign

Due to the conditions of the break from Andersen Consulting, Accenture had just one year in which to introduce its new name to the world and convince its clients and potential clients that more than the name has changed. Given the importance of brand equity in the consulting market and the recognition of Andersen Consulting, successfully completing this task in the shortest amount of time possible would be critical to Accenture's continued success.

> *"Our positioning is also a tool that helps us achieve our vision. If our vision is the internal compass that guides us, our brand essence denotes the position we wish to occupy in the minds of our target audience."* Teresa Poggenpohl, partner and director, Global Brand, Advertising, and Research [9]

---

[6] http://www.accenture.com/, February 17, 2001.
[7] Ibid.
[8] Ibid.
[9] Ibid.

The re-branding effort would need to cover more than 70,000 employees, 178 offices worldwide, and more than 40,000 clients. At the same time, the terms of the settlement allowed Accenture only three months, starting on January 1, 2001, in which to use the Andersen Consulting name in association with its own.

Meanwhile, Accenture is also trying to change the business community's perception of the company, despite the fact that Andersen Consulting had a strong reputation built upon its traditional strengths. The re-branding publicity campaign started in late 2000 with prominent signs in airports and other areas frequented by business travelers hinting at a new name and more coming on 01.01.01.

Conclusion

Joe Forehand, James Murphy, Accenture's other top executives, the branding team, and the marketing team have a lot of work ahead of them. How do they organize a smooth transition to the new name within the company? How do they utilize the three months in which they can still use the Andersen Consulting name (as in "formerly") to let their target audience know about their new name? How do they present clients with their new vision for the company and the capabilities they are developing to support that vision? As the largest consulting company in the world, with $10 billion in revenue in 2000, their very livelihood could be at stake in the new millennium.

Questions

1. Who are Accenture's principal target audiences? Are these audiences different for the re-naming and the re-branding activities?

2. What should Accenture say to each audience, and how can it best convey the message?

3. How should the partnership transfer the brand equity of Andersen Consulting to Accenture? Can it be done?

4. How can Accenture manage doubts and confusion that may arise about their new capabilities?

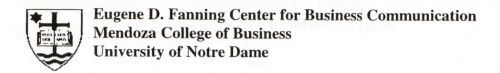
W® Hotels:
Comfortable, Stylish, and Wired for
Today's Savvy Business Traveler

Introduction

Barry Sternlicht, the 39-year-old Chairman and Chief Executive Officer of Starwood Hotels & Resorts (Starwood), followed Theresa Fatino into an office cluttered with piles of designer carpet swatches, draperies, and wallpaper. Fatino, a former designer at Pottery Barn and Ralph Lauren and the current Vice President of design and brand development at W Hotels, had been working on the specs for the launch of the very first W in New York City.

The launch of the new brand of hotels is the culmination of months of market research and strategic investment decisions by Sternlicht and his company. The hotel industry watched closely as the launch date approached. In order for the new brand to be a success, every detail had to be perfect, and it was Sternlicht's mission to ensure that they were.

The meeting with Fatino lasted several hours. Many decisions were finalized regarding the new design of in-room accessories that would differentiate W rooms from the generic hotel rooms in which most business people spent hundreds of hours. Later, Sternlicht reviewed the many details of the launch. He knew that the company was ready and that the market existed for this new, innovative type of hotel.

Nonetheless, there were questions about the strategy to communicate this new brand to its target market. Sternlicht thought of the marketing department and their many ideas to reach the right consumer. Although the design of W was special, Sternlicht thought that they had to do more than simply sell hotel rooms. They had to educate consumers and financial analysts alike about the newest innovations in hospitality efficiency and service.

This case was prepared by Research Assistants Megan Bonifas and Marc Van Neuren under the direction of James S. O'Rourke, Concurrent Associate Professor of Management, as the basis for class discussion rather than to illustrate either effective or ineffective handling of an administrative situation. Information was gathered from corporate as well as public sources.

Barry S. Sternlicht

A graduate of Brown University and Harvard Business School (1986), Sternlicht spent his early postgraduate years working for a real estate investment firm. By the mid-1990's he had thrown himself into the hotel business, acquiring brand names such as Westin and St. Regis. In 1998, Sternlicht stunned the hotel industry when he stepped in to buy ITT Corporation for $14.6 billion, essentially saving the company from a hostile takeover bid by Hilton. Sternlicht's passion for the hotel industry does not stop with the preservation of classic brands, such as Sheraton and Westin, but increases with the idea of revolutionizing the industry for a new market. In response to a visionary idea of combining style and technology, Sternlicht launched a new brand of hospitality, dubbed W. "W Hotels was an attempt to reach a segment of the market that really doesn't have a place to stay," Sternlicht said in a recent news article. "It's a place that speaks to a younger crowd, a slightly hipper crowd."[1]

Sternlicht's idea of a new hotel "style" was a result of his personal experiences as a traveling businessman. His new hotel chain, considered "style" hotels, would have to resonate its chic, hip, and high-tech focus in every one of its communication channels. In naming the new chain, Sternlicht wanted to convey a classy and sleek simplicity, yet a welcoming and warm idea of a good night's sleep. Indeed, the simple one-letter name conveys all of these things: "Warm," "Witty," "Welcoming," and "Wired."

Company Overview

Starwood is one of the world's largest hospitality companies with more than 700 hotels and 210,000 hotel rooms owned, managed, and/or franchised. In addition to W, the Company's proprietary brand names include Sheraton, Westin, The Luxury Collection, St. Regis and Four Points by Sheraton.

Starwood is comprised of two companies. The first is Starwood Hotels & Resorts Worldwide, Inc., a traditional "C" corporation that manages the hotel portfolio, among other things. The second is Starwood Hotels & Resorts, one of the nation's largest real estate investment trusts. The shares of common stock of Starwood Hotels & Resorts Worldwide, Inc. (the Corporation) and the Class B shares of beneficial interest of Starwood Hotels & Resorts (the Trust) are attached and traded together as one unit under the ticker symbol HOT. The attached shares may be held or transferred only in units consisting of one Corporation share and one Class B share.

In 1995, the Corporation and the Trust – known at the time as Hotel Investor's Corporation (HIC) and Hotel Investor's Trust (HIT) – consummated a reorganization with a predecessor of Starwood Capital Group, LLC (SCG), founded by Mr. Sternlicht, and certain affiliates of SCG. Following the reorganization, HIC and HIT were controlled by SCG and its affiliates, and they were renamed Starwood Lodging Corporation (SLC) and Starwood Lodging

---

[1] McGinn, Dan, "The Suite Smell of Success," *MBA Jungle*, November 2000, p. 44.

Trust (SLT). At the time, SLC and SLT combined held less than $200 million in total assets.[2]

Following the reorganization, the Company completed several public offerings, the proceeds of which were used in part to acquire several upscale, full-service hotel properties throughout the United States. By December 31, 1996, the Company had experienced tremendous growth. Total assets exceeded $1 billion, and its market capitalization had grown to more than $2 billion. However, Starwood still had no proprietary brands of its own. Consequently, its properties were flagged with other companies' brand names for which Starwood paid franchise fees. Despite this tremendous growth, not until 1998 would Starwood become a major player in the hospitality industry.

During the first quarter of 1998, Starwood acquired Westin Hotels & Resorts Worldwide, Inc. and ITT Corporation, currently Sheraton Holding Corporation, in transactions valued at approximately $2.0 billion and $14.6 billion, respectively. In addition, the Company changed its name to Starwood Hotels & Resorts Worldwide. By the close of the first quarter of 1998, Starwood's market capitalization soared to more than $7 billion, and it became one of the largest hotel companies in the world. Unlike many of the other large hoteliers, however, Starwood chose to focus almost exclusively on the upscale, full-service lodging industry. The fact that five of the Company's six brand names are directly associated with this segment of the market is clear evidence of this strategy.

As of December 31, 2000, Starwood held $12.7 billion in total assets. The year end revenue increased 13.5 percent to $4.3 billion, and net income grew to $403 million. The company had 129,000 employees and headquarters in White Plains, NY. Institutions owned approximately 83 percent of the company as of December 30, 2000.

Starwood has recently received praise from critics around the world. It was designated as the "World's Best Hotel Company" by *Global Finance* magazine in their September 2000 issue. For the second year in a row, Westin was rated number one in the upper-upscale category of *Business Travel News' 2000 Survey of Top Hotel Chains.* The *Condé Nast Traveler Magazine 2000 Gold List Readers' Choice Poll* included 33 Starwood properties among the top 500 places to stay in the world. In fact, Starwood owns or manages more *Gold List* winners than any other hotel company in the world.[3]

Starwood's loyalty program, Starwood Preferred Guest (SPG), which is available automatically to all Starwood shareholders, has received numerous awards. SPG was awarded the 1999 Hotel Program of the year by consumers in the prestigious Freddie Awards. In addition, it received awards for Best Customer Service, Best Web Site, Best Elite-Level Program, and Best Award Redemption. In April 2001, the SPG program signed an award redemption deal with its former subsidiary, Caesars Palace in Las Vegas, through Caesars' current owner, Park Place

---

[2] Starwood Hotels & Resorts Worldwide Form 10-K, December 31, 1995.
[3] Starwood Hotels & Resorts Worldwide Form 10-K, December 31, 2000.

Entertainment (PPE). This relationship with PPE is remarkable since PPE was actually spun off from Starwood competitor, Hilton, a few years prior.

The Hotel Industry

The hotel industry is made up of hundreds of companies that own, manage, and franchise hotels. The vast majority of hotels are owned by companies that most people have never heard of, but they are managed and franchised by the large, well-known hotel companies like Marriott and Hilton. For example, as of December 31, 2000, Starwood owned only 162, or 22 percent, of its hotel portfolio.[4] The majority of the remaining Starwood hotels are managed and franchised but not owned. This poses a challenge to the large hotel companies because hotel owners rely on the strength of the large companies' brand names and management skills to maximize earnings. This explains why few new hotel brands have been introduced recently. It also explains why most new brand introductions are associated with old brands, such as Courtyard by Marriott.

This, in turn, creates a dilemma for the brand owner. It also creates a problem for existing franchisees who are using the well-known brand that is being associated with the new brand. For the brand owner and existing franchisees, there is a risk associated with attaching a well-known brand to a new, and in many ways, dissimilar brand. This is especially true when brands known to serve an upscale clientele are associated with a brand that intends to cater to a mid-scale market. When, for example, Hilton Corporation introduced Hilton Garden Inn, a brand that Hilton describes as "an upscale mid-priced, focused service hotel concept,"[5] it had to consider the impact the new brand would have on its existing Hilton franchisees. When Starwood launched W, it did not associate this new brand with Sheraton, Westin or any of its other brands.

With hundreds of hotel companies and numerous hotel brands, the hotel industry is very competitive. In 2000, according to world rankings by *HOTELS* magazine, the 300 largest hotel companies had nearly six million available rooms. However, more than half of those rooms were owned, managed, and/or franchised by only ten companies. The ten largest companies, in terms of rooms available, from largest to smallest are: Cendant, Bass Hotels & Resorts, Marriott International, Accor, Choice Hotels International, Best Western International, Hilton Hotels Corporation, Starwood Hotels & Resorts Worldwide, Carlson Hospitality, and Hyatt Hotels/Hyatt International.

These giants of the hotel industry own many of the most popular hotel brands including Hilton, Sheraton, Westin, Marriott, Radisson, Clarion, Ritz-Carlton, DoubleTree, Embassy Suites, Hampton Inn, Crowne Plaza, Holiday Inn, Ramada, Inter-Continental, Red Lion, Days Inn Best Western, and Howard Johnson. Some of the well-known names that operate under smaller, independent companies include Four Seasons, Wyndham, La Quinta, Omni, and Loews. In addition, there are literally hundreds of boutique-style hotels around the world, especially in urban areas such as New York City, London, Paris, and Rome. Because Starwood's W

---

[4] Starwood Hotels & Resorts Worldwide Form 10-K, December 31, 2000.
[5] http://www.hilton.com, April 18, 2001.

emphasizes the global operation of hotels and resorts in the urban, full-service, upscale segment of the market, these boutique hotels may be W's greatest competitors. Among the more famous of these operators is New York City hotelier, Ian Schrager Hotels LLC. In addition, W competes with smaller, but well-known, brands such as Four Seasons, Trump, and Helmsley.

W® Hotels

In 1998 Starwood launched its newest brand, W, as a new, refreshing option for the business traveler. The intent of the launch was to combine the style and personality of an independent hotel with the superior business services of a major business brand. W was initially designed as a "lifestyle" experience for a new generation of travelers and was, therefore, intended to integrate the needs of today's business traveler – high-tech capabilities with a stylish, social environment.

As the first new upscale hotel brand to be launched in the hotel industry in 20 years, W was met with much speculation as well as interest from shareholders, financial analysts, and consumers. The idea was to offer an alternative for the business or leisure traveler that would combine the personality and style of independent hotels with the reliability and substance of a big hotel company. The marriage of these two components gave birth to the successful brand of "style" hotels – quality and functionality of a brand combined with a boutique hotel flair.

"The launch of W Hotels has represented an important evolution in the hotel industry, a union of style and substance," said Barry Sternlicht. "W Hotels offer the hip personality and chic style of an independent hotel, while providing the reliability and comprehensive business amenities and services that savvy travelers expect from large hotels. We call this concept the 'style' hotel."[6]

Starwood opened the first W property in December 1998. The 720-room W New York was in the heart of midtown Manhattan. From the beginning, a team of top designers and restaurateurs had assembled to create an "urban oasis" amidst the jungle of downtown city life.

W Style

In defining its new hotel brand, Starwood organized a talented team of top designers and architects to collaborate on the look and feel of the "W." Starwood Design Group achieved the W look and feel by combining sophisticated urban style with relaxed elegance in modern environments. One of the main priorities of the design group was to ensure unique styling with each property.

Each property presents décor that is reflective of the culture and environment in the surrounding city. Nonetheless, a signature W theme is evident in every hotel. For instance, each

---

[6] Briskin, Diane, "W Hotels – Starwood's Hottest Brand Combines Substance with Style," Press Release, July 2000.

hotel lobby leads to a "Living Room" designed to tempt guests to linger and relax while mingling with other guests who may be enjoying a drink or playing one of W's board games.

Other design elements that have become trademarks of the W style include an oversized desk, upholstered chaise lounge or banquette, natural fabrics throughout, and specially designed room accessories. The focus of all guestrooms is the luxurious W bed, with a pillow-top mattress, 250 thread-count linens, and goose down comforters and pillows. In addition to the amenities one would expect in an upscale hotel, the W guestroom includes a W CD, a coffeemaker with W's own blend of coffee, a lush terry-lined cotton piqué W bathrobe, and custom-formulated Aveda bath products. All of this has created an atmosphere where both function and comfort provide guests with a productive yet relaxing stay.[7]

W Market

The W guest needs and wants to be connected to the modern world, and the hotels provide this at every corner. To truly meet the needs of today's business traveler, guestrooms feature the latest in cutting-edge technology, including a 27-inch color TV equipped with ultra-fast Internet access via an infrared keyboard. Working guests can set up their own home office near the "Living Room" fireplace, in their rooms, or virtually anywhere in the hotel through high-speed data port connectivity at speeds up to 100 times faster than conventional data modems. Guests also can set up their own personal, secure e-mail addresses while staying at W.

Additionally, each room has two phones one with a dataport and speakerphone capabilities and another 900MHz cordless dual-line phone. Nearly any business equipment or service is available upon request to guests, and no fewer than 15 percent of the rooms in each hotel are designated "W Home Offices," offering special amenities geared specifically to the business traveler such as a combination printer/copier/fax/scanner.

Above and beyond the special amenities W offers, the hotels have a service commitment that provides "whatever you want, whenever you want it." Whether it is a laser printer at 2 a.m., a last minute fitting of a tuxedo, or a bath filled with chocolate milk, guests just need ask for their special requests to be fulfilled. Moreover, W guests are rewarded with eligibility to participate in Starwood's Preferred Guest program, lauded as the best hotel loyalty program by *USA Today* and by consumers through *Frequent Travelers Magazine's* "Freddie Award."[8]

"We wanted to target the young business travelers – those in the high-tech, entertainment, fashion, and publishing industries," says Brian Windle, vice president of sales and marketing for W hotels.[9]

---

[7] http://www.whotels.com.
[8] http://www.freddieawards.com.
[9] Khan, Salina, "Plenty of Pampering Define Boutiques," *USAToday*, October 6, 2000.

Conclusion and Discussion Items

In the hotel industry, brand names typically serve one purpose – to distinguish the level of service and cost associated with one brand as compared to another. For example, while Four Points by Sheraton seeks to associate itself with Sheraton, it also seeks to be recognized as more affordable than Sheraton. Guests then infer that Four Points by Sheraton will provide Sheraton-like, but fewer, services as a result of its lower price. In the case of W, however, Starwood Hotels is attempting to create an image of a service that is new and fresh, not just a more or less expensive version of something else. The following issues should be carefully considered:

1. Who are Starwood's stakeholders? How might each be affected by the W launch?

2. What message should be presented to consumers?

3. How should that message be delivered?

4. Who should the message target?

5. How will Starwood convince hotel owners to become W franchisees when W has no track record to date?

6. How will the launch of W affect Starwood's other upscale, full service hotel businesses?

7. How might current upscale Starwood franchisees be affected by the new brand?

Starwood Hotels & Resorts (ticker: HOT, exchange: New York Stock Exchange) News Release - 4/2/1998

STARWOOD HOTELS & RESORTS WORLDWIDE, INC. ANNOUNCES THE LAUNCH OF 'W' HOTELS

Business Hotel Group to Open in U.S. Beginning in Fall 1998,

Combining Reliability, Top Amenities and Distinct Sense of Style

(Phoenix, AZ – April 2, 1998) -- Starwood Hotels & Resorts Worldwide, Inc., will launch W Hotels, a new brand of business hotels to debut nationwide beginning in Fall 1998. The announcement was made today by Barry Sternlicht, Chairman of the Board of Directors of Starwood Hotels & Resorts Worldwide, Inc., and Chairman and CEO of Starwood Hotels & Resorts.

The innovative W group, which will initially comprise 10 hotels opening in major U.S. cities over the next 15 months, is designed to provide discerning business travelers with a comfortable, sophisticated place to stay quite unlike anything they've ever experienced in a business hotel.

Says Sternlicht, "We feel that the launch of W Hotels represents an important evolution in the hotel industry, a unique union of style and substance. All W Hotels will offer the highest level of service to meet every business need and the benefits of our Starwood guest programs, while each property will have its own distinct personality and a strong, very smart sense of style – something which really doesn't exist in the business travel market today."

Featuring a residential feel in the guestrooms and a hip, urban style throughout, W will offer the personality and individuality of an independent, boutique hotel yet also guarantee the reliability and superior level of business amenities and services which business travelers require.

W hotels will be located in major cities across the U.S., the first three opening in New York City. The first W New York will open in Fall 1998 at 541 Lexington Avenue, in what is currently the Doral Inn. Two other properties, currently the Doral Tuscany and Doral Court at 120 and 130 East 39th Street respectively, will debut in early 1999. Seven additional W hotels are scheduled to open by June 1999 in cities to include Los Angeles, Chicago, Seattle, San Francisco and Denver. While sharing a common aesthetic and standard of service, each W will have its own distinct personality, bringing together the best of what each city has to offer. The properties will range in size from approximately 120 to 450 rooms.

The W guestroom will be an oasis of relaxed elegance, designed for exceptional comfort in a sophisticated urban style. W trademarks will include a luxurious bed, oversized mahogany desk, chaise lounge, natural fabrics throughout and specially designed room accessories. Commented Hilary Billings, Senior Vice President of Brand Development and Design for Starwood Hotels & Resorts Worldwide, Inc., "We are taking a very basic, yet completely novel approach to the design of W hotels. I think there are a lot of business travelers who need to get their job done, yet want the same level of style and comfort in hotels that they enjoy in their own homes, and W is going to provide that."

For doing business at W hotels, every need will be anticipated and fulfilled, from E-mail to business services to scanners, printers and the latest computer equipment. Also, all W guests will enjoy the benefits and perks of the upcoming Starwood international reservations system and premier membership program – debuting this fall as the world's largest, encompassing all W, Westin and ITT/Sheraton hotels worldwide.

Among the guest facilities planned at W hotels are a comfortable, active lobby for relaxing or socializing; an intimate café and newsstand open throughout the day and night for a quick bite or drink; a first-class, independent restaurant designed to attract guests and locals alike, and a health club with the most advanced equipment available. In addition, some W hotels will offer spa services.

As for the W name, Sternlicht explains, "W is for witty, warm, wonderful. Essentially, it is for 'wonder why no one has ever done this before.'"

W hotels are managed by Starwood Hotels & Resorts Worldwide, Inc., a hotel operating and management company whose shares are paired and trade together as a unit with Starwood Hotels & Resorts, the nation's largest hotel real estate investment trust (NYSE: HOT).

Source: Michael Doneff, Susan Magrino Agency, April 2, 1998. Reprinted with permission.

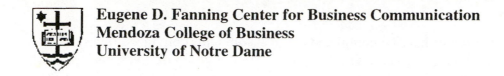
General Motors Corporation and the Death of the Oldsmobile

"We're committed to make every brand a success...All the brands we've got we plan to keep."

-Rick Wagoner, GM CEO, November 2000[1]

The minute the story broke, the finger pointing began. The brand managers blamed the advertising agency for ineffective advertising campaigns. The advertising agency blamed the brand managers for "not being car guys" and for managing the brand to death. The dealers blamed GM executives for making the decision to abandon its core customer base. GM executives blamed dealers for not giving Oldsmobile proper attention in relation to other non-GM brands. Oldsmobile, the 103-year old brand with a history rich in innovation and success stories, was to be phased out.

History of Oldsmobile

As the oldest nameplate in the auto industry, Oldsmobile was a living legend. Founded in 1887 by Ransom E. Olds in Lansing, Michigan, Oldsmobile grew to become one of General Motors' strongest brands. Olds' first cars were powered by steam engines manufactured at his father's company. Soon, Ransom Olds realized that the internal combustion engine provided

---

This case was prepared by Research Assistants J. Berent and J. Meier under the direction of James S. O'Rourke, Concurrent Associate Professor of Management, as the basis for class discussion rather than to illustrate either effective or ineffective handling of an administrative situation. Information was gathered from corporate as well as public sources.

---

[1]"GM Betrayed Oldsmobile Fans," *Automotive News*, November 6, 2000.

more power. With production of his first completed car, Ransom Olds convinced investors to put up capital for mass production of a car. On August 21, 1897, a group of investors formed the Olds Motor Works in Lansing, Michigan.[2]

In 1900, the first Olds Motor Works manufacturing facility was built in Detroit, Michigan. By 1902, the Curved Dash Olds, which sold for $650, quickly gained recognition in the auto-manufacturing world.[3] In March 1902, a fire burned the Detroit factory to the ground. The combination of the Curved Dash Olds' reputation and the news of the fire at Olds Motor Works created a new interest in the auto-manufacturer. To fuel the newborn interest in the Olds Motor Works, Roy D. Chapin, friend of R.E. Olds, decided to drive a Curved Dash Olds from Detroit to New York for the New York Auto Show. Chapin accomplished the goal of driving all 278 miles. At the time it was the longest trip ever taken in an automobile. Thanks in large part to the success of the Curved Dash Olds, the fire at the plant, and Chapin's trip, orders for the Olds skyrocketed. With such demand for his product, R.E. Olds rebuilt the plant.[4]

In early 1904, a dispute between R.E. Olds and investors forced a split in the company. R.E. Olds moved his part of the company from Detroit back to Lansing, leaving the trademark name Oldsmobile behind. Without the trademarked name, R.E. Olds produced cars under the name REO instead. By 1908, R.E. Olds had four times the number of sales (4,105) than the Oldsmobile company back in Detroit (1,055). In the same year however, sales fell and the future looked bleak. William Durant purchased the Detroit-based Oldsmobile manufacturer and folded it into General Motors' Durant. REO sales also fell drastically, and by 1936, Lansing-based REO had stopped producing cars. REO kept the truck division of the Lansing-based business running until White Trucks purchased it in 1957.[5] General Motors eventually reestablished Oldsmobile as a Lansing, Michigan-based company.

Innovation at Oldsmobile

Over the years, General Motors has turned to Oldsmobile to supply cutting edge technology. Oldsmobile had been innovative from its founding in the late 1800s. R.E. Olds became the first mass producer of gasoline cars in the world. In 1901, it was Ransom E. Olds who used an assembly line to mass-produce the Curved Dash. Henry Ford later copied and perfected Olds' concept of assembly line mass-production. In 1926, General Motors' Oldsmobile division became the first automaker to use chrome-plated trim. Eight years later, in 1934, Oldsmobile introduced independent front suspension and hydraulic brakes. The 1940 Oldsmobile lineup revolutionized driving through the introduction of a feature called the Hydra-Matic drive. This $57 option removed the need for a manual transmission, therefore introducing the world to automatic transmissions. Oldsmobile's 1949 "Rocket 88" was the first high

---

[2] Wright, Richard A. "Oldsmobile was America's Oldest Surviving Nameplate," *Detroit News*, November 6, 2000.
[3] Gross, Daniel, "Old Glories," *US Airways Attaché*, April 2001.
[4] Ibid.
[5] Ibid.

compression V-8 engine in the auto industry. In addition, Oldsmobile offered the first domestic diesel engine as part of their 1978 full car lineup.

The most significant innovation by Oldsmobile was the 1966 Toronado. The Toronado was the first U.S. built modern day front wheel drive car. General Motors adapted this technology throughout the company. GM was now able to manufacture front wheel drive cars, which handled better in poor weather conditions and had higher fuel economy rates. By 1974, Oldsmobile offered driver's side airbags in all Toronados.[6]

General Motors Car Divisions

In a 1924 message to stockholders, GM would offer, 'A car for every purse and purpose' with the idea that as customers' economic status improved, they would trade up from Chevrolet to Pontiac to Oldsmobile to Buick to Cadillac. Chevrolet targeted entry-level buyers, while Pontiac, Oldsmobile, and Buick offered models that moved progressively up the price scale. Cadillac offered vehicles for the higher-priced market looking for luxurious cars.

From the 1930s to the late 1950s, each of GM's divisions sold distinct models. Every brand offered a different engine, chassis, and body style to create individual personalities, but the models did share basic components to cut costs. In 1959, GM deviated from this manufacturing philosophy and introduced smaller cars that shared platforms, a practice that became known as badge engineering. Oldsmobile, Pontiac, and Chevrolet models were virtually identical except for their body panels and upholstery. Only small stylistic changes identified a particular car.

Japanese Invasion

From the early 1900s, when Henry Ford's newfangled "horseless carriage" revolutionized the way people traveled, through the Great Depression and the two World Wars, U.S. automakers dominated the U.S. market. Nameplates such as Nash, Ford, Chevy, Studebaker, and Chrysler were parked in driveways, at churches, and on downtown streets. In 1950, domestic carmakers held over 96 percent of the U.S. auto sales.[7] (Exhibit #1).

The oil crisis of 1973 came as a particular shock to Americans. Suddenly, driving a car that only ran ten miles to a gallon was no longer affordable. The government initiated a host of regulations concerning fuel efficiency, clean air standards, and safety. American auto manufacturers found it difficult to design cars that matched these standards. The U.S. automaker dominance ended in the late 1960s and early 1970s. Higher quality and more efficiently

---

[6] Wright, Richard A., "Oldsmobile was America's Oldest Surviving Nameplate," *Detroit News*, November 6, 2000.

[7] Womack, James P., Daniel T. Jones, and Daniel Roos, *The Machine That Changed The World* (Harper Perennial, New York, New York) 1991, p. 45.

manufactured Japanese cars entered the U.S. marketplace, and Detroit felt it. Japanese auto manufacturers' share of the world market grew from less than 3 percent in 1955 to over 31 percent in 1988.[8]

The Japanese produced smaller, lighter, more fuel-efficient cars and focused on customer satisfaction. The Japanese made huge strides in style, including creating glossy paints, friendly interiors with appealing trim, and other features such as internal trunks and gas cap releases. Japanese management practices were lean and flexible without rigid hierarchies or acrimonious labor relations. At the same time, Japanese firms guaranteed employment for life. As a result, quality was built into the system.[9]

The Japanese automakers experienced such tremendous growth around the world and particularly in the U.S. that they established "transplants" in the United States. In 1985, Toyota built two adjoining auto plants including a stamping facility, a plastics plant, and a power train plant in Georgetown, Kentucky. Meanwhile, Nissan built an assembly plant in Smyrna, Tennessee. Honda established a U.S. plant in Marysville, Ohio. These U.S.-Japanese-based production facilities adapted many of the efficient Japanese manufacturing principles, known as lean manufacturing, into their U.S.-based plants. The adaptation of lean manufacturing concepts allowed the Japanese manufacturers to produce vehicles with less waste and to produce higher quality cars. Japanese manufacturers sold these cars for the same price, or less, and made larger profit margins on the vehicles compared to the U.S. makers. The large profits generated from these new sales in the U.S. helped the Japanese to expand their overall market share in a short period of time. In 1989, the Honda Accord became the best selling car in America, a first for a Japanese vehicle.

By the mid 1980s, the major U.S. manufacturers, Ford, GM, and Chrysler, regrouped and fought back. Chrysler introduced cutting edge concepts such as the minivan. Ford moved forward with its "Quality is Job #1" theme to reinforce the idea that American quality was back. General Motors, hoping to learn more about the Japanese manufacturing process, formed an alliance with Toyota. They assembled cars jointly at their New United Motor Manufacturing Inc. (NUMMI) plant in Fremont, California.[10]

The 1980s

Oldsmobile offered over 15 different models for the midsize car market in the 1980s. (Exhibit #2) Oldsmobile models such as the Cutlass, Delta 88, Ninety-Eight, and Cutlass Ciera

---

[8] Ibid.

[9] http://www.thecorporatelibrary.com/cases/cs_gm.html

[10] Womack, James P., Daniel T. Jones, and Daniel Roos, *The Machine That Changed The World* (Harper Perennial, New York, New York) 1991, p. 122.

provided drivers with a ride on a "road sofa" complete with bench seats and column shifts. Oldsmobile gained credibility with buyers of 60 years and over, and these buyers were extremely loyal to Oldsmobile.

In the late 1980s, baby boomers reached their prime earning and spending years. Male baby boomers entering their 40s were different from their fathers at that age. They lived within a perpetual youth culture -- they broke with the past and created a new future. The boomers had a strong appetite for clothes, electronic toys, cars, entertainment, and values. As families became smaller, and as men entered their 40s and 50s, they desired a more fuel-efficient, better designed, more stylish car to meet their families' needs.

As sales of import vehicles like the Honda Accord and the Toyota Camry took off, GM repositioned Oldsmobile as an import fighter. They attempted to capitalize on consumers' changing preferences for more stylish vehicles. Oldsmobile targeted its vehicles toward a younger, more affluent generation of baby boomers. For the first time, Oldsmobiles claimed to be the best car for a younger generation of consumers instead of promoting its cars as the best form of transportation. In 1988, GM called upon longtime advertising agency, Leo Burnett USA, to develop an ad campaign that would change the image of Oldsmobile. Leo Burnett USA developed a television ad campaign called, "This is Not Your Father's Oldsmobile." The ad featured models like the Cutlass, Delta 88, Ninety-Eight, and the Toronado in sporty driving situations. Singers chanted, "This is Not Your Father's Oldsmobile. This is a New Generation of Olds." Older, loyal customers wondered whom Oldsmobile was targeting, and baby boomers mocked the campaign stating, "Olds is Old."[11]

Oldsmobile Gets a Makeover

In 1994, the Oldsmobile division announced "The Centennial Plan," that called for rolling out all-new Oldsmobile models by 1997, just in time for Olds' 100th birthday. GM invested an estimated $5 billion in the project, and engineers developed sleek, aerodynamic designs with windswept lines and sculpted corners—a far cry from the boxy, conservative bench seat and column shift designs of the Ninety-Eight, Eighty-Eight, and Cutlass Supreme. John Rock, General Manager of Oldsmobile, bought 275 foreign-made cars and ordered members of Oldsmobile's product teams to drive them. Their mission was to figure out what consumers found so appealing about the Toyota Camry and the Honda Accord, as well as to find ways to fashion those attributes into a new Oldsmobile. Every Friday the Olds product teams went over, with painstaking detail, what they wanted Olds to be.

The first model launched under the Centennial Plan, the Aurora, featured a silver script "A" logo instead of the traditional Oldsmobile rocket logo. Consumer research conducted during the Aurora development revealed that potential buyers loved the car when it didn't have the

---

[11] http://ad-rag.com/sections.php?op=viewarticle&artid=53

Oldsmobile emblem. They responded negatively when the rocket logo was present on the car.[12] The new vehicle lineup soon made its debut without the Oldsmobile name. The lineup included the entry-level Alero sedan, the premium midsize Intrigue sedan, the Silhouette minivan, the premium 4-door Aurora sedan, and the full-size Bravada sport utility vehicle. Each model was priced and positioned to compete with foreign automobile manufacturers' models. (Exhibit #3) Between 1996 and 2000, Oldsmobile introduced the new models and gradually phased out the older models. (Exhibit #4)

Oldsmobile ran more television and print ads in order to win over the younger, more affluent generation of people interested in import automobiles. One television commercial was a parody of a Gap ad. It featured groups of young adults standing against a white background, singing about being in cars to the tune of Gary Numan's song, "Cars." Another ad proffered former Beatles drummer Ringo Starr and his daughter. Other featured ads in the campaign were quick-paced with edgy images and rock music urging consumers to "Start Something" and "Get out of Neutral."

Brand Management at General Motors

In 1996, during the rollout of the new Oldsmobile models, General Motors formally adopted a brand management system under the advice of John Smale, a retired Chief Executive Officer of Procter & Gamble. Smale believed that if brand management worked for products like soap and toothpaste, elevating companies like Procter & Gamble to the top tier of consumer products companies, it would certainly work for cars and trucks. Smale recruited Ron Zarella, President of sunglass maker Bausch & Lomb, to take over GM's sales and marketing operations. Zarella recruited brand managers from consumer packaged goods companies like Procter & Gamble, Warner Lambert, and Scott Paper Company.

GM implemented the brand management system to create clear and distinct images for each division as well as to eliminate overlap. The system also sought to reduce development time, improve cost competitiveness, and increase profits and market share by assigning accountability to individual brand managers. The brand managers worked closely with design and manufacturing chiefs to match specific customer needs that had been identified through market research. GM believed customers would benefit from this type of management because they would be able to better understand the vehicles. This would ultimately create strong loyalty for the brands.

Under Zarella, GM brand managers developed the following brand positioning statements for each of the GM divisions.[13]

---

[12] http://www.kbb.com/kb/ki.dll/kw.kc.rp?kbb&&11&95aurora

[13] G. Stern. "GM's New Marketing Chief Seeks Clarity Amid Muddle of Overlapping Car Lines." *The Wall Street Journal*, May 1, 1995, A3, A13.

Division	Brand Positioning
Chevrolet	High volume car and light truck division, should offer affordability, dependability, reliability, and widest range of models.
Pontiac	Sporty brand, standing for youthfulness and spiritedness and featuring sleek, athletic, and "in your face styling."
Saturn	Focus on "an overall shipping, buying, and ownership experience" targeting import-buyers and standing for dependability, intelligence, and friendliness.
Oldsmobile	Logical step up for Saturn buyers; medium-priced cars to compete against Audi, Acura, and entry-level Infiniti and Lexus.
Buick	Premium American car with substantial, distinctive, powerful, mature styling targeting baby boomers in their 50s.
Cadillac	Luxury car with innovative, responsive, sophisticated, highly perfected cars; competing against Mercedes, BMW, and Lexus.
GMC	Premium truck brand with differentiated products from Chevrolet.

Oldsmobile Dealer Network

The Oldsmobile dealer network consists of 2,801 dealerships, 63 of which are Oldsmobile-only dealerships. In some instances, dealers sell other GM brands and non-GM models in addition to Oldsmobiles. The dealers enter into franchise agreements, or legally binding contracts, with General Motors to provide sales, service, and support for Oldsmobile models.

In 1996, J.D. Power & Associates conducted a Dealer Attitude Study Survey to give dealers the opportunity to describe their levels of satisfaction regarding their relationships with the manufacturers. The results showed that strong gains in satisfaction among dealer principals went to Toyota Motor Sales, Chrysler Corporation, and Mercedes-Benz. The news was much less positive for General Motors. Six of GM's nameplates—GMC, Oldsmobile, Buick, Pontiac, Chevrolet, and Cadillac had scores far below the industry average. Oldsmobile dealers gave GM the lowest dealer satisfaction rating out of all GM divisions.[14] In contrast, Saturn Corporation, another division of General Motors, had the industry's highest level of dealer satisfaction.[15]

Deteriorating Results

During the early 1980s, Oldsmobile posted record high sales in excess of 1 million cars per year. In 1983, Oldsmobile was the United States' third best-selling brand behind Chevrolet and Ford. In fact, more Oldsmobiles were sold that year than all Chrysler products combined.[16] Oldsmobile continued to prosper into the 1986 model year, and buyers 60 years and over could not get enough of the Oldsmobile bench seats and column shifts. Oldsmobile commanded a ten percent market share, and dealers fared well, earning profit margins of approximately 12 percent-14 percent on each Oldsmobile they sold.[17]   But in 1987, Oldsmobile sold nearly 400,000 fewer cars than it had in 1986. (Exhibit #5)

By 1999, Oldsmobile posted sales just over 350,000 vehicles and commanded a two percent market share of the total North American vehicle market.[18] This blared in contrast to its ten percent market share in the 1980s. Dealer profit margins shrunk to approximately six percent, down from roughly 14 percent in the 1980s. Relative to the steady sales of other GM divisions, Oldsmobile sales fluctuated over the years. (Exhibit #6)

The Announcement

On Monday, December 11, 2000, dealers received phone calls inviting them to watch a closed circuit broadcast the following day. As news of the broadcast leaked out, dealers speculated as to whether they were going to hear news about a new vehicle launch or a new advertising campaign. Instead, on Tuesday, December 12, 2000, GM Chairman Jack Smith and Sales Vice President William Lovejoy, greeted them and stated that the Oldsmobile division would be phased out. Dealers were shocked upon hearing the news and stated that there was "no forewarning, no premonitions."[19] Dealers were even more shocked to learn that the news was revealed to them at the same time as it was to the media.

GM executives were short on details but stated that GM would take a one-time charge of $939 million in the fourth quarter of 2000 for the Oldsmobile phase out, including $583 million to cover payments to dealers and others.[20] CEO Wagoner stated to the media that GM would continue to sell Oldsmobiles "until it is no longer economically viable." He went on to say,

---

[14] http://www.jdpower.com

[15] http://www.jdpower.com/global/jdpaawards/releases/61218car.html

[16] http://www.usatoday.com/money/autos/2000-12-13-olds-sales.htm

[17] Personal interview with Oldsmobile dealer, wishing to remain anonymous

[18] http://detnews.com/1999/autos/9901/16/01150159.htm

[19] Williamson, Doug, "Phase-Out Surprised Auto Dealer," *Reporter-News*, December 14, 2000.

[20] Ellis, Michael, "GM Firmly Shuts Door on Oldsmobile Future," *Yahoo Daily News*, December 12, 2000.

"Despite major investments that resulted in critically acclaimed new Oldsmobile products, the division was still unprofitable, and its sales volume continued to erode. We stretched to find profitable ways to further strengthen the Olds product line, including developing products with our global alliance partners, but in the current environment there was no workable solution."[21]

The shutdown of Oldsmobile was announced as part of a company-wide restructuring that would cut 20 percent of GM models by 2004, would allow GM to deploy resources to its other divisions, would launch new vehicles at a faster pace, and would strengthen the remaining brands in its North American portfolio.[22] Additionally, the phase out of Oldsmobile meant elimination of ten percent of its salaried workforce in North America and Europe. It also meant the permanent shutdown of the Delta engine plant in Lansing, Michigan, as well as production cuts at Saturn plants in Wilmington, Delaware, and Spring Hill, Tennessee. GM announced that the restructuring would lead to a special pretax charge ranging from $1.5 billion to $2.5 billion in the fourth quarter.[23] GM executives admitted that the permanent impact of the phase out on the city of Lansing, Michigan, was not clear, as was the effect on the thousands of Oldsmobile dealerships around the country. However, they suspected no factory closings or blue-collar layoffs since the GM factories that produced Oldsmobiles also made similar cars for other divisions.

Plans for the Dealers

The original offer issued on December 14, 2000, from GM executives to compensate its Oldsmobile dealers included the following:

Support

- The establishment of a toll-free hotline to address issues, concerns, or problems; staffed by contract employees who took messages and passed them along to GM executives.
- The deployment of transition teams in each of GM's five regions who would work with dealers on an individual basis to facilitate a smooth and orderly transition.

Compensation

- $400 cash directly to each salesperson for every Oldsmobile he or she sold.
- 60 days of interest-free floor planning for any Oldsmobiles ordered through April 2001.

---

[21] http://www.generalmotors.com
[22] http://detnews.com/2000/autos/0012/13/a01-161708.htm
[23] http://www.post-gazette.com/businessnews/20001213olds8.asp

- Up to $2,400 per car sold during a dealer's best year of the three years from 1998 through 2000, not including fleet sales.
- The option to take a standard vehicle payout or to argue for payout of "special circumstances" such as recent dealership renovations, new signs and displays, and long-term advertising contracts.
- Repurchase of unsold dealer inventory from the 2000 and 2001 model years.

GM executives increased the franchise buyout offer by 20 percent, to $2,800, in a letter to the dealers on January 26, 2001. The executives hoped to avoid a clash at the scheduled meeting in February at the National Automobile Dealers Association (NADA) convention in Las Vegas. GM Sales Vice President William Lovejoy stated in the letter to the dealers, "We realize this letter does not answer all of your questions and requests. It is part of a genuine effort by GM to work through the Oldsmobile transition consistent with our commitment to gain dealer trust as a top priority of our entire organization."[24]

In return, dealers who accepted the offer had to agree to cancel their Oldsmobile franchises at a later date. Dealers, however, would retain ownership of the buildings and property.[25] Only dealers with exclusive Oldsmobile dealerships or whose overall sales were more than 75 percent Oldsmobile vehicles would receive the higher payout. For dealers whose overall sales were less than 10 percent Oldsmobile, the minimum payout was $1,675 per vehicle. That means an exclusive Olds dealer selling 500 vehicles a year could get $1.45 million.

Upon receipt of the letter containing the revised buyout offer, many dealers still expressed dissatisfaction. Leo Jerome, owner of three Oldsmobile dealerships in Warren and Lansing, Michigan, stated, "What they don't get is you just didn't take away what (the dealership is) worth, you took my life away. I don't think this is over. I don't think they have any conception what they're headed for."[26]

During the week of February 6, 2001, GM executives met with dealers behind closed doors at the NADA conference to provide clarification of the buyout offer.[27] GM executives also advised dealers to expect a warning a year before Oldsmobile would be formally killed off.

Some dealers left the meeting expressing their desire to sell other GM brands even if they disliked the Oldsmobile decision. On the other hand, some dealers vowed to cancel orders for new vehicles and threatened to file class action lawsuits against GM, charging that GM violated existing franchise agreements. Oldsmobile dealers had renewed their five-year franchise agreements with GM approximately one month before the announcement to phase out

---

[24] http://detnews.com/2001/autos/0102/02/b01-182684.htm
[25] Ibid.
[26] Ibid.
[27] Suhr, Jim, "GM, Dealers Discuss Oldsmobile Phaseout," *The Nando Times,* February 6, 2001.

Oldsmobile. Bill Lovejoy warned that if dealers filed suits, the company would stop talking to all dealers about buyout offers.[28]

Ernie Swanson, who had been an Oldsmobile dealer for almost 28 years said, "We were continually told things were going to get better, that Olds was here to stay, that there'd be better advertising. But sales steadily fell. Basically, I'm a used-car dealer masquerading as an Olds dealer." [29]

Plans for Customers

GM offered Oldsmobile customers a certificate worth $1,500 toward the purchase or lease of another GM vehicle to customers who purchased or leased a 1996 model or newer and still retained it. GM also increased its GM Protection Plan for Oldsmobile owners from 3 years/36,000 miles to 5 years/60,000 miles. Warranty on repairs would be honored at any GM dealership in an emergency situation. GM also established a toll-free phone number for customers to call with any questions or concerns.

Qualified buyers interested in purchasing a new Oldsmobile would be offered 0.9 percent financing, up to $3,000 cash back on the 2001 Bravada, or $2,000 cash back on Aurora, Silhouette, Alero, and Intrigue models. [30]

No Change of Heart

When GM announced the sales incentives on new Oldsmobiles, sales for the month of December 2000 were up 10.6 percent from a year earlier, despite slow sales everywhere else in the industry. January 2001 sales were up 30.4 percent from the same month in 2000.[31] Nonetheless, this burst of sales was not enough to change GM's mind about phasing out the Oldsmobile division.

With the launch of the newly redesigned 2002 Bravada on the horizon, GM planned to spend an estimated $400 million in media spending in 2001 to support the vehicle launch and other Oldsmobile events.

---

[28] Welch, David, "Ending Olds: Sticker Shock for GM-and its Dealers," *Businessweek*, February 7, 2001, p. 13.
[29] http://www.aemag.com/printedition/toc2001/features/01jan/out_cold.html
[30] http://www.oldsmobile.com/brandwideNewsReviews.asp
[31] http://www.usatoday.com/money/autos/2001-02-19-olds-deals.htm

Questions

1. What are the critical issues that GM faces in phasing out the longest running brand in its history?

2. Was GM's plan for communicating with its dealers and customers fair? Was GM's plan for compensating its dealers and customers fair?

3. Was GM's reasoning for phasing out Oldsmobile justifiable? Is GM taking the right steps to phase out the division?

4. Was a brand management system appropriate for GM?

5. Who are the key stakeholders affected by the announcement to phase out Oldsmobile?

Exhibit 1
Market Share Rankings
Years 1950, 1970, 1994

Rank	1950	1970	1994
1	GM	GM	GM
2	Ford	Ford	Ford
3	Chrysler	Chrysler	Toyota
4	Studebaker	Volkswagen	Volkswagen
5	Nash	Fiat	Nissan
6	Kaiser-Frazer	Toyota	Chrysler
7	Morris	Nissan	Fiat
8	Hudson	Renault	Peugot
9	Austin	British Leyland	Mitsubishi
10	Renault	Peugot	Honda
			Mazda
			Renault

Exhibit 2
Oldsmobile Models Sold During the 1980s and 1990s

1980s	1990s
442	Eighty-Eight
Eighty-Eight	Ninety-Eight
Ninety-Eight	Achieva
Calais	Alero
Ciera	Aurora
Custom Cruiser	Bravada
Cutlass	Calais
Cutlass Supreme	Ciera
Cutlass Ciera	Custom Cruiser
Cutlass Cruiser	Cutlass
Delta 88	Cutlass Calais
Dynamic 88	Cutlass Ciera
Firenza	Cutlass Cruiser
Omega	Cutlass Supreme
Regency	Delta 88
Toronado	Intrigue
Touring Sedan	LSS
Trofeo	Regency
	Silhouette
	Toronado
	Touring Sedan
	Trofeo

Source: http://cartalk.cars.com/Survey/Results/Demographics/Comments/Oldsmobile/index.html

Exhibit 3
Oldsmobile's Centennial Plan New Vehicle Lineup

Model	Positioning	Price Range
Alero	Oldsmobile's entry-level coupe or sedan	$17,210-$22,190
Intrigue	Oldsmobile's premium midsize sedan	$22,515-$26,635
Silhouette	Oldsmobile's minivan	$26,655-$33,320
Aurora	Oldsmobile's redesigned flagship 4-door sedan	$30,619-$34,794
Bravada	Oldsmobile's premium midsize SUV	$31,635-$34,167

Source: http://carpoint.msn.com/browse/Oldsmobile.asp. Reprinted with permission.

Exhibit 4
Total Oldsmobile Sales
1996-2000

Oldsmobile Cars	1996	1997	1998	1999	2000
Achieva	40.344	63.196	888	0	0
Alero	0	0	28.134	118.907	122.722
Cutlass	434	26.708	53.438	32.677	1.243
Ciera	89.577	4.322	63	0	0
Cutlass Supreme	81.263	40.717	1.601	78	0
Eighty Eight	58.525	67.190	65.877	23.915	477
Ninety Eight	12.626	666	48	0	0
Intrigue	0	23.460	90.563	90.057	64.109
Aurora	23.717	25.404	21.374	16.321	28.250
Total Oldsmobile Cars	**306.486**	**251.663**	**261.986**	**281.955**	**216.801**

Source: http://www.autointell.com. Copyright 2001. Reprinted with permission.

Exhibit 5
Oldsmobile Sales
1984-1999

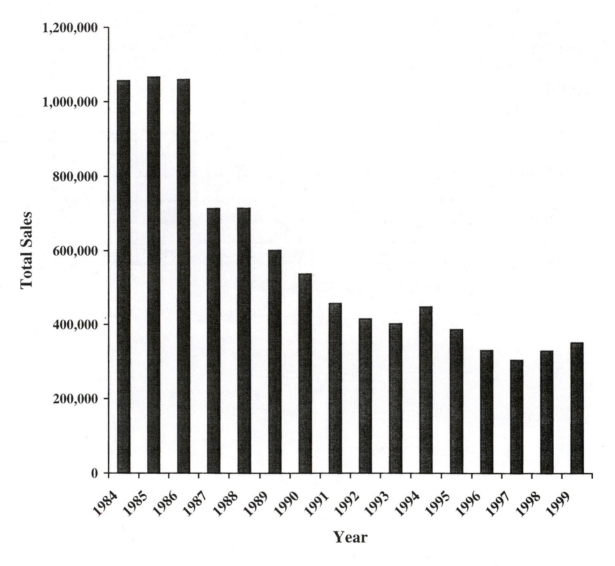

Source: Kiley, David.   "Oldsmobile Might Be Nearing Final Lap."   USA Today, July 13, 2000 pg 2.   Copyright 2000, USA TODAY.   Reprinted with permission.

Exhibit 6
Deliveries of Chevrolet, Pontiac, Buick, Oldsmobile, GMC, Saturn, and Cadillac
1996-2000

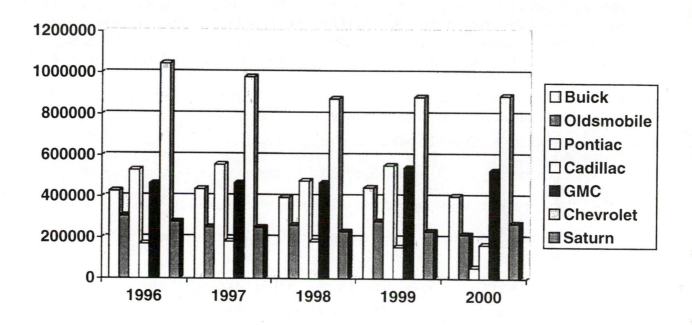

Source: http://www.autointell.com. Copyright 2001. Reprinted with permission.

Exhibit 7

NADA TO GM: DO THE RIGHT THING

NADA officials are calling on GM to do the right thing by Oldsmobile dealers by going beyond the basics spelled out in their franchise termination clauses. In a meeting the day after GM's announcement, top association leaders and Olds dealers told Bill Lovejoy, group vice-president of GM's North American Vehicle Sales, Service, and Marketing, that the automaker had a responsibility to be broad-minded in determining compensation and assistance for its 2,801 Olds dealers.

Compensation should be based on dealers' sales over a 5- or 10-year period and should consider their investments in brand programs. It should also reflect such costs as:

- advertising to assure the public the y're still in business;

- expensive employee training, especially for techs;

- data-processing hardware and software bought to interface with Olds;

- long-term commitments for advertising, employee health insurance, and other benefits; and

- devaluation of used Olds vehicles recently bought or taken in trade.

In a written "Action Statement," NADA also says GMAC should provide low- or no-cost loans to help dealers with LIFO, and give floor-planning assistance for as long as it takes to move inventory. And GM should offer employee-retention programs for techs as well as salespeople. Using this input, GM is in the process of hammering out formulas to ensure that Oldsmobile dealers are fully and fairly compensated.

Source: http://www.aemag.com/, January, 2001. Reprinted with permission.

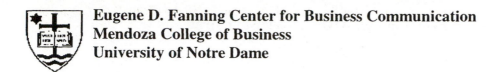
Sears, Roebuck and Co. and
The United Colors of Benetton

Since day one, Arthur C. Martinez's career at Sears, Roebuck and Co. had not been without challenges. The now hyper-competitive retail industry had been flooded with new competitors who positioned themselves in specific segments where Sears had been the market leader for decades. Throughout his tenure, Martinez was constantly faced with the challenge of making strategic decisions quickly. Issues concerning growth and expansion, alliances, earnings, corporate reputation, employee welfare, and marketing came across his desk daily and each action contributed to the massive financial turnaround of Sears that occurred in the late 1990's – a recovery widely credited to Martinez's management expertise.

The morning of February 16, 2000, brought with it an opportunity for yet another strategic decision. What had been hailed as a brilliant alliance for both Sears and Benetton, a cutting-edge Italian fashion label, had turned into a situation in dire need of immediate attention. The sensitive nature of the most recent Benetton advertising campaign, "We On Death Row," had prompted protests from Sears employees who demanded that Benetton merchandise be immediately removed from Sears stores. Should Martinez heed the demands of his employees, who are widely believed to reflect the overall attitudes of Sears' consumers, or remain true to the alliance recently established with the stylish and sophisticated Italian retailer? Would continued protests and publicity negatively impact the successful turnaround efforts? Was it necessary to stop selling Benetton merchandise in order to quell the controversy? Additionally, would Ron Culp, Senior Vice President for Public Relations and Government Affairs, and Tom Nicholson, Director of Public Relations, be able to handle this issue effectively enough to satisfy the many different parties affected by and interested in this issue? Martinez realized the critical need to answer these questions quickly and that careful and appropriate actions would be essential.

This case was prepared by Research Assistants Anne K. Hellwig and Erin E. Loughney under the direction of James S. O'Rourke, Concurrent Associate Professor of Management, as the basis for class discussion rather than to illustrate either effective or ineffective handling of an administrative situation. Information was gathered from corporate as well as public sources.

Sears and Benetton Split Over Advertising Strategies

When Sears entered into an agreement with Benetton in October of 1998 to sell the Benetton USA line of clothing in more than 400 Sears outlets, the company knew that Benetton had a history of producing controversial print advertisements. Sears, however, was assured that the Benetton USA line (exclusive to Sears stores) would carry advertising and signage distinct from that of other Benetton stores and product lines and that this separate advertising campaign would shield Sears against any controversy that arose from other Benetton ad campaigns. Apparel sales at Sears outlets had fallen dramatically over the past few years and a new look and feel to product offerings was the only way to salvage this segment of operations. An alliance with Benetton seemed a logical way to proceed as that company sought to increase U.S. sales in order to supplement its primarily European base. Tom Nicholson, Sears's Director of Public Relations, expressed the situation quite clearly:

> We always knew there was some risk in any type of joint marketing venture with Benetton. They were hip, edgy and were known for a chic urban style. However, everything about this venture was separate from United Colors of Benetton; styles were more mainstream, the merchandise was made by a third party manufacturer, and the marketing message was to be completely different. Quite simply, we knew that at some point Benetton's overall image and advertising would no longer be compatible with that of Sears but we certainly did not expect this to occur so soon, just months after the our agreement was signed.[1]

What Sears did not realize was just how far Benetton would continue to "push the envelope" in terms of advertising designed to stimulate brand awareness and encourage consumers to buy more of its apparel – all under the guise of promoting social and political awareness. Sears found out when Benetton launched its latest campaign, "We on Death Row."

The ad campaign featured 26 men and women who were either facing the death penalty or who had been executed by the time the ads went to press. The advertisements only mentioned the charges of which the individuals were convicted and provided no detail of their crimes. The ads did not display any Benetton clothing in the pictures.

Sears' Corporate Communication staff knew that the company's primary customer base consisted of middle-American people with traditional, conservative values. As demonstrations were held outside Sears' Houston offices to protest Benetton's "We On Death Row" ad campaign, and employees who had lost loved ones to those profiled in the Benetton ads contacted Sears headquarters, Ron Culp knew the company must take action. Not only were employees and customers hurt by the painful memories dredged up by seeing convicted felons on

---

[1] Telephone interview, April 5, 2000.

billboards and in telephone kiosks in New York City, but Sears found themselves in an especially precarious situation of appearing to take a position on the death penalty.

Sears, Roebuck and Company

Sears, Roebuck and Company is a leading U.S. retailer with annual revenues of $41 billion in 1999 generated from apparel sales and home and automotive products and services. The company serves families across the country through more than 850 full-line department stores, 2,100 specialized retail locations, and a variety of online offerings accessible through the company's Web site, **http://www.sears.com**. Founded in the late 1800s as a mail order company that predominantly serviced farmers and rural families, the company has retained strong ties with its Midwest heritage and customers.

Benetton

Benetton Group SpA is engaged in the design, manufacture, and marketing of distinctive casual apparel for men, women, and children, marketed principally under the brand name United Colors of Benetton. The company is traditionally known for knitwear and casual clothing in a wide array of colors and is recognized for fashionable Italian design and a youthful image. Benetton's philosophy has been to offer, on a worldwide basis, product lines with sufficient breadth to accommodate the needs of many markets. Benetton also licenses its trademarks for products manufactured and sold by others, including fragrances and cosmetics, watches, sunglasses, and other fashion accessories designed to complement its core product lines.

The Franchising Contract

In the Fall of 1998, Sears and Benetton executed a contract through which Sears agreed to carry Benetton USA merchandise in approximately 400 Sears stores. In part, this deal was an attempt by Benetton to re-establish itself in the U.S., after years of decline had led to the U.S. market accounting for only 5 percent of Benetton's total business. Likewise, the agreement was an attempt by Sears to reposition itself in the youth clothing market and attract younger consumers to its stores. The deal was lauded as an excellent move for both companies.

Benetton's Advertising History

Although Benetton's early advertisements were rather conventional, focusing on the product and stressing the quality of the wool the company used, Benetton grew accustomed to controversy surrounding its advertising campaigns. The first U.S. advertising campaigns were handled by a small agency and stressed the European origins and international success of Benetton. In 1982, however, Luciano Benetton, chairman of Benetton Group, met Oliviero Toscani, a well-known fashion and advertising photographer who lived in Tuscany and had studios in Paris and New York. Toscani convinced Benetton that the company had to promote its brand as a lifestyle, not as a clothing business.

Benetton's initial campaigns with Toscani were conventional in style. They stressed social status and conformism, and featured groups of young people wearing Benetton clothes. The first real departure from the original styling arrived in 1984 with the concept of "All the Colors in the World." Advertisements in that campaign portrayed groups of teenagers from different countries and ethnic groups dressed in colorful knitwear. While there were some negative reactions to these advertisements, overall the public greeted the campaign with enthusiasm. During the late 1980s, Benetton continued to use multi-racial messages to promote its clothes, a "united" Benetton. The company also believed that it was promoting a message of racial equality. But throughout the years, the advertisements grew more controversial and continued to offend various groups around the world with their shocking nature.

By the 1990s, Benetton campaigns began to tackle issues beyond racism. Also designed by Toscani, the ads had images of a man dying of AIDS, a priest kissing a nun, a newborn child covered in blood, and two horses, one black, one white, copulating. According to Benetton, all the campaigns presumed to offer some social message and the company was trying to promote debate of serious social issues.

In order to increase sales at the United Colors of Benetton retail stores, Benetton introduced the advertising campaign conceived by Toscani called "We On Death Row." In the U.S., Benetton opened the campaign with a 96-page supplement that was attached to the February issue of *Talk* magazine. The campaign included interviews with convicted killers and featured photographs of 26 condemned people in different U.S. states. Only the charges of which they were convicted were mentioned. No details of their crimes were provided, and no photographs or images of Benetton clothing were shown.[2]

The written profiles were mostly sympathetic, focusing on regrets about their plight and offering few details about the crimes they were convicted of committing. The photographs were shot in the photojournalist style of Toscani, who had developed Benetton's branding for two decades. He claimed that his campaigns are all based on the same premise: "We are all equal. There is no reason to slaughter each other, to fight, not even to hate each other. We can wear whatever we want, whatever colours, we want just to live."[3] Toscani also insisted that his advertisements do not exploit sensitive social issues in order to sell knitwear. He asserted,

> It's the other way round. I exploit clothing to raise social issues. Traditional advertising says if you buy a certain product you will be beautiful, sexually powerful, successful. All that [stuff] doesn't really exist. I'm not doing that.[4]

---

[2] Rees, Jon, *Sunday Business*, Sunday Business Group, January 30, 2000.
[3] Adams, Tim, "Focus: Advertising Wars: Cost of a Killer," *The Observer*, February 20, 2000.
[4] Rees, Jon, *Sunday Business*, Sunday Business Group, January 30, 2000.

Benetton also claimed that the portraits, with accompanying interviews, would "give the prisoners back their human face and highlight the present of those without a future."[5]
To create the campaign, Toscani joined forces with the National Association of Criminal Defense Lawyers, which strongly opposes the death penalty. Benetton and the Association told prison officials they were making an "international photo documentary" project sponsored by Benetton. There was no mention of the advertisements and Toscani was described only as a "photojournalist."[6] Ken Shulman, who conducted the interviews for Benetton's magazine was described as a "*Newsweek* magazine contributor."[7] Some prison officials, however, felt they were misled and claim that they did not know the prisoners were being used for advertising.

Benetton has said the following about its communications campaigns:

The choice of new communication channels has prompted advertising campaigns on issues of social and current interest worldwide, such as racism and AIDS, conservation, life and death. Oliviero Toscani's photos for Benetton picture reality but, perhaps because they do, the images themselves become a focus for debate and discussion, transcending the bounds of advertising to enter the realm of artistic expression and depict our era. Exhibitions of Benetton ads have been mounted by museums and cultural institutions throughout the world, including the Old England Museum in Brussels, the Corporate Art Museum in Tokyo, the Bienal in Sao Paulo, Brazil, and the Cable Factory in Helsinki. Communication is complemented by initiatives in support of international humanitarian associations, like SOS Racisme, for whom Benetton organized the first world conference in Treviso in 1996, and FAO (Food and Agricultural Organisation of the United Nations), who invited Benetton to devise a communications campaign for the first World Food Summit held in Rome in 1996.[8]

Negotiations Begin

Fortunately, Arthur Martinez received advance warning of the "We On Death Row" campaign several weeks prior to launch. After previewing the campaign in a marketing trade publication, Martinez immediately realized the delicate implications of such a message reaching the community. He sent an urgent message through Ron Culp to Tom Nicholson and the Public Relations staff saying, "Begin talks with Benetton and review all options from A) how to better differentiate United Colors of Benetton to Z) actually removing merchandise from our stores." Martinez hoped that a compromise could be reached and either production of the Benetton USA merchandise could be stopped or the ad campaign halted.

---

[5] Kerrigan, Michael, *The Scotsman*, The Scotsman Publications Ltd., January 28, 2000 pg.22.
[6] Ibid.
[7] Ibid.
[8] http://www.benetton.com/, Who We Are, Our Communications.

Nicholson explained,

> We had hoped that by approaching Benetton before the Talk magazine insertion, we would be able to avoid the controversy. Soon after talks began however, three things became apparent: 1) There would be no apologies. Benetton stood firmly behind its strategy of using shocking advertising to sell its clothing. 2) There would be no scaling back of production. Third party manufacturers had been contracted with and there was clearly not enough time to unravel these contracts. 3) Finally, Benetton had an agenda. The "We On Death Row" campaign was part of an overall business strategy and the promise of increasing U.S. sales was a minor goal in the overall scheme of things.[9]

What could Sears do? The Public Relations department believed they had achieved a major coup when Benetton agreed to halt all insertions of the advertising campaign past February 2000, and limit the exposure in the United States. Sears soon realized that Benetton never intended to run this campaign longer than February and exposure in the U.S. would be limited to only a few national publications and outdoor advertising in New York City.

The Decision

Benetton's decision to continue increasing the "shock value" of its advertisements in order to sell clothing had appeared to work – until February of 2000. Although Martinez and Sears executives had been aware of the Italian retailer's philosophy and the franchise agreement had been financially successful, the protests by Sears employees against the Death Row campaign were now generating substantial negative publicity and contradicting the original goals of the alliance.

While controversial advertising had worked effectively for decades in the fashion industry, it also had drawn serious objection from political, social, and religious leaders. Martinez was now faced with the decision of whether to be the first to draw the line and denounce profiting from such exploitation.

Questions

1.   From the Sears, Roebuck and Co.'s standpoint, why do they feel they need to separate themselves from Benetton's "We On Death Row" campaign?

2.   How should Arthur Martinez handle the situation?

3.   Should Martinez denounce the campaign?

---

[9] Telephone Interview, April 5, 2000.

4.   Should he pull Benetton products from Sears' stores?

5.   How should Sears handle the publicity?

6.   What should Sears' message be to the public? What about Benetton's message?

7.   In this case, is any publicity good publicity?

8.   How should Sears evaluate the impact of a social controversy in relation to image? To sales?

9.   What ethical issues arise in terms of corporate responsibility to the public and a contractual agreement with another corporation in this kind of scenario?

PART II

Diversity and Corporate Culture

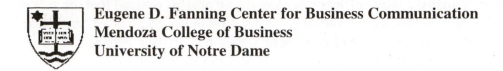
Denny's Restaurants:
Creating a Diverse Corporate Culture

On the morning of February 5, 1995, Jim Adamson walked into the corporate headquarters of Flagstar Companies (renamed Advantica Restaurant Group in 1998) in Spartanburg, South Carolina. As Flagstar's newly hired CEO, he was responsible for the future of the firm – a future he knew would be difficult. After a series of recent events, Adamson knew that Flagstar was in need of serious change. His predecessor, Jerry Richardson, struggled to keep the company alive with $2.3 billion in debt from a series of restructuring attempts in the 1980s. Despite his attempts, the company lost money for five consecutive years from 1989 to 1993.

Adamson also had to consider the issue of discrimination. Flagstar was the parent company of Denny's restaurants, a chain that had become a symbol for racism in the United States. He also had some serious questions about the firm he had just taken charge of. Would he be able to improve the financial performance of the firm? Could he begin to change the pervasive culture throughout the firm that had allowed these events to take place? As he sat at his new desk, Adamson began reviewing the challenges he faced.

April Fool's Day

On April 1, 1993, a group of 21 uniformed United States Secret Service agents stopped at a Denny's Restaurant not far from the Andrews Air Force Base in Annapolis, Maryland. They had a free hour before their detail would assemble and had decided to stop for breakfast. Of the 21 men, seven were African-American. Six of them – Alfonso Dyson, Melvin Fowlkes, Merrill Hodge, Joseph James, Leroy Snyder, and Robin Thompson – sat at a table together. The other 15 agents sat elsewhere.

Many of the agents ordered the All-You-Can-Eat breakfast, a menu feature allowing a customer to choose five items from the menu and eat all he wanted for one price. After 30 minutes, however, the table of black officers had still not been served any food, while the other officers were already eating. Robin Thompson asked their server twice about their meals, but

This case was prepared by Research Assistants M. Jennifer Abes, W. Brent Chism, and Thomas F. Sheeran under the direction of James S. O'Rourke, Concurrent Associate Professor of Management, as the basis for class discussion rather than to illustrate either effective or ineffective handling of an administrative situation. Information was gathered from corporate as well as public sources.

was told to wait. William Winans, a white officer who was sitting nearby, noticed that the server had made a face and rolled her eyes as she left the table. After 45 minutes had passed, the black officers noticed that customers who entered half an hour after they had arrived were already served their meals. Further, their fellow officers were being served second helpings. At this point, Thompson asked to see the restaurant manager.

Given that the group was on a tight schedule, James Sobers, the agents' supervisor, advised that they should file a complaint against the restaurant. When the restaurant manager approached them, the agents asked for his name and the address of the Denny's regional management office. The manager, who did not seem to understand English, only provided them with the address of the restaurant itself.

Alfonso Dyson stated later, "I didn't want to believe it was discrimination. But I couldn't think of what else it would be." [1] The six Secret Service agents, soon after the incident, filed a class action race-discrimination lawsuit against Denny's.

Events That Followed

Some three weeks later, on April 24, 1993, the company released a statement from corporate headquarters regarding the event, stating that after an on-site investigation of the incident, the manager involved was terminated. They also stated their commitment to further investigation of the incident and the elimination of any possible racial discrimination.

The incident involving the Secret Service agents was far from a one-time occurrence. Rather, discrimination against minorities was pervasive throughout the Denny's culture. Discrimination had been previously reported, even before any lawsuits were filed. This incident, however, triggered a growing number of customer complaints and subsequent lawsuits. Denny's had become, in the words of Jim Adamson, "a poster child for racism."[2] One law firm, Saperstein Mayeda, even ran advertisements targeted at minorities, inviting those who thought they had been discriminated against at any Denny's restaurant to contact the firm for information. This led to a strong, negative public image for Denny's and more plaintiffs. Also contributing to negative publicity was the fact that another, similar class-action lawsuit had been filed by a group of young African Americans who were asked to prepay at a Denny's restaurant in California. Ironically, the lawsuit had been settled the same day that this incident had occurred.

Jerry Richardson, CEO of Flagstar companies at the time, quickly settled both lawsuits. By December 1995, Denny's had paid $54 million to 294,000 customers and their lawyers, the largest public accommodations settlement ever.[3] Denny's was forced to sign a consent decree with the U.S. Justice Department, which mandated that Denny's restaurants publicize its nondiscriminatory policies and train employees about diversity issues. Further, a civil rights monitor was assigned to keep tabs on all 1,721 existing restaurants, as well as any future restaurants, for the next seven years.

---

[1] Adamson, Jim, *The Denny's Story*, New York, 2000, pp. 8-9.

[2] Adamson, Jim, *The Denny's Story*, New York, 2000, p. 9.

[3] Rice, Faye, "Denny's Changes Its Spots," *Fortune*, 1996.

Flagstar Companies: Corporate History

In 1961, Jerry Richardson, former wide receiver for the Baltimore Colts, and Charles Bradshaw, his college football teammate, bought the first Hardee's franchise in Spartanburg, South Carolina. By 1969, they grew their franchise into Spartan Food Systems and went public. In 1979, a conglomerate, TransWorld Corporation, acquired the company. Bradshaw chose to leave the company while Richardson decided to stay on and run his division. In 1986, TransWorld spun off many of its non-food related investments and renamed itself TW Services. The following year, TW Services purchased Denny's restaurants, along with El Pollo Loco, a chain of grilled-chicken restaurants, and Richardson became president of the food service company. (In an effort to centralize overall company operations, Denny's corporate headquarters was moved from Irvine, California, to Spartanburg in 1991.) In 1989, the company took on a huge debt as a result of a hostile takeover by the private equity firm of Gollust, Tierney, & Oliver. In 1992, Kohlberg, Kravis, Roberts & Co. (KKR), rescued the company by investing $300 million of equity to restructure its debt. This investment gave them control of the company and a new name in 1993: Flagstar Companies.

Flagstar Companies: Key Leaders

Jerry Richardson, CEO of Flagstar, had mishandled several financial and racial issues during his tenure. In 1990, before any racial issues were publicized, Richardson had hired a consulting firm, Synetics, to help Flagstar develop a strategy to mold the company into a top-ranked food service organization. Following a series of employee focus groups, Synetics' initial observations focused on a lack of diversity within the company. Despite being warned that the firm was in a dangerous position, Richardson saw no urgency to make any changes. His response to Synetics was, "I'm sure you're right about our being behind on diversity, but I never thought about it."[4] When racial problems first arose, Richardson and his management team wrote them off as isolated incidents.

Despite such neglect, Richardson grew Flagstar under his leadership into a $3 billion company, and made Denny's restaurants the nation's largest, best-known family restaurant chain. His goal was to make Flagstar the best food service company in the world by the year 2000. After a 33-year career in the restaurant business, however, Richardson resigned as Chairman of the Board and Director of Flagstar Companies. After relinquishing his Chief Executive title, Richardson turned his attention to the Carolina Panthers, a National Football League team that he owned. The majority owner of the Flagstar Companies, KKR, recruited Jim Adamson from Burger King to replace Richardson as CEO of Denny's parent company. Within months after the Secret Service agent incident, Adamson hired Ron Petty, former head of Burger King USA, as CEO of Denny's to manage the chain's transformation.[5]

Jim Adamson's personal history was a good fit for the job as Flagstar's new CEO. After growing up in the racially mixed environment of Army bases around the world and in the neighborhoods of Washington, D.C., and Oahu, Hawaii, Adamson was sensitive to acts of racial

---

[4] Ibid, p. 4.

[5] Adamson, Jim, *The Denny's Story*, New York, 2000, p. 20.

discrimination. Because of that background, Adamson would be certain not to tolerate them at Flagstar. He had developed a reputation as a calm and approachable leader. A former boss once noted that because of his sincerity, Adamson's team was devoted to him.

Racism within Flagstar

By the early 1990s, racial issues were still common to Flagstar. Many communities in California had already begun to complain about the treatment they had received at Denny's restaurants. Further, the U.S. Department of Justice had begun looking into charges that Denny's demonstrated a pattern of discrimination against customers who were African-American. In fact, Richardson, who was chairman of Flagstar at the time, had begun talking with local NAACP members as early as January of 1992 to find ways to respond to the challenge of diversifying the company.[6]

Although there had never been a deliberate corporate policy advocating discrimination, top executives of Flagstar did not pay much attention to what was happening in their restaurants. Their ignorance allowed many restaurant managers to set their own racist policies. Some managers asked African American diners to show identification before being served, requested that they pay before food arrived, and forced them to wait interminably for their meals.[7] Some were even known for ordering "blackouts," a situation in which employees were directed to lock patrons out of the restaurant.

Flagstar was insensitive to minority business people as well. Samuel Maw, Flagstar's executive vice president and chief procurement officer, claimed that it was extremely difficult to find minority vendors. Minority vendors who called on Denny's, however, claimed they were ignored by the company's buyers.

Key External Factors

Because of the nature of race relations in the United States, any organization that participates or is accused of discriminatory practices will face a number of external challenges, including unwanted press attention, lawsuits, and scrutiny from organizations such as the National Association for the Advancement of Colored People (NAACP) and People United to Save Humanity (PUSH). Denny's faced such a situation on April 1, 1993. The same day that the firm settled a federal discrimination lawsuit, the Denny's restaurant in Maryland refused to serve six African-American Secret Service agents while their white counterparts were served. Because of this incident and the company's checkered past, Adamson knew that Denny's was at a crossroads. He had to fix this or risk losing the company.

During this latest crisis, Denny's endured relentless press coverage of not only the current racial incident involving the six Secret Service agents but also its history of nationwide discrimination. The media coverage included a press conference with the six agents, interviews with disgruntled employees, and other angry former customers. Closely following the media coverage was a class action lawsuit and additional scrutiny from organizations such as the

---

[6] Adamson, Jim, *The Denny's Story*, New York, 2000, p. 14.
[7] Segal, David, "Denny's Serves Up A Sensitive Image," *Washington Post*, 04/07/99, p. E1.

NAACP, PUSH, and the Southern Christian Leadership Conference (SCLC). The class action lawsuit helped prolong damage from the racial problems at Denny's and its parent company. Additionally, these activist groups began using Denny's to help promote their own agendas and organize boycotts of the restaurants. Adamson knew those groups, well intentioned though they may have been, would have the potential to damage the long-term growth of a firm more than any lawsuit.

Can Denny's Hit a Grand Slam?

Adamson stood up and walked to the window. It would take an enormous amount of hard work, innovation, and commitment to turn this company around. Many stakeholders were involved. Could he satisfy each of their needs? Denny's current strategy was somewhat low-key and focused principally on internal change. Would this strategy work to resurrect Denny's name?

Questions

1. As Jim Adamson, what would your managerial approach be in this sensitive situation?

2. List key issues for Jim Adamson to address at this point.

3. How does a company categorize discrimination in order to create an effective corporate policy for diversity in the workplace?

4. How can Adamson and Flagstar Companies effect change and sustain that change in the corporate culture?

5. How can they manage diversity throughout the organization?

6. Is a strong communication campaign needed to ensure the public of Denny's commitment to diversity or is a more subtle approach needed?

7. How can Flagstar Companies go about reaching the public with their message of diversity?

8. How should Adamson respond to the special interest groups?

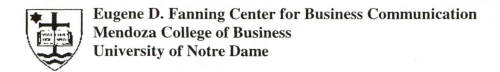
Texaco, Inc.
Racial Discrimination Suit

Amidst pending allegations that Texaco had consistently failed to promote blacks in certain employee groups because of their race and had "fostered a racially hostile environment,"[1] Texaco was hit with yet another allegation. As reported by *The New York Times* on November 4, 1996, Texaco executives were taped discussing a $520 million lawsuit which was filed by six employees in 1994 on behalf of almost 1,500 other minority workers at the firm. In these discussions, "senior Texaco managers made disparaging comments about minorities and discussed destroying documents related to [the] class-action discrimination suit."[2]

Texaco Chief Executive Officer, Peter I. Bijur, now faced a major corporate crisis in just his sixth month at the helm of Texaco. "The tape recording is [the latest] piece of evidence in [the] anti-discrimination lawsuit brought against the company in two years."[3] Texaco's history of hiring and promoting minorities was less than exemplary, even for the oil industry. The written transcripts of the audiotape, as provided to the courts by an ex-Texaco executive, containing racial slurs and stating intentions to destroy evidence, threatened to exacerbate Texaco's already mounting minority-related issues. The once hardly-noticed racial discrimination suit, Roberts v. Texaco, quickly began to attract media and public attention.

This case was prepared by Research Assistants Tanya Goria, DeWayne Reed, and Dan Skendzel under the direction of James S. O'Rourke, Concurrent Associate Professor of Management, as the basis for class discussion rather than to illustrate either effective or ineffective handling of an administrative situation. Information was gathered from corporate as well as public sources.

---

[1] Eichenwald, Kurt. *The New York Times*, "Texaco Executives, On Tape, Discussed Impeding a Bias Suit," November 4, 1996, Section A, Page 1, Column 1.
[2] *Business Week*, "Texaco: Lessons From A Crisis-In-Progress," News: Analysis & Commentary, December 2, 1996.
[3] Eichenwald, Kurt. The New York Times, "Investigation Finds No Evidence of Slur on Texaco Tapes," November 11, 1996, http://www.dorsai.org/.

The Charge

Among the many questions immediately facing Texaco's CEO, Peter Bijur, were these: What action should he take on behalf of the company in response to the newly released tapes? What would the best approach be in managing this public relations disaster? Should employees be addressed separately from the public sector? Is racial discrimination part of the Texaco culture? What, if any, steps can be taken to minimize future discrimination practices? Are reparations necessary? If so, how should it be addressed?

Texaco, Inc. Background

"Texaco Inc., originally known as The Texas Company, was founded in 1902 in Beaumont, Texas, by oilman 'Buckskin' Joe Cullinan and New York investor Arnold Schlaet."[4] In 1996, the time of the case, Texaco ranked number 11 on the *Fortune 500* (Exhibit 1) list and employed more than 27,000 people worldwide.[5] Within the petroleum industry, Texaco ranked third behind Exxon and Mobil. At year's end in 1996, Texaco had assets of $27 billion and revenues of more than $45 billion.[6]

The company's recent employee history had been less than ideal. *The Wall Street Journal* reported that:

> Texaco had been a snakepit of disappointed middle management since the
> 1980s . . . . It went from 11 layers of management to five, dumping tens
> of thousands of employees over the next decade. Last year [1996], in fact,
> was the first in a long time that Texaco's payroll grew instead of shrank.[7]

Middle management discontent may have been an issue, but Texaco claims to have been working earnestly toward a more integrated work force, despite the layoffs. In a November 1996 interview on *Nightline*, Texaco CEO Peter Bijur offered this assessment of Texaco's employment figures: "16.6% of our U.S. work force of 27,426 were minorities in 1991, while as of last June, 22.3% of our 19,554 employees were minorities. Of those employees, the percentage of minorities in supervisory, management and executive positions was 6.8% in 1989, and 9.5% in 1994."[8]

---

[4] Texaco, Inc., Home Page, "A Brief History of Texaco," http://www.texaco.com/.

[5] Bijur, Peter, I. Statement of Chairman and CEO, Texaco, Inc. to Company Employees, Friday, November 15, 1996, http://www.texaco.com/.

[6] Texaco, Inc., Home Page, "A Brief History of Texaco," http://www.texaco.com/.

[7] Jenkins, Holman, W., Jr., "History of a $20 Million Lie, Business World," *Wall Street Journal,* Tuesday, August 12, 1997, p. A15.

[8] Fritsch, Peter, " Texaco's New Chairman Navigates PR Crisis," *The Wall Street Journal*, Friday, November 8, 1996, pp. B1, B5.

In early 1996, the Equal Employment Opportunity Commission (EEOC) reviewed the lawsuit against Texaco and found that black workers seeking promotion were chosen "at rates significantly below that of their non-black counterparts."[9] The EEOC's finding also supported the results of a study of one Texaco division by the Department of Labor. They discovered that minority employees took up to twice as many years as white workers to win promotions and ordered Texaco to pay compensation and revise its company-wide appraisal system.

Another survey, carried out for a rival oil company, found that the proportion of highly paid black workers at Texaco was consistently below the industry average. White senior managers at Texaco outnumbered their black counterparts by more than 80 to one.

The Meeting

During a 1994 meeting between Texaco finance department manager Richard Lundwall and other Texaco finance department managers, recordings were made by Lundwall allegedly detailing derogatory remarks being made by the department managers concerning Texaco's African-American employees. "The transcript filed by Plaintiffs of the pending discrimination lawsuit against Texaco contains four instances of remarks with apparent racial connotations: (1) a statement characterizing African-Americans as "f****** n****rs"; (2) a statement, 'you know how black jelly beans agree,' followed by other remarks relating to jelly beans; (3) references to an event at which African-Americans allegedly sat through the playing of the United States National Anthem and then stood for a song presented as the Black National Anthem; and (4) references to Hanukkah and Kwanzaa."[10] Further comments included: "All the black jelly beans seem to be glued to the bottom of the bag."[11]

The behavior captured on tape revealed discrimination issues within the culture at Texaco. The term "black jelly beans" was used on the tape and Bob Ulrich, an attendee of the meeting and one of the individuals who used the term, through his attorney Jonathan Rosner, stated that the reference on the tape was not in any way intended to be a racial slur. Rosner pointed out that the term "jelly bean" is not, in and of itself, known to be a derogatory term, and Ulrich had no reason to think that the reference carried any such connotations.

Rosner also observed that Ulrich's reference to jelly beans was prompted by a speech given by an African-American at a conference at which the speaker, advocating integration and opposing separatist philosophies, illustrated his remarks by using jars of jelly beans as an analogy for racial integration. "While Ulrich could not remember the name of the speaker to whom he referred, Dr. R. Roosevelt Thomas, Jr. was identified as the probable source of the remarks

---

[9] *The Economist*, "Black Hole: Race in the Workplace," November 16, 1996, v341, n7992, p. 27.

[10] Court TV Library Home Page, Report from Independent Investigator, http://205.181.114.35/library/business/texaco/report.html.

[11] Eichenwald, Kurt, "Investigation Finds No Evidence of Slur on Texaco Tapes," *The New York Times*, November 11, 1996.

alluded to by Ulrich. Dr. Thomas is the founder and former President of the American Institute for Managing Diversity, at Morehouse College in Atlanta, Georgia."[12]

Public Outcry

The public was outraged when it received the initial reports that top executives within Texaco had made derogatory remarks about its African-American employees. Those derogatory remarks seemed to validate the public thought, feeling, and insecurity surrounding Corporate America. At a time when affirmative action was being questioned, and the issues of prejudice and injustice were being debated, tangible evidence was offered that the "good ole boys" network, "glass ceilings" and many other negative Corporate America caricatures did in fact exist. This incident was specific to Texaco, but the public sentiment reflected a wider scope of discriminatory issues.

Rev. Jesse Jackson quickly became the voice of the black community, calling for a boycott of all Texaco products. The public responded by cutting up Texaco credit cards and boycotting independent Texaco dealers. Wall Street recognized the potentially disastrous effects on business and adjusted its stock price accordingly. Texaco stock traded at 99 $^{5/8}$ at the opening on November 4, 1996, and dropped to 97 by the end of trading that day.

Unresolved Issues

At the time of the case, Texaco, Inc. appeared to have disproportionately lower levels of minorities in roles of authority as compared to whites. Also it should be noted that the discrimination lawsuits supported by the tape were pending prior to the meeting in 1996. The U.S. EEOC had begun an investigation into the employment practices of Texaco prior to the taping of the conversation. These and other unresolved issues appeared to support the notion that Texaco had substantive discrimination problems that management would have to address directly.

Questions

1.   What are the critical issues surrounding the newly released tapes?

2.   How should Peter Bijur and Texaco respond to the allegations? How should the company respond to the publicity?

3.   Should the employees be addressed separately from the general public? How can Texaco mend fences with minority employees and customers?

4.   What would be an effective corporate strategy in dealing with encouraging diversity in the workplace?

---

[12] Court TV Library Home Page, Report from Independent Investigator, http://205.181.114.35/library/business/texaco/report.html.

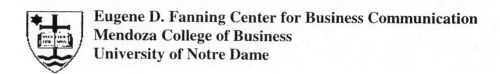

Deerfield Hospital Supply, Inc.

Background Note

Diane Jackson is the new operations manager of the Distribution Center for Deerfield Hospital Supply, Inc., a mid-size, non-union healthcare company located in the upper Midwestern United States. The Distribution Center is a $40 million-dollar-a-year operation that employs 50 people, including 15 minorities (African-American, Asian, and Hispanic) and 18 women in the workforce. Four of the minorities are female.

Jackson, a 25 year-old college-educated woman, was transferred from another operations position in the company to fill this position because of some serious performance problems in the Distribution Center that had resisted previous attempts at improvement. The Center had experienced a very high level of defects (nearly 400 per month) as well as a high rate of errors among orders taken from client hospitals. Jackson accepted the assignment knowing that top management would expect her to improve the performance of the Distribution Center in a relatively short period of time.

Jackson's first few weeks on the job were revealing, to say the least. She discovered that the five supervisors whom her predecessor had selected to lead the Center's workforce had little credibility with the employees. They had each been selected on the basis of their job seniority or their friendship with the previous manager.

The workforce was organized into three categories. *Pickers* identify supplies by code numbers in the storage area, remove packaged items from the shelves, and sort them into order baskets. *Drivers* operate forklifts and electric trucks, moving baskets and boxes of supplies to different locations within the Distribution Center. *Loaders* transfer supplies onto and off of the forklifts and delivery trucks.

This case was prepared by Ms. Kay Wigton with the assistance of James S. O'Rourke, Concurrent Associate Professor of Management, as the basis for class discussion rather than to illustrate either effective or ineffective handling of an administrative situation. Personal and corporate identities have been disguised.

Jackson found that her employees were either demoralized or had tough, belligerent attitudes toward management and other employees. Part of the problem, she soon learned, was a lax approach to background checks and prior job references. Five employees were convicted felons, two of whom had been imprisoned for violent assaults on their victims. The previous manager had made all of the hiring decisions by himself without bothering to check on the applicants' references or backgrounds.

Jackson soon discovered that it was not unusual for employees to settle their differences with their fists or to use verbally abusive language to berate people who had offended them. Her predecessor had unintentionally encouraged these disruptive activities by staying in his office and not being available to the other workers. He had relied largely on his discredited supervisors to handle their own disciplinary problems. Before long, the Center employees felt they could handle their own affairs in any way they wanted, without interference from management.

The Loading Dock Incident

While sitting in her office one morning, planning to make several policy changes to improve the efficiency of the Distribution Center, one of Jackson's supervisors entered and reported that two of the loaders had just gotten into a heated dispute, and the situation on the loading dock was very tense. The dispute was between Edwin Williams, a black, male employee, and Buddy Thomas, a white, male employee, and focused on which radio station to play on the dock sound system. Williams is the only black employee working on the loading dock. The company's policy permits employees to listen to music while they work and, in recent years, workers have considered listening to music a benefit that improves working conditions.

Williams insisted that he couldn't stand to listen to the country-western music that Thomas preferred to play. For his part, Thomas claimed that Williams' rap music was offensive to him and made working conditions difficult. An emotional and angry argument developed between the two men over their choices in music, and each yelled racial slurs at the other. Neither the company nor the division had a policy governing the choice of music permitted in the workplace. Apparently, whoever arrived at work first chose the music for the day.

Both Thomas and Williams were known as tough employees who had previous disciplinary problems at Deerfield Hospital Supply. Thomas had been incarcerated for 18 months prior to being hired by the company. Jackson knew that she should take immediate action to resolve this problem and to avoid a potentially volatile escalation of the conflict. Her supervisors told Jackson that, in the past, the previous manager would simply have yelled at the two antagonists in the conflict and then departed with no further action.

Jackson's objectives in resolving the conflict include the establishment of her own control in the workplace. She knew that she would have to change "business as usual" in the Distribution Center so that employees would respect her authority and would refrain from any further unprofessional conduct.

Deerfield Hospital Supply, Inc.

Resolving the Problem

In determining the most appropriate solution to the situation that Diane Jackson faces, you may wish to consider these questions:

1.   What are the most important issues Ms. Jackson faces today? Of these, which one is most critical?

2.   Can you identify the cause of the conflict?

3.   What should Ms. Jackson do to settle the conflict? Should either or both of the employees be punished for their behavior?

4.   What can Ms. Jackson do over the long term to ensure that incidents such as the one described in this case are less likely to occur?

5.   What role (if any) do gender, ethnicity or age play in this situation?

6.   What can Ms. Jackson do to develop a group of supervisors who can provide the support she requires and who can properly direct the work of the employees in the Distribution Center?

7.   How important is communication in this case? What should Ms. Jackson do to improve the quality of communication in the Distribution Center?

PART III

The Internet and e-Technology

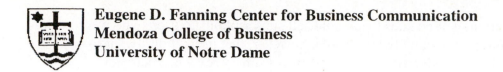

DoubleClick, Inc.

*"I think we took the public by surprise. This is not a DoubleClick problem.
It is an industry problem."* Brenda Mahe, DoubleClick

It was just over six weeks into the new year and just over six months since DoubleClick first appeared on the radar screens of consumer privacy groups. Up until now, privacy groups had certainly been a thorn in the side of the company, but DoubleClick CEO and Founder Kevin O'Connor felt that they would weather this storm no worse for the wear. The battle, however, had now escalated to include consumer lawsuits and an inquiry by the Federal Trade Commission (FTC). Clearly, DoubleClick would have to remove itself from the trenches and launch an offensive strategy.

Company Background

DoubleClick, Inc., is a global Internet company, the largest in New York's so-called "Silicon Alley," and a "leading provider of comprehensive global Internet advertising solutions for marketers and web publishers."[1] DoubleClick uses a combination of technologies, including its DART technology, to aid advertisers and publishers in reaching consumers on the Web with targeted ads.

DoubleClick was founded in Atlanta, Georgia, in February of 1996, by two software engineers, Kevin O'Connor (CEO) and Dwight Merriman (Chief Technology Officer). Prior to forming DoubleClick, 38-year-old O'Connor co-founded a communications software company called ICC, helped fund and build an Internet security software company called ISS, and together with Merriman, co-founded the Internet Advertising Network (IAN). The two created

---

This case was prepared by Research Assistants Will Ho, Ashley Misquitta, and Joe Williamson under the direction of James S. O'Rourke, Concurrent Associate Professor of Management, as the basis for class discussion rather than to illustrate either effective or ineffective handling of an administrative situation. Information was gathered from corporate as well as public sources.

---

[1] http://www.doubleclick.com

DoubleClick as a collection of Web sites that would sell subscriptions to users who were interested in their content. They quickly discovered, however, that users didn't want to pay for subscriptions. Instead, Internet advertising would be their primary revenue generator.

The firm assembled a network of Web sites to which they could deliver advertisements and developed technology that delivered specific advertisements to specific Web pages. Today, DoubleClick is the dominant Internet advertising company with a market cap of $8.5 billion, and they offer six services to help advertisers and publishers. The DoubleClick Network is comprised of 1,500 Web sites ranging from The Dilbert Zone to AltaVista.com, and it aids advertisers in targeting an ad message to a non-specific but demographically-selected audience. DoubleClick's DART technology "matches advertiser-selected target profiles with individual user profiles and delivers an appropriately targeted ad."[2] Other services provide ad management, specific geographic targeting, international advertising, and re-marketing capabilities.[3]

DoubleClick has worked with more than 4,400 advertisers. Companies such as Datek Online, GTE, Firstar Bank, and SK Telecom have all used DoubleClick services for their Internet advertising and brand-building campaigns. These companies have taken advantage of DoubleClick's ability to target consumers with specific ads for their product. DoubleClick's core competency is its ability to track interests and surfing patterns of anonymous Web users through the use of "cookie" files that surfers collect in their online travels.

What is a Cookie?

Lou Montulli, an employee at Netscape, created cookies in 1994 as a way to streamline the process of purchasing items online. Cookies are small text files that are sent and recorded on to a user's hard drive when they visit a Web site to enhance the user's experience. They can be used to tailor Web sites to user preferences by remembering user names and passwords, personalizing stock quotes or news stories, and to deliver personalized advertisements to the user's interests. The cookie assigns a unique identity number to each computer, but no personal data (name, e-mail address, or otherwise identifying information) is included. They have developed into an anonymous vehicle used to track not only products purchased, but also information such as which pages are viewed most frequently, for how long, and which ads were clicked on a particular Web page.

DoubleClick, among other online advertisers, uses the information gathered from cookie files to segment product markets and to provide targeted advertising capabilities to their customers. This new Internet advertising allows product companies to save millions by targeting their products and promotions to specific individuals who are most likely to make a purchase. The use of cookies for this purpose "passed muster with privacy advocates, who were satisfied that surfers' anonymity was being preserved."[4]

---

[2] Ibid.
[3] Ibid.
[4] http://www.msnbc.com, "DoubleClick Faces Scrutiny," February 18, 2000.

Purchase of Abacus Direct Corporation

In November 1999, DoubleClick completed the $1.7 billion purchase of Abacus Direct Corporation, a company that markets consumer purchase data to catalog companies. The Abacus database contains information on millions of consumers gained from years of data collection from direct-mail marketers. It contains such data as names, addresses, phone numbers, e-mail addresses, particular products purchased in the past, favorite stores, and buying habits. Such data has been collected from over 1,100 merchants from Williams-Sonoma to Bloomingdale's.

The purchase of Abacus was prompted by a decreasing rate of effectiveness in online advertising. Click rates for online advertising were falling and DoubleClick saw great value in the possibility of combining the databases of the two companies. If they could combine the data they had on computer user habits, surfing patterns, and ad effectiveness, with Abacus's data on personal consumption and demographics, then they could create a consumer profile that allows marketers to target customers and provide "one-to-one" marketing. DoubleClick figured that this investment would be highly profitable as advertisers and Web publishers would be interested in using their information to market their products to a very well defined and targeted audience.

The Problem

When DoubleClick purchased Abacus Direct Corp., they did so with plans to combine the companies' databases. The company's management didn't foresee a public backlash because they felt that these were much the same issues as with credit cards 25 years earlier. According to Kevin Ryan, the President of DoubleClick, "Some people forget that the No. 1 issue with credit cards 25 years ago was that someone is going to have a record of all my purchases."[5] DoubleClick mistakenly felt that the public and consumers were comfortable with giving personal information online.

The purchase of Abacus Direct was announced in June of 1999 and was soon assailed by privacy rights groups and other organizations as an example of the larger ongoing controversy over consumer profiling. DoubleClick's plan to match personal information from the Abacus databases with their data on Web surfing patterns created a furor among consumer advocacy groups and individual consumers. Many felt that the ability to match names and addresses with online shopping or browsing habits would leave individuals at risk of being exploited by employers, insurance companies, merchandisers, or divorce lawyers. Furthermore, the controversy attracted the attention of government agencies, including the Federal Trade Commission and the Attorneys General of Michigan and New York. Over the next several months, DoubleClick found itself in an ever-escalating controversy and its private dreams were quickly turning into a public nightmare.

---

[5] *Wall Street Journal*, "A Privacy Firestorm at DoubleClick," February 23, 2000, p. B1.

The Privacy Firestorm: Ground Zero

The public was not ready for the convenience Kevin O'Connor felt cookies could provide, nor for the "good news of having online ads that cleverly anticipated just what they wanted to buy." [6] The controversy started when advocacy groups such as the Electronic Privacy Information Center (EPIC) and the Center for Media Education brought DoubleClick's plans to the public light. These groups claimed that DoubleClick was reneging on its previous commitment not to merge the information found in its databases. In fact, EPIC filed a complaint with the FTC requesting an investigation into "unfair and deceptive trade practices by DoubleClick, in failing to properly disclose what information it collects and how it is used."[7]

The situation garnered the attention of the FTC, which threatened government intervention into the growing world of electronic commerce if the industry did not begin policing itself effectively. California State Senator Debra Bowen entered into the controversy by introducing a bill to the state Legislature with the goal of preventing cable and satellite television providers from collecting and selling information on what programs their viewers watch.[8]

Individual consumers also signaled their unhappiness with the controversy. On January 27, 2000, Hariett Judnick filed suit against DoubleClick on behalf of the residents of California. The suit focused on the consent issue, alleging that DoubleClick illegally collected personal information because they didn't have the consent of the computer user to collect that information. The suit called for an injunction against further collection of information, the creation of a simple way for consumers to destroy the dossiers already created on them, and the requirement of an "opt-in" policy. Judnick's attorney, Ira Rothken said, "Even if DoubleClick provides warnings, such warnings give no protection to many unsophisticated Web surfers. One wrong click and the originally anonymous cookie becomes a window into that consumer's private life."[9]

Rothken's comments underscore the insidious nature of the larger privacy issue. Other public debate regarding Internet privacy is with Web sites that automatically create pop-up ads for other sites, including those that contain adult content (and therefore record a cookie file from that site, whether intentionally visited or not). The general public is also concerned about sensitive information relating to personal health or finances that may be revealed through Web sites that they may have visited. The specific concerns center on the possibility of privacy breeches and the exploitation of information gathered from these sites.

With these public concerns in mind, led by Michigan Attorney General Jennifer Granholm, the Attorneys General of Michigan, New York, Connecticut, and Vermont launched investigations and threatened legal action against DoubleClick. In her February 17 filing

---

[6] Ibid.

[7] *New York Times*, "Privacy Advocates Fault New DoubleClick Service," February 15, 2000, p. C2.

[8] http://www.cnet.com, March 9, 2000.

[9] http://www.cnet.com, February 28, 2000.

accusing DoubleClick of violating Michigan's Consumer Protection Act, Granholm said, "Forget Big Brother. Truly, Big Browser appears to have arrived in the form of an Internet corporate giant. Companies like DoubleClick take advantage of the technology to rob people of their privacy."[10] The action goes on to state that the public is not given "meaningful notice and choice" and that DoubleClick has only vague plans about what they will do with the information they collect.

DoubleClick's Response

The controversy first began in June of 1999, when DoubleClick announced that it was in the beginning stages of negotiations with Abacus. The issues regarding privacy and DoubleClick continued to develop throughout the merger negotiations to the November purchase date and further extended into the new year.

By the middle of February, DoubleClick decided that something had to be done to quell the growing debate. On February 14, 2000, DoubleClick used 50 million Internet banner ads and full-page display ads in major newspapers, to announce their "Internet Privacy Education Campaign" and their plan for dealing with the privacy issues.

The crux of the educational campaign is the Web site, **http://www.privacychoices.org**, set up by DoubleClick to explain both sides of the debate and to offer consumers a chance to block the receipt of cookie files. The remainder of their plan included the following points:

DoubleClick will:
- require all sites with which it does business to post clear policies outlining what information is collected on that site and how it is used;

- hire a Chief Privacy Officer;

- create an advisory board to discuss these issues;

- hire PriceWaterhouseCoopers to perform privacy audits.[11]

Consumer groups were still unsatisfied with DoubleClick's actions. Marc Rotenberg of EPIC called the actions, "a desperate attempt to avoid stricter regulations by the government," and Jeff Chester of the Center for Media Education said, "This is a feeble attempt at crisis management. They know that fewer than three percent of the population opts out of anything."[12] The "opt-in" versus "opt-out" controversy seemed to be a contentious issue for many of the groups opposed to DoubleClick's plans. They felt that they still didn't have what they really

---

[10] http://www.cnet.com, February 17, 2000.
[11] http://www.doubleclick.com.
[12] *New York Times*, "Privacy Advocates Fault New DoubleClick Service," February 15, 2000, p. C2.

wanted, a statement from DoubleClick indicating they would not merge the databases.

Looking to the future

DoubleClick has completed the $1.7 billion purchase of Abacus and encountered a public uproar. They attempted to educate the public, but their stock price was still being battered. The public was not satisfied.

Questions

1.   How should Kevin O'Connor and DoubleClick proceed?

2.   What are the critical issues facing DoubleClick?

3.   To whom is DoubleClick responsible?

4.   Other than the outlined efforts to handle privacy issues by DoubleClick, what else do they need to do?

5.   What should the strategy be for handling the opt-in/opt-out debate and related privacy issues?

6.   How can DoubleClick maintain their ability to attract new customers?

7.   Does DoubleClick have a significant role in establishing industry standards for consumer privacy? If so, what is their role?

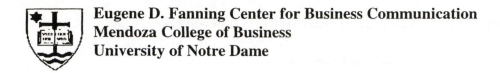
Napster:
Intellectual Property Rights vs. Music for Free

On the afternoon of February 12, 2001, Napster's founder, Shawn Fanning, and its CEO, Hank Berry, listened as the 9th U.S. District Circuit Court of Appeals ruling affirmed that Napster's file sharing system violates copyright law. According to many industry analysts, this was the ruling that would make or break Napster. Fanning and Berry knew that their backs were against the wall, and they needed to make a decision to save their troubled company. They could either continue to fight the Recording Industry Association of America (RIAA) using circumlocutory tactics to skirt copyright laws, or they could compromise to meet the record labels on common ground. The irony is that as the case unfolds, "Record companies reluctantly recognized that the digital distribution of music isn't going away – and (Napster) may represent a singular opportunity to expand their business."[1]

The Evolution of the Music Industry

The recorded music industry has its roots in the nineteenth century when Thomas Edison first recorded the human voice in 1877. Since that famous day, the world of audio transmission and recording has grown exponentially. It's now a $38 billion a year industry. Beginning in the 1920s, the first wire and tape recording devices were emerging in Europe. The devices electronically converted sound waves to pulses of magnetism that were then applied to a metallic medium.

In 1940, new tape recording inventions flooded the industry as plastic was discovered to be the new great recording medium. The late 1950s saw the emergence of the vinyl records and

---

[1] Goodin, Dan. "Can Napster Change Its Tune?" *The Industry Standard*, February 26, 2001.

shortly afterwards in 1966, the eight-track player was invented for use in automobiles. At the same time, Norelco and Philips were developing a smaller cassette with the ability to be played or recorded, eventually driving the eight-track out of the market.

In 1982, the music industry made a giant leap forward with the introduction of digital recording. This came in the way of the Compact Disc (CD), and by 1988, the CD had replaced LPs as the standard recording format. Today's newest technology has given us digital recordings that can be transferred over the Internet and even played on a computer with CD quality sound. This new medium is the MP3.

Technical Background

MP3 Technology

MP3, which stands for MPEG-1 Audio Layer-3, is a standard technology and format for compressing a sound sequence into a very small file, approximately one-twelfth the size of the original file, while preserving the original level of sound quality when it is played. MP3 files are identified by the file name suffix of ".mp3" and are available for downloading from numerous Web sites. These MP3s can be played on most computers since Windows users will find that they have a media player built into their operating system.[2]

Consumers can create an MP3 file by using a program called a 'ripper' to transfer a song from a CD to a computer hard drive. Most people, however, simply download MP3s from P2P networks such as Napster. Since the sharing of these files comes with no transfer of currency, companies like Napster are being accused of encouraging copyright violations. While there are several proposals for how to discourage such piracy, there is currently no secure distribution or copyright management standard that publishers and other parties agree upon.[3]

Peer-to-Peer file sharing

Peer-to-peer (P2P) is a type of transient Internet network that allows a group of computer users with the same networking program to connect and directly access files from one another's hard drives.[4] The best analogy of the traditional client/server model of networking is a classroom where the students ask questions, and only the teacher is allowed to answer them. The teacher is the server and the students are the clients. P2P architecture is like a classroom full of teachers where they all ask each other questions, and they all share their information. Just as every student in this classroom is a teacher, every client is a server in a P2P network.[5]

---

[2] http://www.whatis.com
[3] http://www.napster.com
[4] http://www.whatis.com
[5] http://www.bearshare.com

Napster's Technology

Napster's networking program makes the sharing of MP3 files possible through its P2P network as users talk with one another and share MP3 files. Napster's directory service makes software available that allows users to: (1) search a directory that lists all the MP3 files available to be shared and (2) create file folders on their hard drive to store and share transferred files.[6] All of these stored files then become part of Napster's directory and become available to users when they sign onto Napster. This Internet directory service helps users navigate the available files and locate files of interest.

Perhaps the greatest innovation of the Napster program is the decentralized architecture of its software. The Web site itself, does not hold any of the MP3 files on its servers and thus, acts only as a conduit for the sharing of files. This advance is vastly different from the traditional centralized architecture that most Web sites use today, and it has turned the Internet inside out.

In addition to Napster, there are many other P2P file-sharing program alternatives that include the popular Gnutella, FreeNet, and Aimster. These networking programs are different from Napster in that they have no central server index. This is predicted to cause an even more substantial problem for the music industry, since this absence of a graphical user interface (GUI) makes its system almost impossible to control. At the moment, a critical mass of online users still has not made the transition to these alternative sites because compared to Napster's user-friendly system, these services are still difficult to navigate.

Stakeholders

Shawn Fanning, Hank Berry, and Napster management team: Senior management is determined to make Napster a profitable company. Aside from the monetary incentives, Shawn Fanning and the management team have an emotional stake in the success of this historical breakthrough in music distribution.

Hummer Winblad: San Francisco-based Hummer Winblad, a top-tier venture capital firm, led a $15 million round of financing for the company in March 2000. Napster's public relations firm confirmed that Hummer Winblad partner Hank Barry will take over as CEO, replacing Eileen Richardson. Partner John Hummer also joined Napster's board.

BMG/Bertelsmann: The publishing and media giant will develop a subscription service with the MP3-swapping company. German media-titan Bertelsmann, which owns recording company BMG, established a joint venture with Napster when it gave $50 million in funding to keep the service running. It promised to address many of the recording industry's most pressing concerns about digital distribution. Its vision of a secure, fee-based online service would

---

[6] Opposition of Defendant Napster, Inc. to Plaintiffs' Motion Preliminary Injunction Case Nos. C 99-5183 and C 00-0074 MHP (ARD).

simultaneously respect copyright owners, ensure payment of royalties, and preserve Napster's appealing 'swap-all-you-like' environment.[7]

RIAA/record labels: The RIAA represents 90 percent of all published music. The strength of the RIAA is derived from the financial strength of its members. The "Big Five" record labels, excluding BMG, are involved in this case. They include Warner Music, EMI, Sony Music, and Universal Music. The "Big Five" have contracts with the most popular and successful artists in the industry. The RIAA's interest in this case is to maintain the distribution and control of the music from which its members derive their revenues.

Individual Music Artists: MP3 technology has undoubtedly changed the music distribution landscape. The artists have a vested interest in prohibiting the possibility of illegal copying and distribution of their work.

Consumers: The consumer has benefitted from P2P file sharing and will continue to do so. However, if online P2P file sharing sites such as Napster are found to be illegal because of copyright infringement, the consumer will undoubtedly pay the consequences.

United States Government: The United States legal system cannot create laws fast enough to keep pace with this powerful new technology. Therefore, the legislation resulting from the Napster case will establish a legal precedent from which all future cases will be measured.

Napster's Legal Problems

"To promote the progress of science and useful arts, by securing for limited times to authors and inventors the exclusive right to their respective writings and discoveries"

The United States Constitution
Article I, Section 8

What is Copyright?

Copyright is customarily defined as the "The exclusive legal right to reproduce, publish, and sell the matter and form (as of a literary, musical, or artistic work)."[8] Article I, Section 8 of The United States Constitution provides the first recorded protection to the authors of "original works of authorship."[9] More specifically, copyright laws are under the jurisdiction of title 17 of the U.S. Code. Several amendments are of significant importance regarding the Napster lawsuit which include:

---

[7] Morse, Andrew. "Sleeping With the Enemy," *The Industry Standard,* November 13, 2000.
[8] *Miriam- Webster's Dictionary,* http://www.m-w.com/cgi-bin/dictionary
[9] The United States Constitution, http://lcweb2.loc.gov/const/const.html

·   The 1976 Copyright Act: Provides the basic framework for the current copyright laws.

·   The Audio Home Recording Act (AHRA) of 1992: Provides consumers with protection from copyright lawsuits when they record the music for personal and noncommercial use. (Exhibit 5)

·   The Digital Millennium Copyright Act (DMCA) of 1998: Title II, §512, "Creates limitations on the liability of online service providers for copyright infringements when engaging in certain types of activities."[10] This act creates four 'safe harbors' for Internet service providers that completely bar monetary damages and restrict the availability of injunctive relief. (Exhibit 6)

The Stance of the Recording Industry Association of America (RIAA)

Based on sampling of MP3 files available through Napster, the RIAA contends that the Web site facilitates and enables the piracy of copyrighted music over the Internet at unprecedented levels. Since the inception of Napster, the RIAA has been acting on the behalf of its many members to shut down the Web site using different legal angles that include four specific sections of title 17: §101, §106, §106A, §107, and §512 (DMCA). (Exhibits 2, 3A, 3B, 4, and 6)

Injunctions, Lawsuits, and Consequences

"Injunctions are orders that one side refrain from or stop certain actions and can be temporary, pending a consideration of the issue later at trial (these are called interlocutory decrees or preliminary injunctions). Judges can also issue permanent injunctions at the end of trials, in which a party may be permanently prohibited from engaging in some conduct – for example, infringing a copyright or trademark or making use of illegally obtained trade secrets. Although most injunctions order a party not to do something, occasionally a court will issue a 'mandatory injunction' to order a party to carry out a positive act – for example, to return stolen computer code."[11]

On December 7, 1999, the RIAA filed a lawsuit against Napster in the U.S. District Court, Northern District of California. The suit charged Napster with contributory and vicarious copyright infringement and related state laws. (Exhibit 2) In the lawsuit, the RIAA claimed that Napster created and operated a haven for music piracy.

In March of 2000, the RIAA filed a compliant for a preliminary and permanent injunction against Napster and its employees from: (1) directly or indirectly infringing in any manner on any

---

[10] The Digital Millennium Copyright Act, http://www.loc.gov/copyright/legislation/dmca.pdf
[11] http://www.nolo.com/dictionary/dictionary_alpha.cfm?wordnumber=675&Alpha=I

of the plaintiffs' respective copyrights and from (2) causing, contributing to, enabling, facilitating, or participating in the infringement of any of the plaintiffs' respective copyrights.

On April 13, 2000, the bad boy rock group, Metallica, sued Napster, three universities, and unnamed users of the Napster technology. The suit filed claimed that the sole purpose of Napster was to abet and encourage online music piracy and that the universities could stop the program instead of allowing it expand. The lawsuit sought a permanent injunction against Napster and damages of up to $100,000 per illegally traded song. As Metallica's drummer Lars Ulrich stated, "[It's] sickening to know that our art is being traded like a commodity rather than the art that it is."[12]

The Metallica lawsuit seemed to jumpstart the fury involving Napster and its users. Shortly after the suit became public, schools including Yale, Indiana University, and University of Southern California blocked student access to the Web site. Meanwhile, various other musicians vocalized their concerns about copyright infringement. Most notably rap artist, Dr. Dre, who said, "Napster has built a business based on large-scale piracy,"[13] eventually followed through on his promise to sue if his music was not removed from the Web site. However, with the many critics speaking out against the Web site, other musicians were taking the opposing position. Many artists, including Chuck D of Public Enemy, Fred Durst of Limp Bizkit, and the band Offspring, felt that Metallica's dislike of the Web site was harmful to the industry and to young, aspiring bands who needed the Web site for exposure.

Subsequently, on June 7, 2000, the RIAA formally filed a motion for the preliminary injunction against the Web site. The plaintiffs argued that a preliminary injunction should be issued on the grounds that the music industry will prevail in its original lawsuit because Napster was causing irreparable harm to the RIAA and the music industry.

In response to the RIAA preliminary injunction, Napster's lawyers filed a brief in the San Francisco Superior Court, refuting the RIAA's belief that the Web site was facilitating online piracy. In the rebuttal, Napster lawyer David Boies argued that the 1992 AHRA permits noncommercial use by the consumer and therefore allows Napster to share MP3s. The brief went on to suggest that there are no limits specified by the government on the number of consumers who can make copies of copyrighted material for personal use. The brief also mentioned that the RIAA-sponsored study was erroneous in attributing the decline in CD sales near universities to P2P file sharing. Furthermore, lawyers for Napster cited five other studies that demonstrated how CD sales have increased by 8 percent since Napster went online.

[12]Nelson, Chris, "Metallica Charge Copyright Infringement In Lawsuit Against Napster," http://wwww.sonicnet.com/news/archive/story.jtml?id20903, April 13, 2000.
[13] Nelson, Chris, "Dr. Dre Follows Through On Warning, Sues Napster," http://www.sonicnet.com/news/archive/story.jhtml?id=821423, April 25, 2000.

Throughout the following months, Napster and the RIAA met several times in court. During a hearing in May 2000, Judge Marilyn Hall Patel had ruled against Napster to dismiss the copyright lawsuit. The Judge felt that the RIAA had a strong suit and thus, decided to move the case forward. However, the Judge had also sided with Napster, proclaiming that the Web site was covered under the DMCA.

The preconceived climax to the preliminary injunction was on Wednesday, July 26, 2000. During the court session, Judge Patel said that the RIAA "Showed not just a reasonable possibility of success, but a strong possibility of success"[14] in the copyright suit. Therefore, she ruled that a preliminary injunction barring copyrighted material from Napster for the duration of the case was to take place the following Friday. Lawyers for Napster responded by saying that the Web site would have to be completely shut down because separating copyrighted material from non-copyrighted material would be impossible in the short amount of time given. Furthermore, the RIAA had not been able to provide Napster with a comprehensive list of its copyrighted titles.

However two days later, on Friday, July 28, 2000, the 9th District Circuit Court of Appeals granted a temporary stay to Napster, thus delaying the injunction imposed by Judge Patel. The stay was granted on the grounds that Judge Patel "Wrongly distinguished between personal and noncommercial uses, ignored the council of the Supreme Court by extending copyright law to cover new technologies and ignored evidence that Napster is helping, not hurting, the record industry."[15]

On October 2, 2000, the 9th District Circuit Court of Appeals reconvened to decide whether to permanently uphold the lower court decision. Napster argued that the "First Amendment has never been interpreted to permit the injunction to prohibit the distribution of a directory system."[16] During the trial Chief Judge Schroeder, Judge Beezer, and Judge Paez all questioned the RIAA's complaint that Napster was guilty of copyright infringement.

Until February 12, 2001, the RIAA had been unsuccessful in shutting down the Web site. The preliminary injunctions that had been filed were all over-turned due to the opinions of the court. However, in the 9th District Circuit Court of Appeals, a panel of judges, again including Chief Judge Schroeder, Judge Beezer, and Judge Paez, reversed their stance and affirmed, in part, the earlier decision entered by Chief District Judge Patel. It was the panel's conclusion that the previous injunction was too broad in scope and that a modification was necessary. The modifications to the injunction were as follows:

---

[14] Simon, Richard, "Judge Grants RIAA Injunction Against Napster,"
http://www.sonicnet.com/news/archive/story.jhtml?id=1122499, July 26, 2000.
[15] Simon, Richard, "Appeals Court grants Reprieve to Napster,"
http://www.sonicnet.com/news/archive/story.jhtml?id=1122615, July 29, 2000.
[16] Hiatt, Brian, "Napster Argues Shutting Down Service Would Violate First Amendment,"
http://www.sonicnet.com/news/archive/story.jhtml?id=1124484, October 2, 2000

"Napster may be held liable for contributory copyright infringement only to the extent that Napster knows of specific infringing files with copyrighted musical compositions or sound recordings, knows or should have known that the files are available on the Napster system, and fails to act to prevent the distribution of the copyrighted material."[17]

The 9th District Circuit Court of Appeals
February 12, 2001

The panel agreed to reject Napster's defense that users are engaged in 'fair use' of the copyrighted material. (§107) Additionally, the panel recognized the earlier decision that the AHRA did not cover the downloading of MP3 files, and the DMCA provisions are to be further explored through trial.

Key Issues

The reason for the broad resistance against Napster is that its P2P file sharing allows the free distribution of every song on the Internet, facilitating the piracy of mainstream recordings. For this reason, the RIAA has vehemently opposed Napster, self-proclaimed to be the world's largest MP3 music library, and has taken every effort possible to halt the continuation of its P2P network.

The scope of Napster is self-evident as they "guarantee that you'll find all the music you want, when you want it" on its site. This kind of message has attracted 57 million users, and its popularity is being bolstered at many U.S. college campuses. At the University of Notre Dame, a moratorium was placed on Napster because 2/3 of network traffic came from students downloading songs. A similar moratorium was put in effect at approximately 150 other major college campuses.

If Napster can outlast the legal battles, the difficult assignment for Napster will be to assess a fee to clients. The many Internet consumer sites that have relied upon advertising revenue for financial support have folded in the Internet debacle that began late in the summer of 2001. Those that survived have either switched from a consumer to a business target client or have developed a successful subscription based revenue model. Many prognosticators believe that Napster will have to charge a monthly fee in the very near future to survive. In fact, Hank Berry, Napster CEO, has even indicated that a $4.95/month fee may be added by late 2001.

The copyright lawsuit is only one avenue for exposing the real issue facing Napster. For the RIAA and Napster, the real issue is not copyright, but rather control. Assuming that the free Napster network continues to proliferate, record labels will loose exorbitant amounts of revenues that could have been collected through either traditional record sales or a pay-for music site

---

[17] Ninth Court Decision Summary, http://www.riaa.com/pdf/napstersummary.pdf

developed by the record labels. This fact is apparent in the ongoing discussions between Napster and the RIAA. Napster Attorney, David Boies states, "The recording industry is attempting in this case to try to maintain control over music distribution. By repeatedly refusing Napster's offers of a reasonable license and opposing a compulsory license, they have demonstrated that they are not seeking to be appropriately compensated, but rather to kill or control a technology they view as competition."[18]

Questions

1.   What is the appropriate communications message that Fanning and Barry should enlist to describe the events that unfolded on February 12, 2001?

2.   With whom should Napster look to establish relationships or alliances?

3.   How can Napster utilize their current customers to support the formidable task of keeping its P2P MP3 service alive?

4.   What are some possible strategies that Napster should develop to ensure the long-term success of its Web site?

5.   What steps can Napster take to realign the company with the individual musicians?

6.   In terms of historical significance, how will the Napster case impact the future of the music industry? Furthermore, how will the outcome of the case affect relevant stakeholders?

---

[18] Rohde, Laura, "Napster Sends Written Reply to Appeals Court," *The Industry Standard*, September 13, 2000.

Exhibit 1: Napster Time line

January 1999
Shawn fanning drops out of Northeastern University with an idea and some software. He solicits the services of his uncle, John Fanning, to help him bring his file sharing software to market.

May 1999
Shawn Fanning founds Napster, the first online file-sharing site specializing in music.

December 1999
Recording Industry Association of America sues Napster over copyright infringements.

May 2000
Hummer Winblad, a San Francisco based venture capital firm, funds Napster with $15 million.

June 2000
The RIAA files an injunction against Napster to stop its online file sharing service. Responding to the need for expert legal council, Napster hires attorney David Boies.

July 2000
In response to the June injunction, Judge Marilyn Hall Patel issues her ruling in favor of the recording industry, ordering the Web site to shut down all trading of copyrighted files. Napster files an appeal to the injunction and manages to stay alive. Just prior to the injunction going into affect, the appeals court issues a stay, postponing the injunction for further ruling.

October 2, 2000
The 9th U.S. Circuit Court of Appeals holds session to decide the validity of the earlier injunction. Both sides of the appeal present arguments in an attempt to prove the validity of their respective positions.

October 31, 2000
Napster and Bertelsmann strike a deal to the tune of $50 million. The generous loan from Bertelsmann is to further the development of a legal file sharing software system.

January 2001
Napster develops a strategic alliance with Edel Music of Germany, who agrees to distribute its catalog on the Napster Web site. CDNow, an online music retailer owned by Bertelsmann, cuts a deal with Napster to provide a link to its Web site on the Napster interface. Meanwhile TVT records, a prominent independent label, drops its lawsuit against Napster.

February 12, 2001
The 9th U.S. district circuit Court of Appeals issues its ruling, affirming that Napster's file sharing system violates copyright law.

Exhibit 2: § 101 et seq.

Federal law protects copyright owners from the unauthorized reproduction, adaptation, performance, display or distribution of copyright protected works. Penalties for copyright infringement differ in civil and criminal cases. Civil remedies are generally available for any act of infringement without regard to the intention or knowledge of the defendant, or harm to the copyright owner. Criminal penalties are available for intentional acts undertaken for purposes of "commercial advantage" or "private financial gain." "Private financial gain" includes the possibility of financial loss to the copyright holder as well as traditional "gain" by the defendant.

Where the infringing activity is for commercial advantage or private financial gain, sound recording infringements can be punishable by up to five years in prison and $250,000 in fines. Repeat offenders can be imprisoned for up to 10 years. Violators can also be held civilly liable for actual damages, lost profit, or statutory damages up to $150,000 per work.

Two important legal concepts, especially pertaining to the Internet, should be kept in mind: contributory infringement and vicarious liability.

Contributory infringement may be found where a person, with knowledge of the infringing activity, induces, causes, or materially contributes to the infringing conduct of another. For example, a link site operator may be liable for contributory infringement by knowingly linking to infringing files.

Vicarious liability may be imposed where an entity or person has the right and ability to control the activities of the direct infringer and also receives a financial benefit from the infringing activities. Vicarious liability may be imposed even if the entity is unaware of the infringing activities. In the case of a site re-transmitting infringing programs, providing direct access to infringing works may show a right and ability to control the activities of the direct infringer, and receiving revenue from banner ads or e-commerce on the site may be evidence of a financial benefit.

Source: U.S. Code, title 17

Exhibit 3A: § 106. Exclusive rights in copyrighted works

Subject to sections 107 through 121, the owner of copyright under this title has the exclusive
    rights to do and to authorize any of the following:

(1) to reproduce the copyrighted work in copies or phonorecords;

(2) to prepare derivative works based upon the copyrighted work;

(3) to distribute copies or phonorecords of the copyrighted work to the public by sale or other
    transfer of ownership, or by rental, lease, or lending;

(4) in the case of literary, musical, dramatic, and choreographic works, pantomimes, and motion
    pictures and other audiovisual works, to perform the copyrighted work publicly;

(5) in the case of literary, musical, dramatic, and choreographic works, pantomimes, and
    pictorial, graphic, or sculptural works, including the individual images of a motion picture or
    other audiovisual work, to display the copyrighted work publicly; and

(6) in the case of sound recordings, to perform the copyrighted work publicly by means of a
    digital audio transmission.

Source: U.S. Code. title 17

Exhibit 3B: § 106A. Rights of certain authors to attribution and integrity

(a) *Rights of Attribution and Integrity.* Subject to section 107 and independent of the exclusive rights provided in section 106, the author of a work of visual art:

(1) shall have the right:

(A) to claim authorship of that work, and

(B) to prevent the use of his or her name as the author of any work of visual art which he or she did not create;

(2) shall have the right to prevent the use of his or her name as the author of the work of visual art in the event of a distortion, mutilation, or other modification of the work which would be prejudicial to his or her honor or reputation; and

(3) subject to the limitations set forth in section 113 (d), shall have the right:

(A) to prevent any intentional distortion, mutilation, or other modification of that work which would be prejudicial to his or her honor or reputation, and any intentional distortion, mutilation, or modification of that work is a violation of that right, and

(B) to prevent any destruction of a work of recognized stature, and any intentional or grossly negligent destruction of that work is a violation of that right.

(b) *Scope and Exercise of Rights.* Only the author of a work of visual art has the rights conferred by subsection (a) in that work, whether or not the author is the copyright owner. The authors of a joint work of visual art are co-owners of the rights conferred by subsection (a) in that work.

(c) *Exceptions.*

(1) The modification of a work of visual art which is the result of the passage of time or the inherent nature of the materials is not a distortion, mutilation, or other modification described in subsection (a)(3)(A).

(2) The modification of a work of visual art which is the result of conservation, or of the public presentation, including lighting and placement, of the work is not a destruction, distortion, mutilation, or other modification described in subsection (a)(3) unless the modification is caused by gross negligence.

(3) The rights described in paragraphs (1) and (2) of subsection (a) shall not apply to any reproduction, depiction, portrayal, or other use of a work in, upon, or in any connection with any item described in subparagraph (A) or (B) of the definition of "work of visual art" in section 101, and any such reproduction, depiction, portrayal, or other use of a work

is not a destruction, distortion, mutilation, or other modification described in paragraph (3) of subsection (a).

(d) *Duration of Rights*.

(1) With respect to works of visual art created on or after the effective date set forth in section 610(a) of the Visual Artists Rights Act of 1990, the rights conferred by subsection (a) shall endure for a term consisting of the life of the author.

(2) With respect to works of visual art created before the effective date set forth in section 610(a) of the Visual Artists Rights Act of 1990, but title to which has not, as of such effective date, been transferred from the author, the rights conferred by subsection (a) shall be coextensive with, and shall expire at the same time as, the rights conferred by section 106.

(3) In the case of a joint work prepared by two or more authors, the rights conferred by subsection (a) shall endure for a term consisting of the life of the last surviving author.

(4) All terms of the rights conferred by subsection (a) run to the end of the calendar year in which they would otherwise expire.

(e) *Transfer and Waiver*.

(1) The rights conferred by subsection (a) may not be transferred, but those rights may be waived if the author expressly agrees to such waiver in a written instrument signed by the author. Such instrument shall specifically identify the work, and uses of that work, to which the waiver applies, and the waiver shall apply only to the work and uses so identified. In the case of a joint work prepared by two or more authors, a waiver of rights under this paragraph made by one such author waives such rights for all such authors.

(2) Ownership of the rights conferred by subsection (a) with respect to a work of visual art is distinct from ownership of any copy of that work, or of a copyright or any exclusive right under a copyright in that work. Transfer of ownership of any copy of a work of visual art, or of a copyright or any exclusive right under a copyright, shall not constitute a waiver of the rights conferred by subsection (a). Except as may otherwise be agreed by the author in a written instrument signed by the author, a waiver of the rights conferred by subsection (a) with respect to a work of visual art shall not constitute a transfer of ownership of any copy of that work, or of ownership of a copyright or of any exclusive right under a copyright in that work.

Source: U.S. Code, title 17

Exhibit 4: § 107. Limitations on exclusive rights: Fair use

Notwithstanding the provisions of sections 106 and 106A, the fair use of a copyrighted work, including such use by reproduction in copies or phonorecords or by any other means specified by that section, for purposes such as criticism, comment, news reporting, teaching (including multiple copies for classroom use), scholarship, or research, is not an infringement of copyright. In determining whether the use made of a work in any particular case is a fair use the factors to be considered shall include-

(1) the purpose and character of the use, including whether such use is of a commercial nature or is for nonprofit educational purposes;

(2) the nature of the copyrighted work;

(3) the amount and substantiality of the portion used in relation to the copyrighted work as a whole; and

(4) the effect of the use upon the potential market for or value of the copyrighted work.

The fact that a work is unpublished shall not itself bar a finding of fair use if such finding is made upon consideration of all the above factors.

Source: U.S. Code. title 17

Exhibit 5: The Audio Home Recording Act of 1992 (AHRA)

This 1992 legislation exempts consumers from lawsuits for copyright violations when they record music for private, noncommercial use; eases access to advanced digital audio recording technologies; provides for the payment of modest royalties to songwriters and recording artists and companies; and mandates the inclusion of serial copying management technology in all consumer digital audio recorders to limit multi-generation audio copying (i.e., making copies of copies).

In general, the AHRA covers devices that are designed or marketed for the primary purpose of making digital musical recordings. Digital audio cassette players, minidiscs, and DAT players are devices covered by the AHRA. This law will also apply to all future digital audio recording technologies, so Congress will not be forced to revisit the issue as each new product becomes available.

The AHRA provides that manufacturers (not consumers) of covered devices must: (1) register with the Copyright Office; (2) pay a statutory royalty on each device and piece of media sold; and (3) implement serial copyright management technology (such as SCMS) which prevents copies of copies. In exchange for this, the manufacturers of the devices receive statutory immunity from infringement based on the use of those devices by consumers. To learn more about the administration of the royalties paid on recording devices and media, see the section on AARC.

Multipurpose devices, such as a general computer or a CD-ROM drive, are not covered by the AHRA. This means that they are not required to pay royalties or incorporate SCMS protections. It also means, however, that neither manufacturers of the devices, nor the consumers who use them, receive immunity from suit for copyright infringement.

Source: U.S. Code, title 17

Exhibit 6: The Digital Millennium Copyright Act of 1998

TITLE II: ONLINE COPYRIGHT INFRINGEMENT LIABILITY LIMITATION

Title II of the DMCA adds a new section 512 to the Copyright Act to create four new limitations on liability for copyright infringement by online service providers. The limitations are based on the following four categories of conduct by a service provider:

1. Transitory communications;

2. System caching;

3. Storage of information on systems or networks at direction of users; and

4. Information location tools.

New section 512 also includes special rules concerning the application of these limitations to nonprofit educational institutions. Each limitation entails a complete bar on monetary damages, and restricts the availability of injunctive relief in various respects. (Section 512(j)). Each limitation relates to a separate and distinct function, and a determination of whether a service provider qualifies for one of the limitations does not bear upon a determination of whether the provider qualifies for any of the other three. (Section 512(n)). The failure of a service provider to qualify for any of the limitations in section 512 does not necessarily make it liable for copyright infringement. The copyright owner must still demonstrate that the provider has infringed, and the provider may still avail itself of any of the defenses, such as fair use, that are available to copyright defendants generally. (Section 512(l)). In addition to limiting the liability of service providers, Title II establishes a procedure by which a copyright owner can obtain a subpoena from a federal court ordering a service provider to disclose the identity of a subscriber who is allegedly engaging in infringing activities. (Section 512(h)).

Section 512 also contains a provision to ensure that service providers are not placed in the position of choosing between limitations on liability on the one hand and preserving the privacy of their subscribers, on the other. Subsection (m) explicitly states that nothing in section 512 requires a service provider to monitor its service or access material in violation of law (such as the Electronic Communications Privacy Act) in order to be eligible for any of the liability limitations.   Eligibility for Limitations Generally a party seeking the benefit of the limitations on liability in Title II must qualify as a "service provider." For purposes of the first limitation, relating to transitory communications, "service provider" is defined in section 512(k)(1)(A) as "an entity offering the transmission, routing, or providing of connections for digital online communications, between or among points specified by a user, of material of the user's choosing, without modification to the content of the material as sent or received." For purposes of the other three limitations, "service provider" is more broadly defined in section 512(k)(l)(B) as "a provider of online services or network access, or the operator of facilities therefor."

In addition, to be eligible for any of the limitations, a service provider must meet two overall conditions: (1) it must adopt and reasonably implement a policy of terminating in appropriate circumstances the accounts of subscribers who are repeat infringers; and (2) it must accommodate and not interfere with "standard technical measures." (Section 512(i)). "Standard technical measures" are defined as measures that copyright owners use to identify or protect copyrighted works, that have been developed pursuant to a broad consensus of copyright owners and service providers in an open, fair and voluntary multi-industry process, are available to anyone on reasonable nondiscriminatory terms, and do not impose substantial costs or burdens on service providers.

Limitation for Transitory Communications

In general terms, section 512(a) limits the liability of service providers in circumstances where the provider merely acts as a data conduit, transmitting digital information from one point on a network to another at someone else's request. This limitation covers acts of transmission, routing, or providing connections for the information, as well as the intermediate and transient copies that are made automatically in the operation of a network. In order to qualify for this limitation, the service provider's activities must meet the following conditions:

1.   The transmission must be initiated by a person other than the provider.

2.   The transmission, routing, provision of connections, or copying must be carried out by an automatic technical process without selection of material by the service provider.

3.   The service provider must not determine the recipients of the material.

4.   Any intermediate copies must not ordinarily be accessible to anyone other than anticipated recipients, and must not be retained for longer than reasonably necessary.

5.   The material must be transmitted with no modification to its content.

Limitation for System Caching

Section 512(b) limits the liability of service providers for the practice of retaining copies, for a limited time, of material that has been made available online by a person other than the provider, and then transmitted to a subscriber at his or her direction. The service provider retains the material so that subsequent requests for the same material can be fulfilled by transmitting the retained copy, rather than retrieving the material from the original source on the network. The benefit of this practice is that it reduces the service provider's bandwidth requirements and reduces the waiting time on subsequent requests for the same information. On the other hand, it can result in the delivery of outdated information to subscribers and can deprive Web site operators of accurate "hit" information – information about the number of requests for particular material on a Web site – from which advertising revenue is frequently calculated. For this reason, the person making the material available online may establish rules about updating it, and may utilize technological means to track the number of "hits." The limitation applies to acts of intermediate and temporary storage, when carried out through an automatic technical process for the purpose of making the material available to subscribers who subsequently request it. It is subject to the following conditions:

1.   The content of the retained material must not be modified.

2.   The provider must comply with rules about "refreshing" material, replacing retained copies of material with material from the original location, when specified in accordance with a generally accepted industry standard data communication protocol.

3.   The provider must not interfere with technology that returns "hit"information to the person who posted the material, where such technology meets certain requirements.

4.   The provider must limit users' access to the material in accordance with conditions on access (e.g., password protection) imposed by the person who posted the material.

5.   Any material that was posted without the copyright owner's authorization must be removed or blocked promptly once the service provider has been notified that it has been removed, blocked, or ordered to be removed or blocked, at the originating site.

Limitation for Information Residing on Systems or Networks at the Direction of Users

Section 512(c) limits the liability of service providers for infringing material on Web sites (or other information repositories) hosted on their systems. It applies to storage at the direction of a user. In order to be eligible for the limitation, the following conditions must be met:

1.   The provider must not have the requisite level of knowledge of the infringing activity, as described below.

2.   If the provider has the right and ability to control the infringing activity, it must not receive a financial benefit directly attributable to the infringing activity.

3.   Upon receiving proper notification of claimed infringement, the provider must expeditiously take down or block access to the material.

In addition, a service provider must have filed with the Copyright Office a designation of an agent to receive notifications of claimed infringement. The Office provides a suggested form for the purpose of designating an agent (http://www.loc.gov/copyright/onlinesp/) and maintains a list of agents on the Copyright Office Web site (http://www.loc.gov/copyright/onlinesp/list/). Under the knowledge standard, a service provider is eligible for the limitation on liability only if it does not have actual knowledge of the infringement, is not aware of facts or circumstances from which infringing activity is apparent, or upon gaining such knowledge or awareness, responds expeditiously to take the material down or block access to it. The statute also establishes procedures for proper notification, and rules as to its effect. (Section 512(c)(3)). Under the notice and takedown procedure, a copyright owner submits a notification under penalty of perjury, including a list of specified elements, to the service provider's designated agent. Failure to comply substantially with the statutory requirements means that the notification will not be considered in determining the requisite level of knowledge by the service provider. If, upon receiving a proper notification, the service provider promptly removes or blocks access to the material identified in the notification, the provider is exempt from monetary liability. In addition, the provider is protected from any liability to any person for claims based on its having taken down the material. (Section 512(g)(1)).

In order to protect against the possibility of erroneous or fraudulent notifications, certain safeguards are built into section 512. Subsection (g)(1) gives the subscriber the opportunity to respond to the notice and takedown by filing a counter notification. In order to qualify for the protection against liability for taking down material, the service provider must promptly notify the subscriber that it has removed or disabled access to the material. If the subscriber serves a counter notification complying with statutory requirements, including a statement under penalty of perjury that the material was removed or disabled through mistake or misidentification, then unless the copyright owner files an action seeking a court order against the subscriber, the service provider must put the material back up within 10-14 business days after receiving the counter notification. Penalties are provided for knowing material misrepresentations in either a notice or a counter notice. Any person who knowingly materially misrepresents that material is infringing, or that it was removed or blocked through mistake or misidentification, is liable for any resulting damages (including costs and attorneys' fees) incurred by the alleged infringer, the copyright owner or its licensee, or the service provider. (Section 512(f)). The provider must not have the requisite level of knowledge that the material is infringing. The knowledge standard is the same as under the limitation for information residing on systems or networks:

> þ If the provider has the right and ability to control the infringing activity, the provider must not receive a financial benefit directly attributable to the activity.

> þ Upon receiving a notification of claimed infringement, the provider must expeditiously take down or block access to the material. These are essentially the same conditions that apply under the previous limitation, with some differences in the notification requirements. The provisions establishing safeguards against the possibility of erroneous or fraudulent notifications, as discussed above, as well as those protecting the provider against claims based on having taken down the material apply to this limitation. (Sections 512(f)-(g)).

Source: http://www.loc.gov/copyright/legislation/dmca.pdf

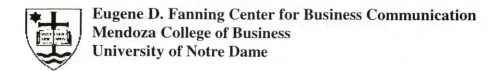
CD Universe and Internet Security

On January 7, 2000, officials at CD Universe learned that credit card information from 25,000 of their customers had been stolen and posted on the Internet. Major media outlets including CNBC, CNN, *The New York Times*, *The Financial Times,* and *The Los Angeles Times* began reporting about the incident shortly thereafter. Brad Greenspan, Chairman of the CD Universe parent company, eUniverse, quickly gathered members of his corporate communication staff and their public relations firm. He knew customer confidence was a key to the company's Internet success and hoped this would not adversely affect their strong reputation.

Key Facts of the Security Breach

In late 1999, a hacker calling himself Maxus was able to obtain customer files for more than 300,000 current and former CD Universe customers. This information included their names, addresses, credit card numbers, and expiration dates. Maxus, who claimed to be a teenager living in Russia, demanded US$100,000 to fix the security problem he had uncovered. On December 25, angry the company ignored his e-mail and faxes, Maxus opened "MAXUS credit cards datapipe." This site featured the credit card information of 25,000 customers and encouraged visitors to use it.

Apparently upset at the lack of response from CD Universe, Maxus e-mailed SecurityFocus.com on January 6, 2000, to inform them of his actions. SecurityFocus.com, a California based computer security firm, then alerted CD Universe and the media about the existence of the site the following day. CD Universe notified the FBI of the situation, and the web site was shut down on January 7. According to the Web site's counter, more than 25,000 credit card numbers had been downloaded.

This case was prepared by Research Assistants Mike Delahanty, Brendon Scott, and Bryce Simms under the direction of James S. O'Rourke, Concurrent Associate Professor of Management, as the basis for class discussion rather than to illustrate either effective or ineffective handling of an administrative situation. Information was gathered from corporate as well as public sources.

Company Profile

CD Universe is an online music retailer and a subsidiary of eUniverse, Inc., which owns a network of popular online interactive community, editorial, and entertainment-focused commerce web sites. Besides CD Universe, its on-line commerce properties include VideoUniverse and GamesUniverse. Leading gaming community and content sites include BigNetwork, Gamer's Alliance, Funone, Case's Ladder, and LivePlace.

The Internet retailing industry grew at an astonishing rate in 1999. On-line sales rose from $1.7 billion per month in 1998 to $3.6 billion per month in 1999. Music was the number two product purchased on-line, behind books. With an estimated customer base of more than 300,000, CD Universe had become a mid-size music retailer. Larger competitors like Amazon.com, barnesandnoble.com, and CD Now dominated this extremely competitive and fragmented sector. Historically, CD Universe had been rated among the top online retailers in both customer satisfaction and service as rated by third party rating services such as Gomez.com and Bizrate.com.

eUniverse is headquartered in Wallingford, Connecticut. The company went public on August 14, 1999, and its stock is traded on the OTC Bulletin Board under the ticker symbol "EUNIE." Revenues for the fiscal year ended March 31, 2000, were $9.1 million and were projected to be $16 million in 2001. The Company lost $6.3 million in the nine months ended December 31, 1999. eUniverse had 6.3 million unique visitors to its Web sites in February 2000, ranking it as the twenty-eighth largest Internet property.

Information Systems and Security

Maxus told the *The New York Times* via e-mail he could breach ICVerify, which is a credit card verification software program used by CD Universe and sold by Cybercash, Inc. Cybercash is an electronic commerce security firm based in Reston, Virginia, and has both retailers and banks as customers.

Scott Collison, a former official at Signio, an Internet payment processing firm and competitor of Cybercash, was quoted in *The American Banker* saying, that "an earlier version of Cybercash's system stored credit card data in a database on the merchant's premises and could be accessed if security measures were not appropriate. There was a big burden on the merchant's side to maintain the system." According to Collison, Cybercash's newer versions of the system maintain the database on its own property.

Daniel Lynch, Chairman of Cybercash, told reporters that Cybercash had discovered a security flaw in ICVerify about a year earlier, but had created a software "patch" for it and notified its clients. He did not know, however, if all the clients had installed the patch. Chuck Riegel, Vice President of marketing at CyberCash, said in press interviews that their product was no longer being used at CD Universe. Officials at eUniverse would not discuss what security measures were used at any of its sites.

This was not the company's first incident with security problems. Previously, CD Universe had sent on-line confirmations for orders placed on the Yahoo! Shopping site. These confirmation notices included the name, address, and credit card information of the customers, and were sent in a plain text format that could be easily intercepted.

MasterCard and Visa developed an Internet security standard in the mid-1990s called the Secure Electronic Transaction (SET) Protocol, which was not used by CD Universe. SET is a protocol used by on-line merchants to secure the submission of customer data to the e-retailer. While SET does not validate the authenticity of either party, it does issue a digital certificate to both the merchant and the cardholder that prevents the transmission of the credit card information over the Internet.

Company Response

After learning of the theft on January 7, the company immediately notified the FBI and Lightrealm, Inc., which shut down the Maxus Web site. Lightrealm is an Internet carrier based in Kirkland, Washington, which was not aware that the hacker was using their system to operate the site. However, thousands of visitors took Maxus up on his offer before the site was closed. Before the site was shut down, a traffic counter indicated several thousand visitors had downloaded more than 25,000 credit card numbers since Christmas Day.

On Monday, January 10, CD Universe publicly confirmed the theft of customer data from its web site. "We take great pains to safeguard the privacy of our customers' information and will take all necessary action to limit any loss or inconvenience to customers which may occur as a result of this unusual occurrence. Refusing to bow to this new breed of cyber-criminals, we have taken a stand against a new form of online blackmail on behalf of all legitimate e-commerce retailers," Greenspan said in a January 10 press release. "We are working with the major credit card companies to limit any losses or inconvenience associated with the theft of the data," said Brett Brewer, director of Investor Relations.

eUniverse also addressed the security issues pertaining to the misappropriated data. While the company confirmed the theft, they did not reveal details on how the security system was penetrated, where the credit card data was stored, or whether the Cybercash systems were to blame. Greenspan stated CD Universe was not ready to conclude Maxus had manipulated the Cybercash system to obtain the customer data. The company retained a major New York technology security firm, Kroll-Ogara, to review its security procedures.

The firm sent an e-mail to individual customers on January 14, one full week after the company learned of the breach, warning that they be aware of and report any unauthorized credit card usage. eUniverse subsequently sent customers a $5 gift certificate for the inconvenience. eUniverse also worked with the major credit card companies to limit customer losses; in what is believed to be the largest credit card recall ever, over 300,000 cards were replaced. Generally, credit card holders are responsible for up to $50 of unauthorized charges.

Questions

1.   In an increasingly competitive electronic marketplace, what would you do if you were Brad Greenspan?

2.   What is at stake for CD Universe?

3.   In light of the other past security breaches at CD Universe, how should they communicate to their customers that Internet transactions are secure?

4.   What is the best strategy in addressing the issues at hand? Is the letter from Brad Greenspan enough?

5.   What responsibility does CD Universe have in setting security standards in this new e-commerce world?

6.   Did CD Universe respond properly to the hacker?

7.   What would be an effective corporate policy for responding to security threats by outsiders?

8.   Can you suggest a list of standards for CD Universe to put in place for future security threats?

9.   What impact will this incident have on consumer confidence in on-line shopping?

Sources

"eUniverse Confirms the Theft of Customer Data From Its CD Universe Subsidiary," *PR Newswire*, Monday, January 10, 2000.

Pollak, Anne. "Technology; Credit Card Data Stolen, Posted on Net," *Bloomberg News* as printed in the *Los Angeles Times*, Tuesday, January 11, 2000.

Kelsey, Dick. "Teen Loots CD Site of Customer Data In Blackmail Plot – Update," *Newsbytes* full text *2000 Financial Times Information Ltd*, Tuesday, January 11, 2000.

Markoff, John. "Thief Reveals Credit Card Data When Web Extortion Plot Fails," *The New York Times*, Monday, January 10, 2000.

Marjanovic, Steven. "Theft of Card Numbers Casts Doubts on Web's Security for Commerce," *The American Banker, Inc.*, Tuesday, January 11, 2000.

Lee, Richard. "Russian Hacker has Local Impact," *Record-Journal*, Tuesday, January 11, 2000.

Kreinin Souccar, Miriam. "SET Protocol Gets 2nd Look After Wave of Web Breaches," *The American Banker*, Tuesday, March 21, 2000.

Kehoe, Louise. "Hacker Forces Card Recall," *Financial Times (London)*, Thursday, January 20, 2000.

Kluger, Jeffrey. "Extortion on the Internet: A Daring Hacker Tries to Blackmail an E-tailer—and Sparks New Worries About Credit-Card Cybertheft," *Time*, January 24, 2000.

"eUniverse Delivers 66% Increase in Revenue over Q299; eUniverse Demonstrates Successful Execution of Business Model with 126% Increase in Advertising Revenue in Q3 Versus Q299," *PR Newswire*, Friday, February 4, 2000.

"eUniverse and Take2 Interactive Forge Partnership to Promote Games Online; Multi-Million Dollar Partnership Includes Ad and Sponsorship Buys Across Premier Entertainment Network as Well as Cross-Promotional Opportunities for Global Interactive Entertainment Software Developer," *PR Newswire*, Friday, March 31, 2000.

Tsuruoa, Doug. "As E-Commerce Insurance Gains But Slowly, as Policy Writers Still Trying to Grasp All of the Liability Issues Associated with Doing Business in Cyberspace," *Investor's Business Daily*, February 16, 2000.

Ceniceros, Roberto. "Managing E-Commerce Risk; New Coverage Introduced to Protect Against First-,Third-Party Risks," *Business Insurance*, Monday, January 24, 2000.

Mitkowski, Ethan D. "Online CD Store Fixes Holes," *Record-Journal*, January 17, 2000.

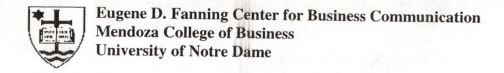
Intel Corporation:
The Pentium III Chip

As Tom Waldrop returned to his cubicle after lunch, he wondered how Intel would respond to possible criticism from the most recent press release. On Thursday, January 20, 1999, they released a statement to the press explaining new technology that would be included in Intel's newest microprocessor, the Pentium III chip. This new technology would allow the microprocessor to transmit unique identification numbers online. Shortly thereafter, Intel found itself under intense criticism from several independent privacy advocate groups. Mr. Waldrop, executive manager of business press relations, was quickly enveloped in this latest crisis.

Intel's executives viewed this new technology as an important step for increased network commerce. The company's personal relations department, however, did not expect such a strong adverse response. The company felt that the new technology would be beneficial to corporate and individual consumers because of its increased security implications. The company was wary of introducing such an advanced product to the marketplace amidst concern and controversy from the public. Furthermore, Intel had made this mistake before. In 1994, Intel was forced to recall its entire product line of Pentium processors because of an application design flaw. Although Intel handled that crisis in an effective manner, a problem with another product line could seriously damage the company's image and reputation.

Company History

Intel was founded with the vision of designing and manufacturing very complex silicon "chips." The company's first products were semiconductor memory chips. In 1996 they celebrated the twenty-fifth anniversary of Intel's introduction of the first microprocessor, an invention which sparked a computer revolution that has changed the world. More than 80 percent of the personal computers in use around the world today are based on Intel-designed microprocessors. Intel currently supplies the personal computing industry with the chips, boards, systems, and software that are the "ingredients" of the most popular computing architecture in the world.

The microprocessor chip, also called the central processing unit (CPU), is frequently described as the "brain" of a computer because it controls the central processing of data. Enterprise systems and file servers use Intel's advanced microprocessors in multiprocessing configurations for network data storage applications. In November 1971, Intel introduced the world's first commercial microprocessor, the 4004, invented by three Intel engineers. Primitive by today's standards, it contained a mere 2,300 transistors and performed about 60,000 calculations a second. Twenty-five years later, the microprocessor is the most complex mass-produced product ever, with more than 5.5 million transistors performing hundreds of millions of calculations each second.

Industry and Market Data

Intel competes at various degrees in different market segments on the basis of functionality, quality, performance, availability, and price. Intel is engaged in a rapidly advancing field of technology. Its ability to compete depends upon its ability to improve its products and processes, to develop new products that meet changing customer requirements, and to reduce costs. Prices decline rapidly in the semiconductor industry as unit volumes grow, as competition develops, and as production experience is accumulated. Many companies compete with Intel in the various computing market segments and are engaged in the same basic fields of activity, including research and development. Both foreign and domestic, these competitors range in size from large multinationals to smaller companies focusing on specialized market segments.

A substantial amount of Intel's financial results are dependent on sales of microprocessors by the Intel Architecture Business Group, and to a lesser extent, on sales of other semiconductor components by the Computing Enhancement Group. The Pentium II processor and the Pentium III processor, introduced in February 1999, compete with existing and future products in the performance desktop and entry-level workstation market segment. Intel's strategy is to introduce ever-higher performance microprocessors tailored for the different segments of the worldwide computing market. The company seeks to develop higher performance microprocessors for each market segment. Intel plans to cultivate new businesses and to continue working with the computing industry to expand Internet capabilities and product offerings. Additionally, they would like to develop compelling software applications that will take advantage of their higher performance chips, thus driving demand toward the newer products in each computing market segment.

Pentium III

This new processor, scheduled for release in April 1999, was constructed with the latest Internet commerce technology. Each chip contains a Processor Serial Number (PSN). Intel developed this technology in order to improve electronic commerce and other net-based applications. According to Intel Vice President Patrick Gelsinger, the PSN will be used to identify users who access Internet Web sites or "chat rooms." The primary advantage of the use of a PSN would be increased personal security with on-line transactions, asset management, and networking capabilities. It would also greatly advance security in Internet commerce through authentication of e-mail and other private documents. The most enthusiastic users of the new technology would be corporations who want greater security of computer use within their internal networks.

An identification number could provide added security for financial transactions. For example, if a person "dials-up" an on-line stock trading service and asks to sell 1,000 shares, the service would have more confidence that the request was not fraudulent if the computer from which the order originated had the correct ID number. In addition, such ID numbers could reduce anonymous on-line pests by stopping people from joining chat groups unless they are willing to be identified.

Whenever a computer with a new Intel chip is turned on, the machine will automatically pump out the PSN if the computer is connected to the Internet or another online network. When a person must "register" and provide details such as name, address, and other preferences, the web site is able to track what the visitor does online. Intel does not plan to keep track of these unique numbers. Prior to the press release, Intel considered shipping the new microprocessor with the PSN in the off position and giving consumers the ability to turn the feature on. Desktop Products executives believed that such a setting would make consumers more vulnerable. If a single click of the mouse turns on the ID feature, then a rogue web site could send virus programs to unsuspecting consumers' computers and secretly turn on the serial number signals as well.

Privacy Advocate Groups

Several consumer privacy advocates spearheaded much of the criticism surrounding the Pentium III. These advocate groups, led by the Electronic Privacy Information Center (EPIC) were calling for a boycott of Intel products. Joining in the boycott were two other privacy organizations, Junkbusters, Inc. and Privacy International. In addition, although not involved in the boycott, the American Civil Liberties Union (ACLU) called the Pentium III "a blow to privacy."

EPIC is a public interest research center in Washington, D.C. The Center was established in 1994 to focus public attention on emerging civil liberties issues. They aim to protect privacy, First Amendment rights, and constitutional values. EPIC's executive director, Marc Rotenberg, has pointed out that people feel as if they are being forced to trade privacy for access, and they do not seem to like it. The message to Internet users from Intel was increasingly clear: "if you want to enjoy the benefits of Web-based services, the admission ticket is your privacy."

At the time of this case, the United States had few legal protections for online privacy. There were no practical limits on what could be collected or used. Advocacy groups worried that the records of many different companies could be merged without the user's knowledge or consent to provide an intrusive profile of the individual. Given the widespread practice of downloading shareware, the lack of legal protection over personal data, and the economic incentives to collect and sell it, widespread abuse of the PSNs appeared likely. It seemed highly probable that once the capability was present in the computer hardware, web sites would begin to require the identification number for access, and PSN use would snowball.

Privacy advocates saw a worrisome potential for government snooping and unwanted commercial exploitation of personal data. "If this goes forward," warned Junkbuster, Inc.'s Jason Catlett, "it's a foregone conclusion that marketers will ultimately have all the information they want about users." What opponents feared was that marketers would be able to accumulate vast amounts of personal information by tracking a user's trail across various web sites, a trail left by the use of an identification serial number. They added that turning it on and off requires shutting down and rebooting each time, a procedure most users will not have the patience for. Thus, if one Web site requires the PSN, users will get in the habit of leaving the feature on.

Intel's Privacy Dilemma

Tom Waldrop and other executives at Intel now face the challenge of deciding how to respond to the advocacy groups and the accompanying criticism. The company believes that the new processor and PSN have value because of the added consumer security it provides. The effects of a boycott from various consumer privacy groups, however, could seriously harm the company's revenues, as well as their image. Waldrop and the other Intel executives have ventured into a dangerous area. In their efforts to improve their existing product line, they have entered into a potential litigation disaster. At a time when the public was already focused on Microsoft and the pending antitrust litigation, further investigations into the industry might continue to diminish its credibility.

While initial efforts were aimed at improving transaction security, this perspective was not delivered effectively to the public. Intel's executives must decide whether they should hold strong in their beliefs that the PSN will increase consumer security or instead, give in to the demands of privacy advocate groups. In either case, Waldrop has the difficult task of clarifying the company's position to the public. He must decide how to convey this message in a manner that will silence the critics and contain any damage done as a result of the negative press.

Questions

1. What are the advantages and disadvantages of the new PSN technology?

2. Who stands to benefit from the new technology?

3. Identify the critics of Intel and explain their effect on the company.

4. Should Intel respond to the growing criticism of advocacy groups?

5. If so, who should speak on behalf of the company when addressing the advocacy groups? When addressing the public?

6. Should Intel modify its technology because of the pressures from such advocacy groups?

7. How can Intel effectively explain the advantages of the PSN technology to the public?

8. Does Intel have a responsibility to set industry standards in regard to consumer privacy?

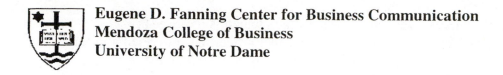
TD Waterhouse Investor Services:
How Easy is This?

Melissa Gitter had been expecting the events that unfolded on January 10, 2001 for some time, but eager anticipation would hardly characterize the sense with which she awaited the news of this day. The global spokesperson for TD Waterhouse Group, Inc. knew that her firm was being investigated by a panel from the New York Stock Exchange for a series of outages to its on-line trading system that left many of the firm's customers unable to make trades for periods at a time. By the time Ms. Gitter received the panel's findings against the firm, she had already been mulling over communication strategies the firm might employ in response to various scenarios. When she finally read that the NYSE was censuring TD Waterhouse and fining the firm $225,000, she knew that a well-crafted media and customer relations plan would be a top priority for company president Frank Petrilli.

TD Waterhouse Background

TD Waterhouse Group, Inc. is a global on-line financial services firm. They provide investors with a broad range of brokerage, mutual fund, and banking services. They also offer consumer financial products and services on an integrated basis. TD Waterhouse is a subsidiary of TD Waterhouse Group, Inc., a publicly traded stock on the New York Stock Exchange and the Toronto Stock Exchange under the symbol TWE. In the United States, TD Waterhouse is the only financial services firm to have branches in all 50 states. Worldwide, TD Waterhouse services 4.4 million customer accounts in the United States, Canada, the United Kingdom, Australia, and Hong Kong. The firm also services customers in Japan and India through joint ventures in those countries. The Toronto-Dominion Bank Financial Group (TD Bank) holds 88 percent of the outstanding share capital of TD Waterhouse Group, Inc.

This case was prepared by Research Assistants John Hudson, Brice Waddell, and William Kehoe under the direction of James S. O'Rourke, Concurrent Associate Professor of Management, as the basis for class discussion rather than to illustrate either effective or ineffective handling of an administrative situation. Information was grathered from corporate as well as public sources.

Since 1979, TD Waterhouse Investor Services, Inc., which is the U.S. brokerage unit of TD Waterhouse as well as the nation's fourth-largest on-line broker, has provided a mixture of products, prices, and services that allow customers to manage their own investments and personal finances. There are over 3.1 million active accounts. TD Waterhouse has over 170 Branch Offices in major cities throughout the United States and through its brokerage subsidiaries, acts as custodian for approximately $136 billion in customer assets.[1]

Industry Overview

Traditionally, brokerage and trading companies have offered a variety of financial services including trading and investment planning. Brokers would share research and analyst information regarding specific companies and investments with existing and prospective clients. In this way they could execute market orders to buy and sell stocks, bonds, and other commodities. The broker handled matching buy and sell orders for these securities. This trading activity allowed brokerage companies to generate substantial fees for these transactions. The thorough research provided by the brokers and the consultation with a full array of services offered justified these significant trading costs. Clients were not able to obtain lower fees due to the virtual oligopoly of large industry leaders who dictated prices and hoarded information.

However, the advent of the Internet in the early 1990s empowered customers and radically changed the investment and trading industry. Internet access greatly increased the ability of investors to research company information on their own. It made data that was heretofore difficult to obtain easily accessible. This information pool reduced the demand for research that traditional brokerage firms provided. This pressured traditional firms to lower their costs and to justify their fees as consumers became more willing to take an active role in their investing. Compounding the situation was the monumental "bull" market that began around this time and seemingly offered large returns with ease for a variety of investments.

The accessibility of information, demand for reduced fees, and desire of investors to handle their own investment activity downplayed the importance of services that traditional firms offered and spawned a surge of new on-line trading companies. These companies, such as E*Trade, Datek, and Ameritrade, offered investors the opportunity to do research on their own, to trade for significantly less money than the industry average, and to execute fast trades over the Internet. Investors flocked to these companies for the opportunity to open accounts and trade for low prices. They wanted to capitalize on quick transactions that maximized earning potential from daily stock fluctuations. This activity prompted the emergence of "day trading" and an increased number of new investors as people looked to capitalize on low fees and high stock gains.

Today, on-line brokerage accounts represent about 25 percent of all retail stock trades while trading activity continues to grow.[2] There are approximately 10 million on-line accounts

[1] http://www.tdwaterhouse.com/home/about/index.html
[2] http://www.sec.com

currently[3], and growth projections indicate that this figure should double by 2003.[4] Furthermore, on-line accounts represent over $500 billion in assets, and projections estimate that on-line account asset values will surpass $3 trillion by 2003.[5] This industry growth has fueled the success of many aggressive online discounters and has increased the appetite of investors for low commissions, quick transactions, and convenient trades.

Competition

The growth and success of on-line trading dramatically altered the competitive landscape of the industry. Traditional full service firms, such as PaineWebber and Morgan Stanley Dean Witter, were forced to offer on-line services to investors and to reduce commissions. Longtime discounters like Charles Schwab and Ameritrade witnessed strong growth and earnings. Furthermore, new companies like Datek and E*Trade flourished and capitalized on low fees with quick service to entice investors. The industry became more fragmented as new companies rushed to join the online investing fray:[6]

- **Ameritrade Holding Corp.** Founded in 1975, Ameritrade is a discount broker that today concentrates primarily on on-line investing. The firm has over $670 million in annual revenues and has a market capitalization of $1.1 billion. From early 1997 to mid-1999, the company's stock appreciated roughly 50 to 1.

- **E*Trade Group, Inc.** E*Trade is primarily an on-line financial services firm. The firm has over $1.4 billion in annual revenues and a market capitalization of $2.2 billion. The company had an Initial Public Offering (IPO) in late 1996. Its stock increased roughly 30 to 1 from its IPO through mid-1999.

- **Charles Schwab Corporation.** Charles Schwab is a leading financial service provider for over 6.6 million accounts. Roughly 3.3 million of these accounts are on-line. Annual revenues are over $5.7 billion, and the firm has a market capitalization of $22.8 billion. Its stock appreciated over 20 to 1 from early 1997 to early 1999.

- **Morgan Stanley Dean Witter.** The traditional brokerage firm offers both full service and on-line trading accounts. It is a global company that provides multiple services and professional consulting in addition to trading. It has annual revenues of over $46 billion and a market capitalization of over $55 billion. Its stock appreciated roughly 2 to 1 from early 1997 through early 1999.

- **Merrill Lynch.** The full service and traditional brokerage firm provides research and investment planning, as well as on-line service. The global firm offers a broad array of services and consulting. The company has revenues of approximately $45 billion and a

---

[3] Ibid.

[4] Personal Communication. Interview with Matt Petty, Morgan Stanley Dean Witter.

[5] Ibid.

[6] http://www.yahoo!finance.com

market capitalization of $46.6 billion. From early 1997 to early 1999, the company's stock increased almost 2 to 1 in value.

TD Waterhouse Runs Afoul of the NYSE

Member Firm Regulation (MFR) is a division of The New York Stock Exchange which conducts an annual evaluation of supervisory standards and sales practice procedures for member firms. MFR also has responsibilities to conduct financial, operational, and supervisory standards and procedures. These are standardized examinations to which members of the NYSE are subject, including TD Waterhouse and other on-line discount brokerage firms. Upon examination of TD Waterhouse, MFR issued a report which identified certain deficiencies in the firm's procedures. In a September 1999 letter, the Enforcement Division of the NYSE notified TD Waterhouse that an investigation would follow.

During the period from November 1998 through early April 2000, TD Waterhouse was unable to process on-line orders on 33 different trade dates. The *webBroker* system used by the firm was unable to process orders ranging in time from two minutes to one hour and 51 minutes on the dates noted. While the customer was prompted by temporary notice to call and have the trades executed, the NYSE investigation found that this action was not adequate in advising customers of their alternatives. The findings also noted that the firm did not maintain adequate telephone routing systems to handle orders that otherwise would have been placed on-line. This resulted in lengthy holds on telephone orders.

While the *webBroker* and the telephone routing systems were experiencing these problems, TD Waterhouse nonetheless continued to open new on-line accounts which would have access to these trading vehicles. On-line customer accounts with access to *webBroker* increased by roughly 600,000 from December 1998 to February 2000 (Exhibit 2). TD Waterhouse also continued to advertise, although ads related to *webBroker* occurred at a reduced rate.

As Waterhouse tried to keep pace with the technical and operational problems, response to customer complaints was lacking. A review of the e-mailed customer complaints regarding *webBroker* revealed that Waterhouse did not adequately respond to some of these complaints. The findings were reviewed in light of Exchange Rule 351(d), Reports of Customer Complaint Statistics, which requires member organizations to report statistical information regarding customer complaints to the Exchange. Interpretation of this rule essentially means that oral, written, or e-mailed complaints must be conveyed to the Exchange with reporting codes on at least a quarterly basis. From October through December 1998, TD Waterhouse reported approximately 400 operational and sales practice complaints. However, it did not report any of the approximately 2,300 e-mail or 18,000 verbal complaints.

The firm also allowed five individuals who had not complied with the continuing education requirements to perform duties requiring registration, therefore in violation of Exchange Rule 345A. A review of the Firm's 1998 compliance with the continuing education requirements disclosed 17 individuals whose status as registered had been inactive due to their failure to complete training requirements.

Questions

1.   How should TD Waterhouse respond to the findings of the NYSE panel?

2.   Should the firm appeal the fine levied against it by the NYSE or quietly admit guilt and pay the fine?

3.   If you were Melissa Gitter, with which constituencies would you be concerned in drafting a communications strategy?

4.   Would the desired message differ among various constituencies?

5.   What is the key issue at stake for TD Waterhouse?

PART IV

Protecting the Environment

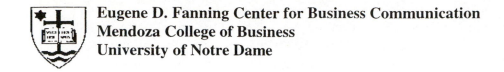
Shell Oil Company U.K.
and The Brent Spar

The proposed sinking of the Brent Spar became a major controversy for Shell U.K. and the British Government in June 1995. The planned sinking was canceled at the last moment after a wave of protest spread across Europe expressing concern about the environmental impact of the sinking. The decision sent a shock wave through the oil industry as companies realized the potential implications of the decision for future environmentally sensitive issues. The company also recognized the power that pressure groups could exert through public campaigns of protest.

Worldwide Platforms

The disposal of decommissioned production platforms is a worldwide concern for oil companies. The industry estimates that 7,300 platforms are located in oceans around the world. Two-hundred nineteen of these installations are located in the U.K. Continental Shelf area. The estimated cost of disposal for these platforms is around US$40 billion.[1]

The average life of a platform is contingent on its size, as well as on the field and reserves where it operates. Smaller facilities are normally designed for a 15-year life, while larger facilities will last approximately 30 years. However, the reserves are usually the deciding factor in a platform's life.

Once a platform has reached its economic limits and is no longer profitable, it is decommissioned and disposed of according to the regulations in effect at the time or in accordance with existing lease stipulations. It is normally up to the platform's operator to decide the best and most cost effective method for disposal.

This case was prepared by Research Assistants Mark Hales, Nikolay Nikolov, and Joshua Parker under the direction of James S. O'Rourke, Concurrent Associate Professor of Management, as the basis for class discussion rather than to illustrate either effective or ineffective handling of an administrative situation. Information was gathered from corporate as well as public sources.

---

[1] *Financial Times,* September 4, 1995.

The decommissioning of North Sea structures is controlled by guidelines established by the International Maritime Organization (IMO) and the Oslo and Paris Convention (OSPAR or OSLO Convention). Companies wishing to decommission and dispose of a platform must submit, as part of their abandonment and decommissioning program, a comparative assessment which evaluates the practicability, risks, environmental impact, effects on other users of the sea, and cost effectiveness.[2]

The Brent Spar platform ceased to operate in September 1991, after 14 years of service. The sheer size, weight, and structure of the Spar and its unique design as a storage and transfer facility called for special consideration in terms of decommissioning. Shell completed a three-year research study of the decommissioning alternatives available to the company for disposing of the Spar. After considering the alternatives and consulting with independent authorities, Shell proposed that the best practicable environmental option (BPEO) was a deep-sea disposal operation in 2,000 meters of water off the Outer Hebrides in Northern Scotland. Shell U.K. submitted the final draft of the BPEO to the British Government in October 1994.

In February 1995, the British Government announced its intention to approve the deep-water disposal. The announcement was accompanied by a notification, as required by the OSLO Convention, to the 13 signatory parties of the convention (12 nation members and the European Union). A period of two months followed in which member nations could submit objections. No replies were received in this time period.

On April 30, 1995, Greenpeace responded to the announcement by boarding the Spar and commencing a campaign to protest the decision. Four days later, the German Ministry of the Environment lodged a formal protest in response to the decision. This objection came as a complete surprise to the British Government and to Shell, having never received a response from the German Government during the time period allocated by the OSLO Convention.

A Campaign of Protest Begins

When the British Government had made the decision to approve the deep-sea disposal, Shell immediately implemented plans to tow the Spar to the designated disposal location in the Atlantic. The heat, however, was being turned up in Europe, as a major campaign was underway challenging the Shell decision.

Greenpeace

The Greenpeace organization was the catalyst for the protest movement, which ultimately resulted in Shell's decision to compromise. An article in the *Financial Times,* June 21, 1995, describes the abandoning of the Spar sinking project as one of the greatest triumphs in the 25-

---

[2] *Financial Times*, September 4, 1995.

year history of Greenpeace. The article describes the tactics and effectiveness of the Greenpeace campaign with its powerful ability to use images and life threatening stunts to capture the world's attention. This particular campaign followed a period of internal division over the future direction of Greenpeace. The internal conflict may have been attributable to the dramatic drop in "causes." Mr. Peter Wilkinson, a former Greenpeace board member is quoted as having said, "Greenpeace now has a fleet of ships running around the oceans looking for something to do."[3]

The campaign that Greenpeace ran between April 30, 1995, and June 20, 1995, however, was a well-orchestrated and powerful machine which achieved the desired results. The campaign took three approaches. The first involved a direct assault on the Spar by having protesters land on the platform; Greenpeace also arranged for a ship and amphibious craft to interfere with the towing flotilla. The second involved a major information campaign in Europe seeking support and sympathy for the cause. This included leaflet drops and advertisements in major newspapers. Press releases accompanied by photos and images of the protesters engaging Shell on the Brent Spar made for dramatic impact with the media. The third approach involved a call for a major boycott of Shell products and services. The firebombing of a Shell garage in Hamburg, although not planned or associated directly with the Greenpeace campaign, was nonetheless a result of the call to action that was made by Greenpeace and the environmental activists who became involved in the campaign.

The European Community

The German Government was the first to lodge a formal protest against Shell and the U.K. government. This challenge initiated a growing storm of protest from Europe.

"In Germany, where opposition to the plan has been greatest, the boycott of Shell gained further momentum yesterday. For the first time in many years, Germany's political parties put aside their differences to unite in opposition to the dumping of the Brent Spar. It coincided with a swelling grassroots movement involving churches, trade unions, and local politicians to boycott Shell's 1,700 petrol stations."[4]

The protest regarding the Brent Spar quickly spread throughout Europe, and an increasing number of top-level government leaders from the continent joined Germany's condemnation of the sinking.[5] Official protests were also received from the Danish, Belgian, and Icelandic governments.

The public clash over the Brent Spar climaxed at the G7 economic summit in Halifax, Nova Scotia, the weekend before the planned sinking was to take place. Germany's Chancellor, Helmut Kohl, challenged British Prime Minister, John Major, over the U.K.'s resolve to proceed

---

[3]*Financial Times*, June 21, 1995.
[4]*The Times Weekend*, June 17/ June 18, 1995.
[5]*Financial Times*, June 21, 1995.

with its support for the sinking of the Spar. Mr. Major was unmoved by the criticism and recommitted his government's position that the deep-sea disposal was the best practicable environmental option.

British Government Response

The Department of Trade and Industry had granted Shell the initial permission to sink the Brent Spar platform in the North Sea. All technical, environmental, and legal issues were carefully examined, and the British Government was satisfied that Shell had followed the appropriate procedures outlined by the OSLO Convention. As the controversy unfolded, the British Government was very supportive of Shell in all of its public briefings. Many high-level British Government officials spoke favorably of both Shell and its plan to dispose of the oil platform.

Mr. Tim Eggar, the U.K.'s energy minister, personally garrisoned Shell's proposal in both British and European newspapers. He was quoted in the *Times* on June 19, 1995, as defending Shell's decision and attacking Greenpeace for "grossly exaggerating the problem." He added that dismantling the platform on land, as protesters were demanding, would cause "very significant environmental damage." British Prime Minister John Major also became involved in the public debate by openly supporting the deep-sea disposal. He went so far as to engage the German Chancellor Helmut Kohl in a major difference of opinion at the G7 summit just prior to the planned sinking.

It was this major role in defending Shell that became a cause of great embarrassment to the British Government when Shell withdrew from the planned disposal.

Shell's Response

Shell was taken by complete surprise when the wave of protest erupted. The initial response from Greenpeace had been the tip of the iceberg, as the company faced a growing level of criticism that had found its way to the highest levels of European government. *The Times* ran an article entitled "Shell Stunned by Brent Spar Anger" on June 17, 1995, which described the shocked reaction of the Shell Oil Company in dealing with the opposition to the sinking. The article suggested that many members of the oil industry considered Shell's handling of the issue disastrous and the result of insufficient planning and sensitivity to European reactions.

Initially Shell showed little sympathy toward the Greenpeace campaign. They did not anticipate the media impact of the clash between the company and protesters, as the flotilla began to make its way to the disposal site. There was also evidence to suggest that the company had failed to plan a corporate strategy of crisis management since Shell Executives around Europe failed to communicate with any sense of solidarity on the issue. *The Times* reported on June 20, "In Germany, some senior Shell officials have voiced bitterness about their British sister company, and distaste for the U.K. government's seemingly arrogant attitude towards the affair."

It also appears that Shell did not give its employees the advance warning which could have given them a firmer grip on events. In an interview with *Der Spiegel*, the weekly German news magazine, Mr. Peter Duncan, Chairman of Shell Germany, said he first heard about the planned sinking of the Brent Spar from the media.[6]

The Deep-Sea Disposal Is Canceled

Shell gave in to the overwhelming international pressure and abandoned the plan to sink the storage platform only hours before it was to be sunk. Shell justified its withdrawal with the following comments found on its Internet home page.

"Shell UK aborted the operation because the Shell position as a major European enterprise had become untenable. The Spar had gained a symbolic significance out of all proportion to its environmental impact. In consequence, Shell companies were faced with increasingly intense public criticism, mostly in continental northern Europe. Many politicians and ministers were openly hostile and several called for consumer boycotts. There was violence against Shell service stations, accompanied by threats to Shell staff."

The U.K. Government Responds Angrily

Shortly after the news, energy minister Tim Eggar accused Shell of abandoning three years of detailed discussion with the Department of Trade and Industry, which licensed the disposal under the OSPAR Convention. *The Financial Times* reported on June 22, 1995, that John Major had privately characterized Shell management as "wimps." The Prime Minister was also understood to be furious with the heads of European governments who had exerted pressure on Shell to reverse the decision to sink the Spar.

In retaliation to the decision, the British Government informed Shell that it would not grant the company a license to dismantle the platform on land unless they were able to prove that it was a better option than the deep-sea disposal.

Shell Issues an Apology

Shell officially apologized to the Prime Minister for the embarrassment the company's actions had caused. Despite the apology, Shell's actions had seriously damaged the reputation of the British Government both at home and abroad. By abandoning its plan to sink the platform, Shell discredited the government's approval of the firm's initial plan.

---

[6]*The Times*, June 20, 1995.

The Brent Spar is Towed to a Norwegian Fjord

With debate still raging about the decision, Shell commissioned the Norwegian certification authority Det Norske Veritas to conduct an independent audit of Spar to verify its contents and re-check Shell U.K.'s previous inventory. Just prior to this, on July 7, 1995, Shell received permission to moor the Spar in the deep waters of Erfjord in Norway while new disposal options were considered.

Questions

1.   What did the company fail to consider in terms of public reaction?

2.   How did the lack of communication between the European divisions of Shell contribute to the problem?

3.   How responsibly did Shell handle its relationship with the U.K. government over the issue of the Brent Spar disposal?

4.   How important is it for companies to understand and anticipate the reaction and impact of interest groups? How would you have handled the situation with Greenpeace?

5.   Was the backdown by Shell a compromise that has implications for other companies dealing with controversial business decisions?

Mitsubishi Corporation

Background

In December of 1997, horrified fishermen discovered 94 black sea turtles, an endangered species, floating lifelessly in the Laguna Ojo de Liebre. The lagoon is near the Exportadora de Sal S.A. de C.V. (ESSA) salt production facility in Baja, Mexico. Following a six-month scientific investigation, it was announced that the turtles had been poisoned by a toxic salt brine waste spill — the fault of the ESSA. This disaster prompted the Mexican government to order an investigation of the company's proposed expansion at the Laguna San Ignacio. The ESSA insisted that their facilities and processes were not detrimental to the environment. To all other interested parties the ESSA operation, heralded as working in perfect harmony with nature, seemed to be having a devastating effect on the local marine life.

Despite the outrage surrounding the death of the turtles, the ESSA pressed on with their proposal for a new salt facility at Laguna San Ignacio, a pristine lagoon in Baja, Mexico. The ESSA claimed that it was one of the few suitable sites in the world for solar salt production. However, it was also an ideal mating ground for numerous California gray whales. As the investigation continued, both the ESSA and the environmentalists dug in their heels and anticipated a long battle.

Exportadora de Sal S.A. de C.V. (ESSA)

The ESSA was formed in 1954 by the Mexican government. In 1976, it became a joint venture with the Mitsubishi Corporation of Japan. At the time of this case, the Mexican government owned 51 percent, and Mitsubishi held the remaining 49 percent of the venture.

The sole business purpose of the ESSA is the production and exportation of solar-produced salt. The by-product of the process is salt brine, a highly solidified toxin. In 1997, salt sold for $13 per ton. During that year, ESSA produced seven million tons of salt, resulting in revenues of $91 million for the year.

This case was prepared by Research Assistants Erika Bonner and Justin Schaefer under the direction of James S. O'Rourke, Concurrent Associate Professor of Management, as the basis for class discussion rather than to illustrate either effective or ineffective handling of an administrative situation. Information was gathered from corporate as well as public sources.

The major competitors for salt exportation were France and Australia. In fact, the ESSA feared that Australia could become a threat to their own exportation in the near future, thus intensifying the need to increase capacity.

The ESSA's original solar production facility is located in Guerrero Negro near the Laguna Ojo de Liebre on the west coast of the Baja California Sur. This facility employs 1,000 people, most of whom are locals from the nearby town of Guerrero Negro. The company has a very low turnover rate and is a very popular place for residents to work because of generous benefits including profit sharing. Most of the salt produced at Guerrero Negro is exported to Japan, but exports are also made to the United States, Canada, and Taiwan. This facility has been adequate until recently. With a growing world population more salt is needed, and the Guerrero Negro plant has reached its capacity.

Why Laguna San Ignacio?

The Laguna San Ignacio, like Guerrero Negro, is located on the west coast of Baja California Sur. It possesses all the characteristics that the ESSA needs for solar salt production. It has safe access for ships to load the salt, and it is near a natural salt water source, the Pacific Ocean. The high salinity of the water in this lagoon provides the process with more salt than in other areas. High temperatures, windy conditions, barren salt flats, and impermeable soil which holds water and helps evaporation, are exactly the conditions that the ESSA requires.

The Solar Salt Production Process

The area surrounding the Laguna San Ignacio is ideal for solar salt production because of the impermeable clay surface and series of natural ponds. Ocean water flows to a two kilometer canal (to be dredged upon approval), through a series of pipes in the canal, and into the natural ponds. The floors of the ponds do not allow water and salt to seep into the ground, creating sealed pools where evaporation of the water can take place. The result of the evaporation is salt. After all of the water has been evaporated, the salt is removed and transported via conveyor belt to a waiting ship. This process requires no buildings or other such structures.

Environmental Situation

Following the discovery of the dead turtles near the ESSA's Guerrero Negro production site, the wrath of environmentalists descended upon the venture. Major newspapers such as the *Los Angeles Times* printed commentaries on the situation, criticizing Mitsubishi Corporation, since they were involved in the joint venture, for negligence and for purposely ignoring the magnitude of the situation.

Both the Guerrero Negro and the proposed San Ignacio facilities are located within the El Vizcaino Biosphere Reserve. This reserve was created to provide legal protection for the various ecosystems in the area. It is the largest reserve in Latin America, covering 2.5 million hectares of land.

Within the area of Laguna San Ignacio reside various species of wildlife, plant life, and marine life. Peregrine falcons and golden eagles rule the skies, with mountain lions and coyotes prowling the land searching for a dinner that could include a pronghorn antelope. Giant black sea turtles and fish claim the ocean. The main issue for environmentalists in this case is the threat to the gray whales.

Gray whales were recently removed from the endangered species list, but any type of calamity, such as what happened to the sea turtles in 1997, could land them right back on the list. Laguna San Ignacio is one of the last untouched breeding and calving grounds for gray whales left in the world. The warm water and high salinity are very important because the salinity buoys newborn whales so they can nurse from their mothers.

Environmentalist Claims

The major environmentalist group leading the fight against Mitsubishi and ESSA's proposal for a new facility is the Natural Resource Defense Council. The environmentalists disagree with nearly every statement that ESSA makes. They claim that the salt production damages the environment and is potentially harmful to creatures, in this case gray whales. Jean-Michel Cousteau, son of Jacque Cousteau, is quoted as saying "the proposed project threatens to disrupt the delicate ecological balance among the mangroves, birds, whales, and other species in the lagoon." Whether this, or any other statement, is true regarding the impact that ESSA had on the environment, such words coming from powerful activists will not be taken lightly by the public.

Environmentalists feel that the proposed facility will affect the whales, and there are some strong arguments on their side. Public opinion is that the death of 94 black sea turtles was the fault of ESSA. This opinion does not improve the company's environmental track record regardless of the facts. The gray whale was removed from the endangered species list just two years prior. Releasing the gray whale from the endangered species list is considered one of the greatest victories of animal conservation. Public opinion would not look kindly upon a business that unfeelingly disregards this animal when making a decision about where to locate a potentially harmful processing facility.

A final advantage the environmentalists have is that the Mexican National Ecology Institute (Mexican counterpart to the U.S. Environmental Protection Agency) rejected ESSA's expansion proposal. An independent environmental committee is studying the question as to whether the facility would harm the lagoon's environment. The committee consists of Mexican and American researchers and professors, a member of the U.S. National Marine Fisheries, and the Chairman of the International Whaling Commission.

Mitsubishi and Steve Wechselblatt

Mitsubishi Corporation of Japan was a 49 percent owner of the ESSA joint venture at the time of this case. ESSA is one of over 500 subsidiaries of the Mitsubishi Corporation, whose 1997 revenues exceeded $127 billion. ESSA is considered to be part of Mitsubishi's chemical division, which earned revenues of $9 billion in 1997. The $91 million earned from salt sales was only ten percent of chemical revenues, and less than one percent of Mitsubishi Corporation's total annual revenue. Regardless of the comparatively small amount of revenues, the salt business is a very important part of the chemical division, according to Mitsubishi International's public relations director Steve Wechselblatt. Mitsubishi is not about to give up its joint venture without a fight.

Steve Wechselblatt heard about his current job from a friend in a Japanese public relations firm. He had been working for Mitsubishi for the previous four years. He has been in charge of communications regarding the Laguna San Ignacio project since the initial proposals. Mr. Wechselblatt has had a very open door communication policy — he visited the San Ignacio site with Natural Resource Defense Council representatives, showed them around, and discussed ESSA's proposal. He has been available to those with questions of any nature regarding the Laguna San Ignacio project.

Questions

1.   What is the most serious problem facing Mitsubishi in this case?

2.   Who are Mitsubishi's advocates, and how can they help the cause for the construction of the Laguna San Ignacio salt production facility?

3.   How should Mitsubishi react to the environmentalist claims against the production facility? What further impact should they anticipate from these environmental interest groups?

4.   Should Mitsubishi respond to any further bad press about the endangered species in the Laguna San Ignacio area?

5.   How can Mitsubishi effectively explain to the public and to key stakeholders the advantages of maintaining the salt production facility?

6.   Should Mitsubishi continue the project, regardless of protests, or halt all proposals?

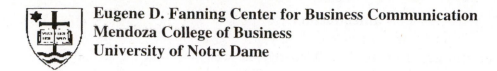
American Electrical, Inc.:
Managing an Environmental Crisis

Background Note

In preparing a statement for the press, managers must keep in mind that they are speaking on behalf of an entire organization. They are, for all purposes, the organization itself in the eyes of those who see the message.

Managers must also keep in mind that they are speaking to a very diverse and complex audience. Those whom the message will reach will have varying backgrounds, reading abilities, educational levels, knowledge of the subject, political views, prejudices, and interests.

In many ways, the mass audience reached by radio, television, newspapers, and magazines encompasses several smaller audiences. It may be helpful to think of the larger audience as comprised of shareholders, customers, suppliers, employees, competitors, politicians, local, regional, and national government officials, potential investors, neighbors, community members, and so on.

In some cases, managers might well consider drafting separate messages for separate audiences, designing their words and pictures for the backgrounds, needs, interests, inclinations, and potential reactions of each. Shareholders, for instance, might have a greater interest in knowing how an event or announcement affects their investment than do members of the surrounding community. Employees might have a keener interest in how an event will affect jobs in the organization than would others.

Keep in mind that managers should never use the mass media to communicate with an audience that they should address directly. Medium, in many ways, can be just as important as message in communicating a manager's views, feelings, and intentions.

This case was prepared from public sources and personal interviews by Professor James S. O'Rourke as the basis for class discussion rather than to illustrate either effective or ineffective handling of an administrative situation. Personal and corporate identities have been disguised.

Introduction

As Walt Martinson returned from lunch on Thursday, he sensed trouble. The visitors' spots in the parking lot outside American Electrical, Inc. (AEI) headquarters were filled with vehicles from the Georgia Department of Environmental Protection (GDEP). Martinson had seen them before. In fact, the GDEP Hazardous Materials Crew had been on American Electrical property three times in the past six weeks.

This visit came without warning. "Whatever they want," Martinson thought to himself, "it can't be good."

Angela Curran, his secretarial assistant met him as he came through the door. "They're in the Conference Room. Todd McLemore, George Willett, and Terry Salter are with them."

"How long have they been talking to the Executive Committee?" Martinson asked.

"Most of the morning," she replied. "I've cancelled your one o'clock and postponed the Department Meeting. I've told them you would join them just as soon as you could."

"Thanks, Angela. Call Roger Mullins and tell him I'll reschedule our meeting. And get me the GDEP file, please." Miss Curran was already two steps ahead of American Electrical's chief executive. "Here's the file, sir. I've already called Mr. Mullins."

Walt Martinson's Company

American Electrical, located in Marietta, Georgia, a suburb of Atlanta, is a stable yet growing firm in a mature industry. The company produces industrial-grade electrical equipment, including transformers, voltage regulators, power converters, and electrical transmission devices. The firm, founded by Martinson's father, was held as a family enterprise for over 30 years. Five years ago, however, Martinson sought additional capital to expand production and broaden both his product line and customer base. After listing the $36 million firm on the NASDAQ, he saw its stock price double within 24 months.

Then, six months ago, American Electrical bought out Multi-Phase Equipment, Inc., a small competitor in the Atlanta area. It seemed like the perfect move at the time. In exchange for $6.5 million in stock and cash, AEI swallowed Multi-Phase Equipment, Inc.'s assets, inventories, and balance sheet. AEI acquired additional plant capacity, a relatively new collection of buildings and equipment, and a small but promising list of customers.

Multi-Phase Equipment was a small, local firm that specialized in rebuilding electrical transformers. Their client base included large utilities such as Georgia Power and Light, as well as smaller customers, such as Kennesaw State College, which operated its own power generating station on campus. The firm used PCBs (polychlorinated biphenyls)[1] in dry, micro-pellet form as insulators within the inner casings of electrical transforming and transmitting equipment.

As transformers were disassembled for re-winding or replacement armatures, the old PCB insulating material was dumped into polyvinyl chloride (PVC)-lined 55-gallon drums for temporary storage. Eventual removal of the discarded PCB drums was contracted to a firm known as Wiregrass Disposal, Inc. of Dothan, Alabama. The contractor was responsible for packaging, loading, transporting, and properly disposing of the PCBs in a federally-licensed toxic waste facility. Wiregrass Disposal was also responsible for maintaining both state and federal records regarding the materials removed from the Multi-Phase Equipment site.

Prior to purchasing the Multi-Phase Equipment plant, Martinson had hired a group of bioenvironmental consultants to perform a survey of air, water, and soil quality. Independent Laboratories, Inc. of Atlanta, which came highly recommended from many of his business associates, gave the Multi-Phase property a clean bill of health just eight months ago. Based in part on their report, American Electrical's board of directors approved the purchase and stock swap.

The GDEP Case File

Before joining the meeting of the GDEP Task Force and his Executive Committee, Martinson briefly reviewed the case file that had been building over the past eight weeks. Among the issues that concerned him most was possible pollution of the local water supply. In response to complaints about the water from residential customers ("tastes funny, smells bad"), officials of the Water & Sewer Authority (WSA) of Cobb County began testing water samples for contaminants. Despite persistent reports of unusual taste and odor in the Marietta water supply, Cobb County WSA officials were unable to link changes they had observed in the local water supply to any particular source.

Following two weeks of water sampling and lab testing, Cobb County WSA called on the state GDEP for assistance and advice GDEP officials, led by Dr. Charles Puckett, followed-up on an anonymous tip that the source of local water contamination might be the old Multi-Phase Equipment yard, located just 300 meters from the Chattahoochee River. The Cobb County WSA treatment plant, which provides all fresh water supplies to the City of Marietta, is located on the Chattahoochee River, just two miles downstream from the Multi-Phase Equipment site on Roswell Road. (The river itself is fed by Lake Lanier, some 45 miles to the northeast; water volume and runoff are regulated by Buford Dam, located at the southeast corner of the lake.)

The anonymous tip, which Martinson suspected came from a former Multi-Phase employee, alleged that the company had improperly stored PCBs on company property. Early last month, the GDEP requested permission from American Electrical to excavate several parcels of land on the former Multi-Phase Equipment site. Martinson agreed, knowing that the department could force the company's cooperation with a court order. He wondered to himself how long he could keep this out of the papers. The GDEP promised a confidential report to the company and its directors in advance of any public announcement, but nothing had been forthcoming.

Martinson Meets with GDEP Officials

As he headed into the conference room, Martinson was greeted by Todd McLemore, AEI's executive vice president. McLemore had been a friend and confidant of Martinson's since they were undergraduates together at Georgia Tech. They had been through a lot together, including the IPO[2] that took the sleepy, little electrical supply firm public five years ago.

McLemore spoke softly. "I'm afraid we've got some bad news, Walt." Turning to the others he continued, "You know these gentlemen from the D.E.P."

Martinson forced a smile. "I sure do, Todd. I can't say it's good to see you fellas. I hope you're close to concluding your work here."

The GDEP's Northern Field Chief, Damon Ledbetter, responded quickly. "Mr. Martinson, our work here may have just begun. Here's a copy of our preliminary findings from the Multi-Phase Equipment site. There's an executive summary on page three that re-caps our findings."

The GDEP Preliminary Findings

Walt Martinson quickly scanned the executive summary. The bad news was up front: the GDEP Preliminary Report in the matter of American Electrical, Inc. revealed that a "relatively serious pattern of abuse appears to exist with regard to the storage and disposal of hazardous materials at the former Multi-Phase Equipment site." The pattern, according to the report, has continued for several years and involves the improper packaging and storage of polychlorinated biphenyls.

"What's your assessment of the situation, Dr. Puckett?" asked Martinson, flipping through more pages.

"Well, Mr. Martinson, the potential for damage is certainly present, but I do think that we can recommend a course of action that will help clean up the Multi-Phase site and contain whatever harm has already occurred."

Martinson suddenly stopped at an appendix in the GDEP Report. "It says here that you've uncovered 200 drums of PCBs on the Multi-Phase site. Twenty-five of them appear to be 'compromised.' What does that mean?"

"It means," replied Dr. Puckett, "that they were either improperly sealed when they were buried or they've undergone corrosive perforation."

"Corrosive perforation?" asked Martinson.

"Rust," said McLemore. "The barrels have rusted through."

"That's not half the problem, Mr. Martinson," Puckett continued. "Those barrels should never have been buried at Multi-Phase in the first place."

"He's right," said McLemore. "Multi-Phase Equipment contracted with an outfit from Alabama called Wiregrass Disposal. They were supposed to dispose of all PCBs removed during the rebuilding and refitting process."

"Where, exactly, did you find them?" Martinson asked.

"We found them on the far northeast corner of the Multi-Phase site," Dr. Puckett replied. "They appear to be clustered in a fairly small area about 350 meters from the river. We're not done, of course, but the location appears to be contained and clearly defined."

"How far is that from the plant?" Martinson inquired.

Todd McLemore could sense his partner's concern. "The manufacturing facility is better than half-a-mile away. Dr. Puckett tells me that he doesn't see any way the PCB leakage could have spread beyond the immediate burial site."

"What do I say to our employees out there?" he asked.

"Tell 'em not to worry," said Puckett. "The damage is significant, but it's confined to a relatively small area. I've seen no evidence of leeching into the water supply and the PCBs aren't airborne. There is no immediate danger to anyone working at your manufacturing facility out there."

"Well, that's a relief," said Martinson. "But . . . I'm really puzzled. Why in the world would the contractor bury the stuff right there at the plant? They surely must have known it was dangerous and illegal."

"Who knows?" offered Puckett. "The most likely reason is money. Properly packaging, transporting, and disposing of hazardous materials in a federally-licensed facility is expensive. If you're greedy and unscrupulous, you just charge the customer, bury it where you please, and keep the money."

"Has anyone spoken with these fellas from Alabama?" Martinson inquired.

George Willett, American Electrical's attorney spoke up. "Chapter 11," he said cryptically. "They filed for protection under federal bankruptcy laws eight months ago. Our contacts over in Birmingham tell us the courts have yet to dispose of the assets. We can certainly queue up behind the rest of the creditors in this case, but I've gotta tell you Walt, there isn't much there."

Martinson's reaction was swift but measured. "Look, George, I'm interested in recovering what we can from the contractor, but I'd also like to talk with the people at Independent Laboratories. They told us the place was clean. They said we'd have no problems with that property . . ."

Dr. Puckett interrupted. "We have already begun our investigation of their records, Mr. Martinson. From what we've seen thus far, they performed a satisfactory, nominal review of the soil and water at Multi-Phase." He paused for a moment. "Keep in mind we have been out there for two months and just recently found those barrels. I'm not sure we can fault Independent Labs for their work. Their core samples just missed the burial site."

"And we're still responsible for clean-up," said Martinson. "Am I right?"

"Yes," Puckett replied. "That's the bad news. The good news is that we have been able to establish no link between the PCBs on the Multi-Phase property and the drinking water complaints. And, even though we've found 25 barrels that are compromised in some way, the damage appears to be contained, since the PCB micropellets aren't water-soluble and they won't dissolve or spread contamination."

"Will you work with us to help select someone reliable to remove them?" Martinson asked. "We can provide a list of licensed contractors and can assist in documenting their work," Puckett replied. "The rest is up to you."

"I'm still curious about the water," said McLemore. "If these barrels of PCBs aren't the culprit, then what's the reason for all the uproar in Marietta about bad water?"

Damon Ledbetter spoke up. "Well, it wouldn't be PCBs to begin with." GDEP's Field Chief explained that PCBs are essentially tasteless and odorless, and are not water-soluble. "Taste and odor problems are proportionally more common," he added, "in surface water than in ground water largely because of the presence of algae. That's what we're looking into right now. Autumn leaves, surface runoff, and agricultural drainage provide ample nutrients for microorganisms that can often generate taste- and odor-producing compounds."

"You think it's algae?" Martinson asked.

"That's most likely," Ledbetter replied, "and that's what we're looking for right now. *Anabaena* and *Oscillatoria* are blue-green algae. *Ceratium* is a flagellate algae, and *Asterionella* is a diatom responsible for septic odors and bitter taste problems at a number of locations." He paused for a moment and added, "It certainly isn't the PCBs."

"Once again," said Martinson, "that's a relief."

"By the way," he added, "we plan to issue a public statement on Monday. That gives you a couple of days to draft plans of your own."

As each of the GDEP Task Force members filed out of the conference room, Martinson shook hands. "Thanks for your help," he said.

"What now?" asked McLemore.

Martinson looked up and responded, "We go to work. We need to figure out how to get the message out to our customers, our shareholders, the community, the city government, the press, and above all, our own employees."

Notes

1.   Highly toxic, PCBs are any of several compounds produced by replacing hydrogen atoms in biphenyl with chlorine. These compounds have various industrial applications but are poisonous environmental pollutants which tend to accumulate in animal tissues.

2.   An IPO is an initial public offering of a stock.

ASSIGNMENTS

A Communication Strategy Memo.

You are the Vice President for Operations and report directly to Walt Martinson, the Company's President and CEO. The executive committee has asked you for a *comprehensive communication strategy*. Don't dwell on the operational details of an environmental clean-up, or the finer points of pending litigation over the bankrupt subcontractor. Among the audiences you should consider in this case are these:

Employees. What should you tell them? How should you go about conveying the message? What's their proper role in dealing with the press and members of the community? Should you encourage them to speak up or to remain silent?

Shareholders. What would they like to know? What's your obligation to equity holders? How about creditors, or debtholders?

Customers. What do you suppose their concerns are? How should you go about communicating with them? How much do they need to know?

The Community. How can you allay their fears? What sorts of things are they worried about? What's the best approach to them? Should your message to them be telemediated or direct?

Your strategy memo should be directed to the company president and should probably not be longer than three pages. Keep in mind that even "confidential," internal memos often become public through leaks by disgruntled or attention-seeking employees.

Keep in mind also that American Electrical, Inc. *does not have a department devoted specifically to public relations or corporate communication.* You cannot simply delegate anything you don't feel like writing or thinking about to such a department. Please assume that the Office of the Executive Vice President employs a person whose tasks include internal information distribution and relations with investors. Among the products that employee regularly produces are a monthly employee newsletter and a quarterly newsletter to shareholders, clients, suppliers, and others with an interest in the firm.

A Corporate Press Release.

The executive committee has also asked you to prepare a press release. As you draft this release you may wish to consider these questions:

The facts of the case. What do we know for sure? What do we *not* know? What are we unlikely ever to know?

Assumptions. What's reasonable to assume here? Should your public statement deal with assumptions? If so, how should they be identified?

Expert opinion. Are the opinions of any experts available for you to cite? Can you use any direct quotes in your press release?

The official speaker. Who should speak on behalf of the company? Whose "voice" should the press release cite? Should it be a disembodied third person (as in a newspaper account or news report), or should you identify a source for the information you provide?

Your press release should be properly formatted, ready to transmit, and roughly 400-to-600 words in length.

Discussion Questions.

1.   What's the most serious problem Walt Martinson faces in this case? How should he go about solving it?

2.   What role should American Electrical's attorney play in this case?

3.   Should the company hold a press conference to explain its position, or will a printed release for the media be sufficient?

4.	If the company holds a press conference, who should be present? Who should act as the official speaker for the firm?

5.	The burial of PCBs on the Multi-Phase Equipment property was clearly not American Electrical's fault. What's the advisability of simply shifting the blame to the former owners of Multi-Phase?

6.	What's the advisability of naming Wiregrass Disposal, Inc. as a culprit in this case? Aren't they principally responsible for what's gone wrong?

7.	What role does Independent Laboratories, Inc. of Atlanta have in this case? Should they be named as contributorily negligent in their examination of the Multi-Phase property eight months ago?

8.	Should the American Electrical press release attempt to explain the preliminary findings of the Georgia Department of Environmental Protection? Should AEI simply let the GDEP speak on its behalf?

9.	Who should be invited to a press conference, if AEI decides to hold one? How should the company arrange for that? Where should it be held?

10.	Should local citizens or Marietta civic officials be invited to participate in the press conference? What attempt should the company make to deal with their concerns?

11.	What about the concerns of the American Electrical, Inc. shareholders? How should the company deal with them?

12.	What approach should AEI take with its customers? How about suppliers?

13.	Does the company owe anything special, by way of an explanation, to its employees? If so, how should the company communicate with them? What's the timing involved in such an explanation? In other words, who should the company talk with first, and how should they do it?

PART V

Crisis Management

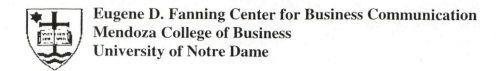
Bridgestone/Firestone, Inc. and Ford Motor Company
Crisis Management and a Product Recall

Before the Turmoil

Two years before a massive recall of more than six million tires produced by Firestone and widely used by Ford Motor Company in the United States, a Ford Explorer was traveling on an expressway in Riyadh, Saudi Arabia, when it experienced a blowout. In a country where tire failures aren't uncommon due to "extreme and unusual" driving conditions that include temperatures reaching 120 degrees or more, the accident itself wasn't what raised concern in 1998. This incident was unique because the secretary to the president of one of Saudi Arabia's largest Ford dealerships, Al Jazirah Vehicle Agencies, Inc., drove the vehicle. Also, the tire was in an unusual condition. Unlike most tires that shredded and were destroyed, the tread had simply peeled away from the tire.

The increasing complaints about the Firestone tires in Saudi Arabia led John Garthwaite, the Al Jazirah Vehicle Agencies national service manager in Riyadh, to examine consumer reports about Firestone tires on Ford vehicles in the Middle East. Beginning in 1997, complaints had been filed regarding the tires. Firestone claimed that the problems were "a customer usage issue" according to James Benintende, Ford's executive director for Middle East and North Africa. With little data to back up their claims, Ford Motor Company didn't investigate further at the time.

Garthwaite was dubious about Firestone's reluctance to take responsibility for what seemed to be more than simply rough road conditions. As he investigated reports in the Middle East accidents, he found that several deaths had been associated with Firestone's tires in Saudi Arabia, Qatar, and Kuwait. An internal Ford memo from the regional office in Dubai, dated

January 1999, raised concerns about the tires. It indicated that "we owe it to our customers and our shareholders to make our own analysis of the tires." Another memo from March of 1999 outlined a plan to replace the allegedly defective tires on Ford Explorers. Unsold Explorers in Saudi Arabia would receive upgraded tires and recent purchasers of Explorers would be given the option of replacing their tires. Firestone, however, was hesitant to offer to replace the tires in the Middle East, perhaps because they might have to notify United States officials, encouraging consumer outcry.

In July 1999, Al Jazirah decided to take action. Without organizing an official recall, the dealership began replacing the Firestone tires on Explorers that were on the lot with upgraded Firestone tires. Additionally, when customers brought their Explorers in for service, the tires were checked by Firestone-trained tire inspectors and consumers were offered a 75 percent discount on new Goodyear tires.[1] Garthwaite hired supplemental employees to call Explorer owners, asking if they would like to bring their SUVs in for a complimentary inspection.

Halfway around the world, a similar scene was being played out in Venezuela involving the same tires on the very same vehicles. According to a *Wall Street Journal* article dated September 11, 2000, Venezuela has "attributed at least 46 deaths to crashes involving Firestone tires on Ford Explorers." In August 1999, Firestone engineers investigated the incidents by driving at speeds reaching 95 mph for extended periods of time but found no defects and experienced no tire failures. Further research later revealed that Ford Motor Company replaced nearly 47,000 Firestone tires on SUVs in the Middle East, Venezuela, Thailand, and Malaysia.

The Companies Involved

The Firestone Tire & Rubber Company was founded in 1900 by Harvey S. Firestone in Akron, Ohio. The company began with only twelve employees and manufactured rubber tires and products for automobiles. In 1990, the U.S. operations of Firestone merged with Bridgestone Corporation of Japan to become Bridgestone/Firestone, Inc. The merger has resulted in the company becoming a leader in tire technology, developing more than 8,000 different types of tires for vehicles ranging from passenger cars to earth-moving agricultural equipment to race cars. Bridgestone/Firestone employs more than 100,000 people worldwide with revenues of more than US$20 billion in the 1999 fiscal year.

Henry Ford founded the Ford Motor Company in 1903 in Dearborn, Michigan. Ford was responsible for revolutionizing the car manufacturing industry by developing the first moving assembly line to produce automobiles. Since the beginning, Ford has been a leader in the automobile industry and today is the number one truck maker in the world and the number two overall manufacturer behind General Motors. Ford produces passenger cars, light trucks, and commercial vehicles in addition to owning other vehicle manufacturers such as Lincoln, Aston Martin, Jaguar, Volvo, and Land Rover. Employing more than 360,000 people, Ford's 1999 revenues were more than US$160 billion.

---

[1] Pearl, Danny, "Isolated Traffic Accident in Saudi Arabia Helped Ignite Ford-Firestone Contention," *The Wall Street Journal*, September, 11, 2000, pp. A3, A8.

The Firestone Tire Recall

On August 9, 2000, Firestone and Ford Motor Company announced a recall of 6.5 million tires in the United States, saying, "The safety of consumers is the company's first concern."[2] Estimates on replacing the tires ranged from $500 million to $4.4 billion.[3] Questions continued to arise, however, as more information became available about why it took so long for this serious matter to finally reach consumers.

The recall included original equipment and replacement tires, regardless of the vehicle manufacturer. While the tires in question were used throughout the automotive industry, Ford Motor Company was the manufacturer who most widely used the tires. The two types of tires announced in the Firestone safety recall included:

Firestone P235 75R15 ATX or ATX II tires installed on the following light truck and SUVs:
- 1991-1996 Ford Explorers.
- 1991-1996 Rangers.
- 1996 Mercury Mountaineers.
- 1991-1994 Broncos.
- 1991-1994 F-150.

Firestone P235 75R15 Wilderness AT tires produced at the Firestone Decatur plant installed on the following vehicles:
- 1997-2001 Ford Explorers [Excludes 1999-2001 Eddie Bauer and Limited editions].
- 2001 Ford Explorer Sport Trac.
- 1997-2000 Mercury Mountaineers.
- 1997-2000 Ford Rangers.[4]

Dejá vu at Firestone

Prior to its more recent mishaps, in November 1978, Firestone had found itself immersed in a pool of customer dissatisfaction after it manufactured faulty tires. The company had to recall more than 13 million tires following numerous reports of accidents and deaths involving tread separation on steel-belted radial tires. Although that situation required a recall twice that of the number targeted this time, the current situation held many parallels. In both instances, Firestone was caught off guard by the concern circulating among its customers and had blamed them for not properly maintaining their tires. Most recently, Firestone failed to react in a timely manner, causing customers to question the company's consumer loyalty and corporate integrity. In the 1970s, the company argued with the government for months before agreeing to replace the tires.

---

[2] "Bridgestone/Firestone Announces Voluntary Recall," http://www.ford.com, August 12, 2000.

[3] "An Open Letter to Firestone Recall Customers," *The New York Times*, August 20, 2000, p. Y21.

[4] "Questions and Answers From the Ford Call Center for Firestone Inquiries," http://www.ford.com, August 12, 2000.

Critics have claimed that Firestone knew about the tread separation problem years before taking action. The tread separation of 2000 was said to be of a different nature than that of the 1970s; Congressional hearings, however, prompted remedial action in both circumstances. In the 1978 recall, Firestone outraged some consumers, saying that they might have to wait up to a year before replacement tires would be available. In 2000, the company proposed a three-tier recall, beginning in Arizona, California, Florida, and Texas, where eighty percent of the incidents occurred.[5] During the 1970s, Firestone added Resorcinol in increased levels to its rubber compounds that, over time, decreased the adhesion. Resorcinol was mixed into the rubber to hold the steel belts together.[6] Industry observers have speculated, however, that during 1990 operations, a disproportionate amount of benzene was added to the rubber compound which affected the adhesion in the years to follow.

Tire Regulations

After the 1978 recall, numerous proposals favoring more stringent federal tire standards were brought forward. During the first Reagan Administration, all proposals were dropped because one of the administration's goals was to lighten the regulatory burden on business. One proposal suggested either a red button that would pop out of the stem of a tire or a dashboard light that would inform drivers when the tire pressure on their vehicle was dangerously low. Low psi levels have arisen as an issue in the latest recall. This proposal was dropped because the industry believed it was inaccurate and costly.

Another proposal that was dropped would have required tire manufacturers to print identification numbers on the exterior sidewall instead of the interior, so it would be easier for consumers to identify where the tires were made. Had this requirement been in place today, consumers could have conveniently and accurately determined if their tires were included in the recall. Instead, they had to drive to an automotive dealership or tire replacement center to have the identification numbers checked. As demonstrated in an NBC Nightly News clip, mechanics have often erroneously identified the tires included in the recall, allowing customers to drive on faulty tires.

Off-Road Utility or Luxury

During the 1990s, sport utility vehicles became safer as auto manufacturers made them heavier and their frames less stiff in response to customers' demands that they be more luxurious. This created a surge in demand for SUVs among business professionals, and Ford responded by maintaining a rugged "off road" image while offering finer amenities on its Explorer.

Shortly after the recall, Firestone accused Ford of faulty vehicle design, related to the Explorer's suspension system, as the primary cause of vehicle rollovers. The suspension system refers to vehicles' handling ability and rigidity of ride. Ford had used the "twin I-beam" heavy-

---

[5] "Ford Motor Company Responds to the Firestone Tire Recall Statement," http://www.ford.com, August 12, 2000.

[6] "Firestone Has Been Here Before," *The Wall Street Journal*, September 6, 2000, p. A16.

duty suspension since 1960, which required that a vehicle's engine be mounted slightly higher than its competition. This raised the height and center of gravity of the vehicle and allowed for more clearance underneath the vehicle but less stability. A 1990 Ford stability memo stated, "The relative high engine position of the Explorer, unchanged from Bronco II, prevents further significant improvement in stability" unless there were to be "extensive suspension, frame, and sheetmetal revisions."[7]

Ford redesigned the Explorer's suspension for the 1995 model to improve front-end crash protection but not stability. This lowered the engine and center of gravity by two-tenths of an inch. Don Tandy, a former Ford engineer who now works as an independent consultant and expert witness for the company in lawsuits involving Explorer rollovers, explained that "Ford wanted to preserve the SUV's high ground clearance for rugged off-road driving."[8]

Since the recall, Firestone has also criticized Ford for recommending that drivers inflate their tires to 26 psi to provide a smooth ride. At a lower air pressure, a tire will bounce less on the road. Firestone says that tires for the Explorer should be inflated between 30 and 35 psi. They argued that under-inflation could put too much pressure on the tire's belt, causing it to separate. Prior to the recall, Firestone had never discussed the difference in recommended tire inflation with Ford.

Ford argued that low inflation should not have contributed to the tread separation unless the psi was below 20 pounds.[9] They stated that at no other time did Ford have any safety issues associated with the Explorer when a competitor's [Goodyear] tires were installed on the vehicle.

Within the industry, it is known that heat generally deteriorates a tire's performance. It has been documented that 97 percent of the accidents related to the Ford Explorer and Firestone tires occurred in high temperature areas.[10] During life-testing trials, Firestone tires did not withstand these conditions as well as its competitors, and was given a "C" grade.[11] Tires are classified in three levels, A, B, and C, with "A" having premier quality and "C" meeting minimum federal mandates. Although a "C" tire is not classified as unsafe, investigators noted that it did not deliver maximum performance in warm climates. Ford maintains that as long as a tire meets Ford performance standards, the automaker does not concern itself with other ratings.

---

[7] Aeppel, Timothy, Clare Ansberry, Milo Geyelin, and Robert Simison, "How Ford, Firestone Let Warnings Slide By As Debacle Developed," *The Wall Street Journal*, September 6, 2000, pp. A1, A16.

[8] Ibid.

[9] Ibid.

[10] "Lessons From Firestone - And Ford - In Massive Recall. First Rule Violated: Always Begin By Saying You're Sorry," *PR Reporter*, August 21, 2000, Vol. 43, No. 33.

[11] Aeppel, Timothy, Clare Ansberry, Milo Geyelin, and Robert Simison, "How Ford, Firestone Let Warnings Slide By As Debacle Developed," *The Wall Street Journal*, September 6, 2000, pp. A1, A16.

A National Scandal Uncovered

Anna Werner, a reporter for KHOU-TV in Houston, first reported in February 2000 that possibly defective Firestone tires on Ford Explorers may have caused a number of deaths across the United States. She first heard about the case in the autumn of 1999, after she approached a lawyer while in search of a news story. He told her that he had been working on a civil case that alleged a defective Firestone tire caused a fatal accident. Firestone was quoted in Werner's story as saying, "it had full confidence in its tires." Her story also quoted Firestone, blaming "driver error" for the accidents. On February 10, 2000, Firestone wrote the station manager a letter exclaiming, "This series has unmistakably delivered the false message that Radial ATX tires are dangerous."

Prior to Werner's story, the National Highway Traffic Safety Administration told her that it had not received any complaints about Firestones on the Explorers. Ms. Werner prompted consumers who had experienced problems to contact NHTSA, and in May 2000, after it received dozens of complaints, NHTSA launched a preliminary investigation. Both NHTSA and Ford CEO, Jacques Nasser, credited the station with prompting its investigation into the tire problem. Mr. Nasser was quoted saying, "They deserve a medal, actually. Channel 11 started everyone to think maybe there really was something there."[12]

Who Knew What and When?

More than four years before Firestone gave Ford or NHTSA any hint of a problem with its tires for sport utility vehicles, the company's engineers had been alerted by the State of Arizona that the tires' treads tended to separate in hot weather. Firestone blamed poor tire maintenance. Two years before Firestone recalled the tires, its financial staff was aware of increasing warranty claims. Moreover, beginning in 1997, Firestone had received more than 1,500 legal claims for property damage, injuries, and even some deaths resulting from failures among the 6.5 million tires being recalled.[13] Nearly a year before the recall, most of Ford management was told about deadly failures of Firestone tires on Ford Explorers overseas. Despite this information, both companies concluded that they did not have a problem.

In 1998, Ford began increasingly pressuring Firestone about the tire problems and pending litigation. Firestone continually reassured Ford noting, "It and other tire makers had been giving plaintiffs [to] lawyers for years. Some tires inevitably fail, and the usual culprit is abuse by customers who do not inflate the tires properly or overload the vehicles." In a memo dated August 9, 1999, Firestone engineers noted that in a recent trip to Venezuela they drove vehicles at speeds in excess of 95 mph, for extended periods of time and there were no tire

---

[12] Rutenberg, Jim, "Local TV Uncovered National Scandal," *The New York Times*, September 10, 2000, p. PW.14.

[13] Bradsher, Keith, "Documents Portray Tire Debacle as a Story of Lost Opportunities," *The New York Times*, September 11, 2000, pp. A1, A23.

failures. Although no tires failed during the engineers' tests, the Venezuelan government had attributed more than 46 deaths to crashes involving Firestone tires on Ford Explorers.[14]

Among the documents circulated was a memo dated September 15, 1999, drafted by Carlos Mazzorin, Ford's group vice president for purchasing, and addressed to CEO Jacques Nasser; Wayne Booker, vice chairman for international operations; and six vice presidents responsible for sales, manufacturing, quality control, vehicle engineering, Asian operations, and public relations. The memo described a problem with Explorers in Saudi Arabia, Oman, Qatar, and Venezuela, where the tread sometimes separated from the tire when the vehicle was driven for long periods of time at high speeds. Mr. Mazzorin also noted that there had been 19 rollovers and some deaths in the Middle East, where Ford had recalled the tires, and an unspecified number of deaths in Venezuela. Mr. Mazzorin summarized his issues stating that "No known instances have occurred in other markets."

Because Ford executives had no other data, they claimed they could not declare that a problem existed. However, two key executives not named on the distribution list could have offered a different perspective. John Rintamaki, Ford's general counsel, had already been involved in several lawsuits against Firestone. Ford paid little attention to this information because automakers are routinely involved in lawsuits seeking damages after crashes. Also missing was Helen Petrauskas, Ford's vice president for safety and environment issues. The safety engineers who reported to Ms. Petrauskas were aware of the rollover issue in sport utility vehicles.[15]

Recall Creates Tire Shortage

Owners of the 15-inch Firestone tires under recall were told they would have to wait several weeks for replacements because the recall created a nationwide shortage. Nearly all dealers around the country were short of the 15-inch tires and many were completely out. Bridgestone/Firestone and Ford had decided to direct the limited supply of replacement tires at four states, Arizona, California, Florida, and Texas, where 80 percent of the accidents occurred. The second phase was to include Alabama, Georgia, Louisiana, Mississippi, and Tennessee, with the remaining 42 states to be covered in the third phase by the end of 2001.[16] Ford had authorized its dealers to replace tires immediately with models from Firestone competitors, including Goodyear, General, Michelin, and Uniroyal. Ford spokesman Mike Vaughn said, "We've scoured our supply base. We're asking all our suppliers to see if they can supply more. We're looking for tires around the world." Meanwhile, Ford told dealers that if they could not find replacements right away, they should check customers' air pressure, and wear and contact them when tires became available.[17]

---

[14] Ibid.

[15] Bradsher, Keith, "Documents Portray Tire Debacle as a Story of Lost Opportunities," *The New York Times*, September 11, 2000, pp. A1, A23.

[16] "Ford Will Let Dealers Use Non-Firestone Tires," *South Bend Tribune*, August 13, 2000, p. A4.

[17] Hyde, Justin, "Firestone Recall Creates Tire Shortage," *South Bend Tribune*, August 17, 2000, p. A5.

Ex-Firestone Workers Testify in Suit

Retired employees of the Firestone plant in Decatur, Illinois, provided testimony for lawsuits against the company that the plant inspectors were pressed to examine 100 tires an hour, which they believed were too many for them to do an adequate job. The testimony was filed during a deposition for a Florida personal injury case against the company. Darrell Batson, who worked for Firestone from 1965 to 1995, disclosed that with the number of tires passing by inspectors, tires often received little to no inspection. Mr. Batson also discussed the use of benzene to refresh the adhesiveness of raw tire material that had lost its tack when left standing too long. Excessive use of benzene can damage the quality of the tire material.

Three other employees testified about the working conditions at the Decatur plant, including how tire builders were paid an hourly rate based on meeting tire-production quotas. In court documents, Bridgestone/Firestone acknowledged that workers could earn additional compensation for building tires above a specified rate.[18]

Communication Strategy

On September 3, 2000, Fleishman-Hillard resigned from its $2.5 million a month Firestone account. Fleishman had worked on the account for just eight weeks prior to their resignation stating, "It became evident that we could no longer be of service." Industry observers speculated that the breakup resulted from a disagreement over communication strategy. The agency is thought to have counseled Firestone to take positive, dramatic steps to address the crisis, and Firestone appears to have ignored the advice.[19]

Firestone then hired the Washington office of public relations firm Ketchum to help restore its image. Ketchum had handled crises for FedEx Corporation and Wendy's International. FedEx's problem involved a plane crash, while Wendy's hired Ketchum after a restaurant shooting. Christine Karbowiak, Firestone's vice president for public relations, said, "Ketchum matched our personality, our overall business, the best. They also have a very strong presence in Washington, which is very important to us." Mark Schannon, a partner with Ketchum, was confident Firestone would be willing to make changes. "I really believe Firestone will do what it says it's going to do. It's determined to be more responsive, to move more quickly, open up the process," he said. Still, he cautioned, "It's a very large company. I think it's not going to happen overnight."[20]

---

[18] Aeppel, Timothy, "Ex-Firestone Workers to Testify in Suit," *The Wall Street Journal*, August 23, 2000, p. A3.

[19] "Fleishman Drops Firestone, Loses $2.5m a Month," *PR Reporter*, September 11, 2000, p. 1.

[20] Kranhold, Kathryn, Stephen Power, "Bridgestone Turns to Ketchum to Ride Tire Image After the Recall," http://www.wsj.com, August 17, 2000.

Damage Control

As pressure continued to mount, the destiny of Firestone remained unknown. Analysts speculated whether Firestone could withstand the costs associated with the recall, having its stock price fall nearly 50 percent, decreasing its cash reserves by $10 billion. What would become of the Ford/Firestone relationship? Would all ties be severed? Rather than dwelling on their partnership and maintaining an alliance, both Firestone and Ford focused on saving their brand name and corporate image.

On July 28, prior to the recall, Ford set up a "war room" at its Michigan headquarters. A crisis response team tried to find a common denominator in the incident reports, such as a tire-manufacturing plant or a geographic region. Others began canvassing tire makers worldwide to see if enough tires would be available to accommodate a recall. The "war room" last occupied eight conference rooms spread across the eleventh and twelfth floors of Ford headquarters in Dearborn, Michigan. In addition to the 500 people directly assigned to the crisis, 4,000 to 5,000 employees were involved, including those monitoring the 24-hour customer hotline. Separate groups began work on logistics, data analysis, technical issues, tire procurement, communications, legal and government affairs, and customer and dealer issues.[21]

For Ford CEO, Jacques Nasser, the damage-control effort had become his top priority and was expected to either make or break his career. He took it upon himself to pose as a concerned customer to evaluate Ford's customer service efforts and went on-line to see what people said about Ford in the Internet chat rooms. Ford ran a series of apologetic commercials, which featured Nasser, trying to exonerate Ford and reassure customers. He authorized Ford Explorer body and assembly plants to shut down for three weeks to make an additional 70,000 tires available for the recall. Ford also ran a series of newspaper ads that explained in detail which tires were being recalled and told consumers how to read the serial numbers labeled on their vehicles' tires. Most importantly, he authorized dealers to use Firestone competitors to provide replacement tires for its customers.

Firestone's efforts were, in many ways, similar to Ford's. John Lampe, Corporate EVP and President, Bridgestone/Firestone Tire Sales Company, was also featured in several television and newspaper advertisements expressing Firestone's commitment to product quality and consumer safety. Firestone had tires flown in from its parent company, Bridgestone, in Japan and ramped up its own tire production to increase product availability. The company posted information to its Web site hourly to keep customers informed and hosted a 24-hour customer service hotline. Firestone also provided each customer affected by the recall with an option to purchase competitors' tires and be reimbursed up to $100 per tire.[22]

---

[21] "Damage Control Is 'Job One' For Ford CEO," *The Wall Street Journal*, September 11, 2000, pp. A1, A8.

[22] "Ford Points at Tire Plant Strike," http://www.msnbc.com, August 14, 2000.

Congressional Hearings and Critical Issues

As Congressional hearings began in Washington, D.C., in September 2000 to investigate the claims related to Firestone tire failures on Ford SUVs, many questions arose. Why did the tires fail?[23] Why didn't Firestone and Ford recognize that there was a problem earlier? Is it possible that cultural differences between the Japanese-owned Firestone and the U.S.-owned Ford Motor Company were to blame? Were the defective tires produced during a Union labor strike at a Decatur, Illinois, plant? Did Ford Motor Company put consumers' comfort and marketability of the vehicle ahead of safety by choosing tires that would give a softer ride but that might be more prone to failure? Why didn't the National Highway Transportation Safety Agency (NHTSA) recognize a pattern when consumers called the government agency to report tire blowouts and SUV rollovers in Ford vehicles? Should the government increase safety regulations or did Firestone just ignore existing regulations? Research also indicates that communication problems within both organizations may have kept the information about the tire problems from some of the executives who could have brought this situation to light earlier.

Ford CEO Jacques Nasser and Firestone CEO Masatoshi Ono gave initial statements to Congress in September 2000 and the finger pointing began. It may be years before all of the memos, research and findings are assimilated and organized. But the critical issues remain: This isn't the first time Firestone has been involved in a major tire recall. As early as July 1996, the State of Arizona reported tire tread separation in hot weather. In the summer of 1998, reports were sent to NHTSA outlining a pattern of flaws in Firestone ATX tires. During this same time period, Firestone financial staff recognized increasing warranty claims on the same tires. Ford replaced Firestone tires in the Middle East, Venezuela, Malaysia, and Thailand in 1999 and 2000, yet no one seemed to notice in the United States. It wasn't until February 7, 2000, when CBS affiliate KHOU-TV, Channel 11 in Houston, Texas, broke the story on the Firestone tires that the U.S. began to take heed. Their finding, that more than 30 deaths in some two dozen cases involved Ford Explorers and Firestone tires, prompted consumers to report their accidents to the NHTSA and initiated the massive recall.

By September 20, 2000, government investigators with NHTSA had received more than 2,200 complaints of tire tread separation, blowouts, and other problems with Firestone tires. Those reports involved more than 400 injuries and 103 deaths directly linked to Firestone tire failures.

---

[23] Pearl, Danny, "Isolated Traffic Accident in Saudi Arabia Helped Ignite Ford-Firestone Contention," *The Wall Street Journal*, September, 11, 2000, pp. A3, A8.

Discussion Questions

1. How should Ford and Firestone proceed? Which company should assume responsibility for the fatal accidents and critical injuries?

2. What are the most important issues facing Ford and Firestone?

3. Who are the principal stakeholders to whom Ford and Firestone have responsibilities?

4. Aside from bolstering federal regulations governing tire performance standards, what should be done to ensure consumer safety?

5. Which priorities should Mr. Nasser and Mr. Ono pursue first? Which issues could wait for attention at a later time?

6. Who should speak on behalf of Ford and Firestone? To which audience(s) should they direct their remarks? Which media should they use to reach these audiences?

7. What message should Ford and Firestone send their audiences?

8. Can the tire maker ever hope to recover from the lost business, bad publicity, angry customers, and the damage to its corporate reputation? Is the Firestone brand dead?

Early Signs of a Major Malfunction

Mounting evidence shows that Ford and Bridgestone/Firestone knew about tire-tread separation problems years before the recall was announced last month.

NOVEMBER 1978: Firestone recalls 13 million tires following escalating reports of accidents and deaths involving tread separation on steel-belted radial tires.

MAY 1988: Bridgestone, the world's No. 3 tire maker, completes its $2.6 billion acquisition of Firestone, the No. 2 tire maker.

FEBRUARY 1989: Ford enlists an independent research lab to measure the performance of 17 Firestone tires. The lab reports there were problems with tires experiencing belt-edge separation on five of 17 test runs.

MARCH 1990: The Ford Explorer is introduced as a 1991 model, overlapping with the discontinuation of the Bronco SUV model.

JANUARY 1995: The newly redesigned 1995 Ford Explorer is introduced to the SUV market.

JULY 1998: State Farm Insurance researcher Sam Boyden sends an email  to the National Highway Traffic Safety Administration outlining a pattern of flaws he sees in a study of 21 cases of tread separation on Firestone ATX tires. Mr. Boyden continues to file periodic information to NHTSA about subsequent accidents involving tread separation.

OCTOBER 1998 : In Venezuela, Ford notes problems of tread separation on Firestone tires mounted on Ford's popular Explorer SUVs and other light-truck models, and sends examples of such failed tires to Bridgestone/Firestone for analysis.

AUGUST 1999: Ford begins replacing Firestone tires on Explorers sold in Saudi Arabia after it received information about tread-separation problems. Ford does not highlight safety concerns, but instead calls the replacement program a "customer notification enhancement action.""

MAY 2000: In Venezuela, Ford changes tire brands to Goodyear as it waits for Firestone's U.S. offices to come to a resolution on the mounting tire problems. Ford's replacement action covers about 39,800 vehicles.

MAY 8, 2000: NHTSA launches a formal investigation into alleged tread separation on Firestone ATX and Wilderness tires.

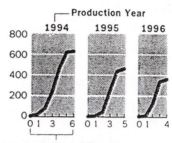

JULY 28: Ford sets up a "war room" at its Michigan headquarters. The team tries to find a common denominator in the incident reports, such as a tire-manufacturing plant or a geographic region. Others begin canvassing tire makers world-wide to see if there would be enough tires available to accommodate a recall.

AUG. 4: Ford finds a pattern in data pointing to 15" ATX and ATX II tire models and Wilderness AT tires made at the Decatur, Ill. plant, and calls in Firestone experts: the two firms work through the weekend verifying all findings. Ford's data analysis showed that older tires produced at the Decatur plant received more claims against them as the production year decreased.

Production Year

1994	1995	1996

Age of Tire, in years

AUG. 9: Bridgestone/Firestone announces a region-by-region recall of more than 6.5 million tires, the majority of them mounted as original equipment on Ford Motor Explorers and other Ford light trucks. The Firestone brands affected include 15-inch ATX, ATX II and Wilderness AT tires.

SEPT . 1: NHTSA announces it has found another 24 Firestone tire models of various sizes that showed rates of tread separation exceeding those of the recalled tires. The announcement came just as the agency boosted to 88 from 62 their estimate of U.S. deaths allegedly linked to Firestone tire failures.

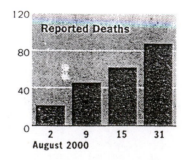

Reported Deaths

August 2000

Walt Handelsman
The Times-Picayune
Tribune Media Services

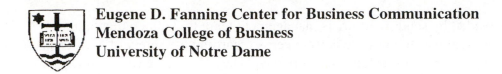
McDonald's Corporation and Mad Cow Disease in Europe

A crisis is awash in Europe due to heightened concerns over the hazards of eating beef and other red meat. Documentation of outbreaks of foot-and-mouth disease and an increase in deaths attributable to mad cow disease have Europeans and travelers questioning the safety of their red meat. Some Europeans have given up meat entirely. According to the United States Department of Agriculture beef consumption has dropped by 30 percent since 2000. Tourism to England has also waned since the headlines about the European beef scares first appeared.

In 2000 McDonald's added 517 restaurants in Europe to strengthen their competitive position. Europe accounted for about 30 percent of McDonald's $3.3 billion operating profits. Capital expenditures in Europe were $797 million, nearly twice of that in the US. (Exhibit 1)

Mad Cow Scare 1996: McDonald's and the Beef Industry

On Sunday, March 25, 1996, headlines across England read "McDonald's suspends sales of British beef products in all its restaurants in Britain." A few weeks earlier, Bovine Spongiform Encephalopathy (BSE) or mad cow disease, was found in some British cattle. This was not the first time mad cow disease had been discovered in England. The government acknowledged that more than 158,000 cases of mad cow disease had been confirmed at 34,211 farms since the previous outbreak in November 1986.[1] McDonald's, however, did not suspend the use of British beef until the British government acknowledged for the first time that scientists had found a possible link between mad cow disease and Creutzfeldt-Jacob disease. This revelation created a public health crisis resulting in the European Union's suspension of all British beef exportation.

This case was prepared by Research Assistants Rebekka Formwalt, Patrick Sackley, and J. B. Mackenzie under the direction of James S. O'Rourke, Concurrent Associate Professor of Management, as the basis for class discussion rather than to illustrate either effective or ineffective handling of an administrative situation. Information was grathered from corporate as well as public sources.

---

[1] "Mad cow Figures." *The Independent* – London, January 24, 1996.

McDonald's responded by sending its crisis management team to dampen this public relations nightmare. Their goal was to alleviate any concerns regarding the safety of McDonald's food that the approximately 1.8 million Britons ate every day. They also had a financial issue to deal with. They spent about 25 million British pounds per year on British beef that was used domestically and throughout Europe. McDonald's first focus was to stop using British beef and to remove any fear the public had regarding their products.[2] The second step was to market alternative products such as the McVeggie Deluxe and McChicken Sandwich in Britain.[3] Third, McDonald's tried not to mention mad cow disease and McDonald's in the same sentence, hoping that customers would not link the two together. They did not view mad cow disease as a McDonald's problem; rather, they viewed it as a beef industry problem.

If there was a silver lining to McDonald's worries, it was that the outbreak of mad cow disease was only in England. No other European nations had an outbreak of the disease at that time, which prompted the European Union to quickly suspend the export of all British beef. While McDonald's expected a decline in revenues in England, they did not foresee the same result in the rest of Europe.

The programs that the crisis management team implemented were successful in protecting McDonald's image. The alternative products such as the McChicken Sandwich and McVeggie Deluxe provided customers with perfect substitutes to hamburgers. Furthermore, since McDonald's was the first of the fast food companies to pull British beef, it provided them with an opportunity to increase their 72 percent market share.[4] While overall sales did in fact decrease in England, it was not as drastic as predicted. Their ability to deal with this potential public relations nightmare had dampened the overall effect on the company.

On June 27, 1997, McDonald's ended its fifteen-month ban on British beef.[5] This was the first real victory for the British government in trying to convince the world that British beef was safe. More than a year later on November 23, 1998, the European Union lifted its ban on British beef exports when Britain agreed to follow the Date Based Export Scheme (DBES)[6] (Exhibit 3). Unfortunately for the beef industry, sales had dropped 15 percent in the prior month due to the 1.4 million households that stopped buying beef as a result of the mad cow scare.[7] This was approximately the same percentage drop seen in the late eighties, the last time mad cow was on the front pages. Industry spokesmen believed once media fatigue and the public misunderstanding of the problem had cleared, sales would increase. The British government

---

[2] Phone Interview – Mr. Dick Starrmann – McDonald's Crisis Management. March 27, 2001.
[3] Ibid.
[4] "Meanwhile, back at McDonald's…" *The Independent* – London, March 27, 1996.
[5] "15-Month Ban on British Beef Lifted by McDonalds." *The Irish Times*, June 27, 1997.
[6] "USDA Report on Lifting of United Kingdom Beef Export Ban." *Dow Jones Commodities Service*, December 9, 1998.
[7] "Mad Cow Disease Scare Causes 15pc Decline in Sale of Beef." *The Guardian*, December 29, 1995.

supported this thought. British Health Secretary Stephen Dorrell stated, "It isn't the cows that are mad; it's the people that are going mad."[8]

Mad Cow Disease

Bovine Spongiform Encephalopathy (BSE), otherwise known as mad cow disease is a degenerative central nervous system disease in cattle. Cattle infected with the disease have difficulty standing and exhibit mood changes such as agitation and nervousness. The disease was first diagnosed in cattle in 1986 in Great Britain. The first known disease of this sort, scrapie, was found in sheep in the 1800s.[9] Similar diseases have been detected recently in deer and elk herds in the Western United States and Canada.[10]

Scientists believe the disease was transmitted to the cattle via rendered sheep remains that were fed to cattle in the form of protein-rich supplements. Such practices of feeding animals ruminant protein feed were banned in the U.K. in 1988 and the U.S. in 1997.[11]

BSE has occurred in such countries as France, Portugal, Germany, Spain, the Republic of Ireland, Canada, and the U.K. due to the importation of livestock and food supplements. The United States, which imports a small amount of live cattle, has not had a diagnosed incidence of the disease.[12]

Unlike most diseases that are caused by viruses or bacteria, mad cow disease is thought to be caused by a protein-like agent called a prion. The prion is actually a misshapen protein of unknown origins. Prions are naturally occurring in many animal cells and typically do not cause problems. A build-up of misshapen proteins is also typical in diseases that effect the elderly such as Alzheimer's disease and Parkinson's disease.[13] Because prions are considered proteins, scientists do not believe that they are alive, but this does not mean they are easy to get rid of. Scientific experiments have found that standard disinfection procedures used in labs, such as steam, dry heat, and chemicals, are ineffective in reducing the infectivity of the BSE prion. Difficulty in destroying the prions has raised concerns beyond mere consumption issues by adding the possibility of contaminated surgical instruments and other necessary sterile equipment.

CJD's Relation to Mad Cow

Since 1996, evidence has increased that links BSE with a disease in humans called new variant Creutzfeldt-Jakob disease (nvCJD). Creutzfeldt-Jakob Disease is a rare and fatal brain

---

[8] Barbash, Fred. "Calming the Mad Cow Clamor British Cattlemen Urge Culling of Suspect Herds to Reassure Public." *Washington Post Foreign Service*, March 26, 1996.

[9] http://www.my.webmd.com/content/article/1728.70732

[10] "FDA Will Weigh Risk of 'Mad Deer' Disease to Humans." *The Wall Street Journal*, January 19, 2001.

[11] "Mad Cow: Can It Happen Here." *The Wall Street Journal*, January 19, 2001.

[12] http://www.cdc.gov?ncidod/eid/vol7nol/brown.html

[13] "Mad cow Disease Answers May Lie in Prions." *The Wall Street Journal*, March 8, 2001.

disorder in humans. The disease is characterized by progressive dementia and associated neuromuscular disturbances. CJD affects men and women between the ages of 50 and 75. The disease can be inherited, occur sporadically, or be transmitted through infection. CJD is caused by a transmissible agent but is not considered to be contagious in the traditional sense. At the time of this case, the only proven manner for transmitting the disease between humans is via contaminated surgical equipment used in medical procedures that involve neural tissues. Approximately 15 percent of CJD cases are inherited through a mutation in the gene coding of the prion protein. Scientists have struggled to ascertain the link between BSE and the new variant form of CJD. Once symptoms have set in, the duration of CJD is usually one year or less.[14] The disease attacks the brain, wasting it away to leave a spongy mass. Early symptoms in infected persons include depression and unusual sensory sensations like a sticky feeling to the skin. Victims slowly lose their sight, hearing, speech, and eventually their minds before the disease leaves them in a coma. Usually an infection like pneumonia ultimately kills the bedridden, unconscious individual.[15] New variant Creutzfeldt-Jakob disease and BSE are both fatal brain diseases with unusually long incubation periods of many years.[16] In contrast to CJD, the new variant form is found in people under the age of 42. Currently, no method exists for diagnosing the disease beyond a post mortem confirmation examination of the brains of individuals with nvCJD symptoms. Humans are suspected to become infected with the disease after eating contaminated beef.

On March 21, 2001, a team of British government experts announced the first clear demonstration of an association between nvCJD and BSE through the diet. Five of the over 80 suspected deaths associated with mad cow disease have occurred in the village of Queniborough, Britain. Of the victims studied, all had purchased meat from local butchers. The study confirmed that people with the disease were 15 times more likely to have bought and consumed beef from a butcher where contamination of BSE was possible, compared to people living in the same area who did not develop the disease. The slaughterhouses in this region utilized a method of killing the animals called "pithing." Pithing occurs by ramming a rod through the animal's brain and into the spinal cord. This method allows brain and spinal fluid to leak out onto other tissues. Another common practice in the area was the consumption of cow brains, which required butchers to separate the brains from the rest of the body with the same knife used for carving other cuts of meat, an obvious source of cross-contamination.

This study also provided the first hard evidence for the incubation period of nvCJD, which was estimated to be as long as 10-16 years between the consumption of the infected meat and the onset of their symptoms.[17] Research indicated that muscle tissue had not been shown to carry the infection, leading investigators to suspect that infection probably results from meat contaminated with nervous system tissue. Contamination of meat with spinal fluid can happen in several ways including: contact between the muscle and saws or other tools used in the slaughter,

---

[14] http://www.cjdfoundation.org/CJDInfo.html

[15] http://www.abcnews.go.com/sections/world/DailyNews/britain010116_madcow.html

[16] http://www.cdc.gov/ncidod/diseases/cjd/bse_cjd.htm

[17] http://www.economist.com/displayStory.cfm?Story_ID=540797

inclusion of spinal parts in cuts of meat near the vertebral tissues such as T-bone steaks, and presence of residual spinal cord or spinal tissues in the recovered meat used for products as sausages and various canned beef products.[18]

As of February 6, 2001, 92 people had died infected with the nvCJD. Eighty-eight of these cases were in Britain. Up to this date, Britain had confirmed diagnoses of over 180,000 cases of mad cow disease in cattle.[19]

Foot-and-Mouth Disease

Foot-and-mouth disease, also known as hoof-and-mouth disease or Aftosa, is a severe, highly contagious viral disease of cloven-footed mammals including cattle, sheep, deer, swine, and goats. Horses are resistant to the virus. Humans cannot contract the disease.

The disease has an affinity for the covering of skin and mucous membranes of the gastrointestinal tract. It debilitates animals, causing blisters on the tongue, lips, mouth, teats, udders, and around hooves. Within the first 24 to 48 hours of infection, the virus enters the bloodstream and causes fever. During this period it is also excreted in the saliva, milk, urine, and feces of infected animals. As blisters begin to form on the mouth and tongue, the animal develops a characteristic smacking of the lips which is followed by a rupture of the blister vesicles, leaving painfully raw and inflamed surfaces. The sores last between one and two weeks. During these weeks, the animal refuses to eat, resulting in a sharp decrease in milk production and meat development. Mortality ranges from 5 to 50 percent in infected animals. No effective treatment exists for the disease.[20]

Foot-and-mouth disease is endemic throughout most of Europe, Asia, and South America. It is spread easily to susceptible animals through contact with contaminated water, clothing, garbage, storage facilities, hay and feed, semen, and vehicles. Because of the contagious nature and long viability of the virus, it is difficult to control infections from spreading to other susceptible animals.[21] Animals confirmed or suspected to be infected with the disease are typically quarantined, slaughtered, and their carcasses are burned.[22]

Restrictions on the shipment of all live cattle, sheep, goats, and pigs as well as import bans on unpasteurized cheeses from the area were imposed in early 2000. This was to prevent the spread of foot-and-mouth disease to the United States and to the countries in the European Union. Such restrictions have been highly publicized and have added to public confusion between mad cow disease and foot-and-mouth disease. The latter poses no risk to humans.[23]

---

[18] http://www.cdc.gov/ncidod/eid/vol7no1/brown.htm
[19] "Europe Is One-Until Disaster Strikes." *The New York Times*, February 6, 2001.
[20] http://www.britannica.com/seo/f/foot-and-mouth-disease
[21] http://www.aphis.usda.gov/oa/pubs/fsfmd.html
[22] http://www.britannica.com/seo/f/foot-and-mouth-disease
[23] http://www.nytimes.com/2001/04/18/living/18WELL.html

History of McDonald's

The year was 1954. At the age of 52, Ray Kroc mortgaged his home and invested his entire life savings to become the exclusive distributor of a five-spindled milk shake maker called the Multimixer. After hearing about the McDonald's hamburger stand in California operating eight Multimixers at a time, Ray Kroc packed up his car and headed west. When he arrived, he was amazed at the number of customers and the speed at which they were served. He pitched the idea of opening several of these restaurants to Dick and Mac McDonald. Ray Kroc opened his first McDonald's in Des Plaines, Illinois, in 1955, with first day's revenues of $366.12.

In 1965 McDonald's went public with the company's first offering on the stock exchange. A hundred shares of stock costing $2,250 dollars that day would have multiplied into 74,360 shares today, worth over $2.5 million on December 31, 2000. In 1985 McDonald's was added to the 30-company Dow Jones Industrial Average. Today, McDonald's is the largest and best-known global foodservice retailer with more than 28,000 restaurants in 120 countries. Average daily revenues in 2000 were $38.81 million.[24]

Food quality and safety

Over the years, McDonald's has been a leader in setting and strictly enforcing high quality and safety standards – often exceeding those established by industry and governments. Quality and safety are the most important items on their menu, so customers can have confidence in McDonald's. McDonald's is aligned with world-class suppliers that share these high standards.

McDonald's Quality Assurance Board provides strategic global leadership for all aspects of food quality and safety. Their quality assurance and supply chain specialists around the world work with McDonald's suppliers to ensure compliance with their standards. McDonald's operates quality assurance labs around the world, where ongoing product reviews and enhancements take place. In addition, they work closely with their suppliers to encourage innovation, assure best practices, and drive continuous improvement.

Further reinforcing their commitment to quality, McDonald's has been recognizing exceptional excellence among their suppliers since 1990 with the Sweeney Quality Award. The award is named in honor of a supplier who exemplified a commitment to McDonald's high standards. The 1998 Sweeney Quality Award winner – Sunny Fresh Foods, a supplier of egg products to the McDonald's System – won the prestigious Malcolm Baldrige National Quality Award the following year.

High standards are also essential to the operations of McDonald's restaurants. Proper storage, handling, and cooking practices are an integral part of their training materials, and a food safety check list is used daily in their restaurants to validate that food safety standards and

---

[24] http://www.mcdonalds.com/corporate

procedures are in place. McDonald's restaurants are also inspected for safety compliance.

Mad Cow & Foot and Mouth: The Sequel

When McDonald's and the European Union decided to lift their bans on British beef, the scientist who first warned of a BSE danger to humans publicly renounced the decision. Dr. Lacey said, "if British beef is safe now then there was no reason not to use it (in 1995). The situation has not changed."[25] This proclamation was ignored by most, and unfortunately it proved to be true in 2000. This time not only England was afflicted with the outbreak but much of Europe was as well. As the European Union scrambled to deal with this problem, an outbreak of foot-and-mouth disease soon followed. Even though the diseases are completely different, the public has confused many of the details regarding the diseases. As such, McDonald's has seen a decrease in sales, and the beef industry is expected to take losses twice as large as those in 1996.

On January 16, 2001, *The Wall Street Journal* reported that the Italian Health Ministry found a possible case of mad cow disease at a plant run by an Italian meat processor, a supplier of McDonald's patties. The cow was found at the Italian meat processor in Cremonini. A McDonald's spokeswoman in Milan said that the plant where the cow was found is not the Cremonini factory where McDonald's patties are made. Cremonini also exports processed meat to the US.[26]

McDonald's European Operations and the Financial Impact of Mad Cow

Public fears over mad cow disease caused a nine percent drop in McDonald's European sales and a seven percent drop in 2000 fourth quarter earnings. "These results were tempered by the recent decline in consumer confidence in the European beef supply. By educating customers about our strict product specifications that assure our beef is safe from BSE, communicating our industry leading safety and quality standards, and introducing additional menu variety, we partially offset the negative impact," Jack Greenberg, McDonald's Chairman and CEO claimed.[27]

McDonald's Corp announced 2001 first quarter earnings would fall more than expected because of slumping sales in Europe, where consumers are buying less hamburgers due to fear of mad cow disease. (Exhibit 2) McDonald's announced earnings of 29 cents a share for the quarter. This was below the 33 cents a share one year earlier, and was also lower then analysts' expectations of 32 cents a share. "The effect of consumer concerns regarding the European beef supply has persisted longer then expected,"[28] according to Greenberg. January and February 2001 sales were flat compared to a 14 percent gain over the same period in 2000. During a

[25] "15-Month Ban on British Beef Lifted by McDonalds." *The Irish Times*, June 27, 1997.
[26] Trofimov, Yaroslav and Winestock, Geoff."McDonald's Reassures Italians About Beef." *The Wall Street Journal*, January 16, 2001.
[27] Hood, Julia. "Euro health fears on McDonald's PR menu." *PRWEEK*, January 29, 2001.
[28] Gilpin, Kenneth N. "Citing Europe, McDonald's Cuts Forecast For Quarter." *The New York Times*, March 15. 2001.

conference call with analysts, Michael Conley, CFO of McDonald's, also acknowledged that the spread of foot and mouth disease might hamper sales. Greenberg added, "In Europe, we are optimistic that lingering concerns about beef will continue to lessen as the year progresses."[29]

Discussion Questions

1. Did McDonald's act effectively in 1996?

2. What are the most important issues facing McDonald's?

3. What should McDonald's course of action be in light of April 2001 reported earnings? What message, if any, should they convey?

4. Who are the concerned parties, and what priority should McDonald's give them?

5. Is there a threat to the McDonald's brand name and global operations?

---

[29] http://www.mcdonalds.com/corporate

Exhibit 1: McDonald's 2000 Annual Report

IN MILLIONS	2000	1999	1998
U.S.	$ 5,259.1	$ 5,093.0	$ 4,868.1
Europe	4,753.9	4,924.9	4,466.7
Asia/Pacific	1,987.0	1,832.3	1,633.2
Latin America	949.3	680.3	814.7
Other	1,293.7	728.8	638.7
Total revenues	$14,243.0	$13,259.3	$12,421.4
U.S.	$ 1,773.1	$ 1,653.3	$ 1,201.4 (1)
Europe	1,180.1	1,256.5	1,167.5
Asia/Pacific	441.9	421.9	359.9
Latin America	102.3	133.0	189.2
Other	94.1	117.4	120.3
Corporate	(261.8)	(262.5)	(276.4)
Total operating income	$ 3,329.7	$ 3,319.6	$ 2,761.9 (1)
U.S.	$ 7,876.7	$ 7,874.3	$ 7,397.8
Europe	7,083.7	6,966.8	6,932.1
Asia/Pacific	2,789.7	2,828.2	2,659.7
Latin America	1,855.6	1,477.5	1,339.6
Other	1,069.3	979.3	678.7
Corporate	1,008.5	1,057.1	776.5
Total assets	$21,683.5	$20,983.2	$19,784.4
U.S.	$ 468.6	$ 426.4	$ 392.4
Europe	797.6	881.8	870.2
Asia/Pacific	224.4	188.4	224.0
Latin America	245.7	213.2	236.8
Other	161.2	112.3	102.8
Corporate	47.6	45.7	53.1
Total capital expenditures	$ 1,945.1	$ 1,867.8	$ 1,879.3
U.S.	$ 417.6	$ 399.7	$ 375.9
Europe	296.5	305.2	268.0
Asia/Pacific	120.5	114.9	97.3
Latin America	69.4	45.5	42.9
Other	60.8	46.2	40.6
Corporate	45.9	44.8	56.4
Total depreciation and amortization	$ 1,010.7	$ 956.3	$ 881.1

(1) Includes $161.6 million of Made For Your costs and the $160.0 million special charge related to the home office productivity initiative.

Source: http://mcdonalds.com, Annual Report

Exhibit 2: McDonald's First Quarter 2001 Financial Release

Key highlights - Consolidated *Dollars in millions, except per common share data*			Percent Increase/(Decrease)	
Quarters ended March 31	**2001**	2000	As Reported	Constant Currency*
Systemwide sales	**$9,649.7**	$9,506.7	2	6
Total revenues	**3,511.7**	3,343.8	5	10
Operating income	**695.2**	768.6	(10)	(6)
Net income	**378.3**	450.9	(16)	(12)
Net income per common share – diluted	**.29**	.33	(12)	(9)

*Information on a constant currency basis excludes the effect of foreign currency translation on reported results, except for hyperinflationary economies, such as Russia, whose functional currency is the U.S. Dollar.

Systemwide sales *Dollars in millions*			Percent Increase/(Decrease)	
Quarters ended March 31	**2001**	2000	As Reported	Constant Currency*
U.S.	**$4,676.5**	$4,505.0	4	n/a
Europe	**2,178.2**	2,305.7	(6)	2
Asia/Pacific	**1,687.5**	1,785.6	(5)	4
Latin America	**455.3**	434.1	5	11
Other	**652.2**	476.3	37	42
Total Systemwide sales	**$9,649.7**	$9,506.7	2	6

Operating income Dollars in millions			Percent Increase/(Decrease)	
Quarters ended March 31	2001	2000	As Reported	Constant Currency*
U.S.	$402.7	$388.7	4	n/a
Europe	222.8	276.4	(19)	(13)
Asia/Pacific	115.5	118.2	(2)	8
Latin America	22.3	31.7	(30)	(27)
Other	11.7	20.8	(44)	(38)
Corporate	(79.8)	(67.2)	(19)	n/a
Total operating income	$695.2	$768.6	(10)	(6)

Source: http://www.mcdonalds.com, Corporate Financial.

Exhibit 3: Date-Based Export Scheme

Five Required Criteria:

1. **Selective slaughter program**: cattle which might have developed BSE have been identified and destroyed.

2. **Identification and traceability**: all cattle born/ imported after 1 July 1996 must have a passport and be registered on a database.

3. **Removal of meat and bonemeal from feed**: all feed contaminated with meat and bonemeal has been traced and disposed of.

4. **Over Thirty Month Scheme**: accounts for 2.7 million cattle removed from the food chain.

5. **Removal of specified risk material**: tight slaughterhouse controls have ensured compliance. The UK is one of the few members states which has already adopted the terms of Commission Decision 97/534 on the prohibition of the use of material presenting risks in regard to transmissible spongiform encephalothies (TSEs).

Source: USDA Report on Lifting of United Kingdom Beef Export Ban, Dow Jones Commodities Service, December 9, 1998.

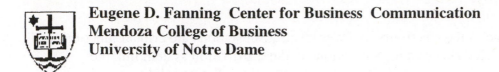
Pacific Gas and Electric Corporation: Energy De-Regulation in California

PG&E Background

Pacific Gas and Electric Company (PG&E) is a wholly owned subsidiary of PG&E Corporation and is one of the largest combined natural gas and electric utilities in the United States. The company provides natural gas and electricity to approximately 12 million people in Northern and Central California, which is about one in every twenty Americans. PG&E covers a 70,000 square mile service area, stretching from Bakersfield in the south to Eureka in the north, and from the Sierra Nevadas in the east to the Pacific Ocean in the west. Based in San Francisco, the utility company employs over 21,500 people. It controls over 131,000 circuit miles of electric lines and 43,000 miles of natural gas pipelines. It has approximately 4.5 million electric customer accounts and 3.7 million gas customer accounts.[1]

Electrical System[2]

There are three distinct stages, or phases, in the electrical system process: generation, transmission, and distribution. The process starts with a diverse mix of generating sources such as hydropower, gas-fired steam, coal, combined cycle, turbine-gas, turbine-oil, geothermal steam, and nuclear power. The energy is then sold to companies for transmission. In this stage, electricity is transmitted across several states. It is carried in bulk over a network, or grid, of high-voltage transmission lines that connect power plants to substations. At this juncture, substations are connected to the transmission/distribution system, which supplies electricity to various regions throughout the country. The transmission system includes transformers that

---

This case was prepared by Research Assistants Nicole Coons and Calvin Daniels under the direction of James S. O'Rourke, Concurrent Associate Professor of Management, as the basis for class discussion rather than to illustrate either effective or ineffective handling of an administrative situation. Information was gathered from corporate as well as public sources.

---

[1] http://www.pge.com/009_about/
[2] http://www.pge.com/006_news/

"step down" the voltage of the electricity to lower levels. Substations are critical junctions and switching points in the electric system. Substations in the distribution system link the transmission system to most customers. It includes both main or "primary" lines, and lower voltage "secondary" lines. The lines deliver electric energy either overhead or underground to customers. Also included in the distribution system are distribution transformers that lower voltage to usage levels, as well as switching equipment that permits the lines to be connected together in various combinations and patterns. Finally, individual services or "drops" connect the distribution system to the customer—industrial, commercial, agricultural, or residential.

Industry Overview

The electric power industry is one of the largest industries in the United States and accounts for approximately four percent of the gross domestic product (GDP). In fact, investor-owned electric utilities generated over $325 billion in revenues in 1999, surpassing the telecommunication and airline industries combined. Individual household users are the largest class of electric utilities users, at 87.7 percent. The industrial sector only accounts for 0.4 percent of electric utilities customers, yet it consumes 31.4 percent of all electricity sold. The residential sector consumes approximately 35.2 percent of all electricity sold. There are three primary electricity suppliers: investor or shareholder-owned companies, cooperatively-owned utilities, and government-owned utilities. Investor-owned utilities (IOUs) are the main service providers of electricity, and they serve 74 percent of American consumers.[3]

Today, the electric utilities industry is undergoing immense change. The first regulation of the electric industry came in 1935 with the passing of the Public Utility Holding Company Act (PUHCA) and the Federal Power Act (FPA) of 1935. These two acts "established a regime of regulating electric utilities that gave specific and separate powers to the states and the federal government."[4] Until the 1970s, electric utilities saw little change in regulation. In fact, electric utilities were able to keep up with the increasing demand for electricity while achieving large economies. During the 1970s, however, electric utilities began to face slowing growth, increasing costs due to higher oil prices, tripled interest rates, and the passage of the Clean Air Act of 1970.

While the industry was trying to recover from these blows, Congress designed legislation to stimulate competition in the electric industry with the Public Utility Regulatory Policies Act of 1978 (PURPA). PURPA allowed non-utility facilities to enter the wholesale electricity market if these facilities met certain ownership, operating, and efficiency criteria established by the Federal Energy Regulatory Commission (FERC). The growth of non-utilities was advanced by the Energy Policy Act of 1992 (EPACT), which was designed to further increase competition in the sector by removing several regulatory entry barriers into electricity generation.

The EPACT created a whole new category of power producers named exempt wholesale generators (EWGs). EWGs are wholesale electricity producers that do not sell electricity in the retail market but may charge market-based rates. EWGs do not own transmission facilities and

---

[3] www.eei.org
[4] A. Abel, L. Parker. "IB10006: Electricity: The Road Toward Restructuring," February 16, 2001, http://www.cnie.org/

therefore, are not regulated.[5] This new legislation also assured the transmission of EWGs wholesale power to its wholesale purchasers, but did not require utilities to transmit EWG power to retail consumers.

In April of 1996, the FERC issued Orders 888 and 889, in an attempt to remedy the discrimination of transmission services between EWG electricity and utility company generated electricity. Order 888 requires transmission line owners to offer both point-to-point and network transmission services under comparable terms and conditions that they provide for themselves. Although not a requirement under the order, the rule encourages the creation of Independent System Operators (ISOs) to coordinate intercompany and interstate transmission of electricity. Order 889 requires utilities to separate their wholesale marketing and transmission operation functions in an attempt to establish a level playing field and create standards of conduct. Order 889, however, does not require utilities to unbundle their assets. Utilities can still own transmission, distribution, and generation facilities, but they must maintain separate books and records.[6]

California Deregulation and Assembly Bill 1890 (AB 1890)

Until 1996, PG&E and other investor-owned utilities operating in California were regulated and controlled by the California Public Utilities Commission (CPUC). In September 1996, California passed The Electric Utility Industry Restructuring Act (Assembly Bill 1890) that deregulated the state's power markets. The deregulation came after the FERC had put Orders 888 and 889 in place.

During the summer of 1996, a Joint Conference Committee of the California Legislature commenced an intensive series of hearings and negotiations with respect to the electric industry restructuring. This resulted in Assembly Bill 1890 which was passed unanimously by both houses of the California Legislature in late August 1996 and was signed into law by Governor Wilson on September 23, 1996 (chapter 854, California Statutes of 1996). The bill was created to allow competition in the California electric service market and in turn, reduce electricity rates throughout the state, which at the time exceed the national average by nearly 40 percent.

A variety of technical corrections and consumer protection provisions were added in August 1997, by Senate Bill 477 (California Statutes of 1997). AB 1890 was the first comprehensive electric industry restructuring legislation passed by any state. Restructuring legislation has also been enacted in seven other states, with major industry restructuring proposals pending in several other states.[7]

The Bill AB 1890 introduced several new mandates, including the establishment of an Oversight Board to oversee California's newly restructured electricity industry. The board's primary objective was to create the ISO and the Power Exchange (PX). Before the restructuring bill, single IOUs, including PG&E, Southern California Edison, PacifiCorp, Sierra Pacific

---

[5] "The Changing Structure of the Electric Power Industry 2000: An Update – Chapter 2."
[6] A. Abel, L. Parker. "IB10006: Electricity: The Road Toward Restructuring," February 16, 2001, http://www.cnie.org/.
[7] http://www.orrick.com/news/elect/electric/4.htm

Power, and Bear Valley Electric, provided customers with generation, transmission, distribution, metering, and billing of electricity. All IOUs would continue to own transmission lines and facilities and continue to be responsible for their maintenance and upkeep. However, under the new system, all electricity transmission in the state of California would be out of the hands of the IOUs. Instead, it would be controlled and operated by the ISO. The new structure was designed to encourage new power producers to enter the market and in turn, to allow customers in most electric utility service areas to choose their electric generation supplier as of March 31, 1998.

The ISO now operates all of the state's electricity transmission and ensures that all standards for transmission are met. The ISO is also responsible for ensuring that no particular buyer or seller of electricity blocks access of others. The ISO became responsible for maintaining overall electricity system reliability as well, although it was originally intended to maintain only reserve generators in the event that a generator owned by an energy service provider failed or could not provide sufficient power. As such, the responsibility of the ISO became acquiring electricity from power plants and generators and then transmitting it to the distributors.

The PX was designed to operate as a commodities market where power producers would compete, selling their electricity to bids submitted by buyers. The PX solicits bids from buyers and generators. Then they choose the lowest generation bidders until the PX has enough supply to meet the power requests. In other words, the PX serves as a spot price market for electricity in the same manner that the stock exchange serves as a market for stocks.

In addition, AB 1890 authorized all IOUs to sell many of their power generating assets and their remaining power to the Power Exchange for resale to distributors, essentially themselves. However, the greatest "power" blow against IOUs was the laws, as mandated by AB 1890, that forbade utilities from passing along the wholesale power cost increases to customers and restricted them from negotiating long-term supply contracts.

Financial Collapse of PG&E

Governor Gray Davis's predecessor, Pete Wilson, enacted AB 1890 to deregulate the electricity industry. Deregulation was intended to protect consumers by promoting competition at the generation stage, keeping retail electricity rates low and forcing producers to compete. However, while the wholesale power costs were free to fluctuate, retail electric rates were frozen.

The initial plan was conceived when wholesale prices were low and were expected to go lower, but wholesale electricity prices dramatically and unexpectedly increased. This was a result of unexpected growth in demand for electricity, a lack of new generating facilities, lower imports from other states, and a drastic increase in natural gas prices. There was also some speculation that suppliers behaved strategically to manipulate wholesale prices. In addition, as demand for electricity was increasing, capacity was actually decreasing. Average wholesale prices more than tripled from 1999 to 2000. In January 2001, those prices were up ten-fold from a year earlier.[8]

In the meantime, PG&E began to lose money on electricity that they were buying for resale to their customers, but their hands were tied. Under deregulation, they had no control over the price they paid for electricity or the price they charged their customers. Under deregulation, PG&E was required to sell all electricity they generated to the PX. They were also required to buy their electricity for resale to customers exclusively from the California PX.

After reporting net losses of $73 million in 1999, it became evident that PG&E would continue to face significant financial distress. In addition, since the company had failed to pay many of its past debts to power generators, a number of wholesalers were reluctant to provide electricity to PG&E. In November 2000, PG&E filed to raise rates by 16.5 percent in order to cover the cost of wholesale prices, effective January 1, 2001. The request was denied, but by December 7, 2000, the California ISO issued its first Stage Three alert, the highest-level, indicating the threat of rolling blackouts. Rolling blackouts were averted, however, when the federal government took direct emergency action and forced generators to sell power to PG&E in order to boost power supplies.[9]

By December 15, 2000, the FERC issued an order, which removed the requirement that California IOUs buy and sell their power through the California PX. The order allowed the IOUs to negotiate long-term supply contracts with wholesale generators. On January 3, 2001, the CPUC also temporarily increased residential electricity rates by 9 percent for customers of PG&E. Both orders came too late for PG&E. They reported a 2000 net loss of $3.36 billion and were still struggling to buy and supply power. By January 19, 2001, the CPUC required PG&E to provide service to all of their customers even if it forced the company into bankruptcy. This caused a vicious cycle. Since PG&E was unable to meet its debt, wholesalers refused to sell power to them. When the Federal government forced generators to sell power to PG&E, wholesalers charged a higher price to compensate for the extra risk they were enduring. Wholesale prices continued to rise, and PG&E plunged further and further into debt.

California's Rolling Blackouts

Throughout the month of January, PG&E took several steps to ensure that they could supply their customers with electricity. Unfortunately, the combination of the company's severe debt, lack of cash, high wholesale rates, and wholesaler resistance to sell was too much to bear. To make matters worse, PG&E requested help from Governor Davis and the state of California to buy natural gas, but California also lacked the funds to help rescue PG&E and their customers for more than a few days. On January 16, 2001, PG&E's credit rating was cut to low junk status, putting them in immediate default of bank loans and credit lines. Bankruptcy seemed inevitable.

In the meantime, California declared a statewide Stage Three alert for the third time. Although the state managed to avoid rolling blackouts on January 16, the small triumph was

---

[8] "Crossed Wires: Major Kinks Emerge in Governor Davis's Plan to Power California," *Wall Street Journal*, February 8, 2001.
[9] Chronology – California Power Crisis, http://www.yahoo.com/news/ , February 8, 2000.

short lived. A day later, rolling blackouts were ordered statewide for the first time ever. At the same time, PG&E announced it would default on $76 million in commercial paper. On January 18, 2001, PG&E customers endured a second day of rolling blackouts.

Primary Stakeholders

- Agricultural, commercial, residential, and industrial customers alike – The energy crisis directly affects all customers. They pay the price through higher rates and/or blackouts. Essentially, they are at the mercy of the industry.

- California Power Exchange (PX) – The PX serves as the state's new spot price market for electricity, similar to the stock exchange. The PX is directly involved in the electrical system. It serves all classes of customers. It was created in an effort to deregulate the California electricity industry.

- California Public Utilities Commission (CPUC) – The CPUC regulates California's investor-owned utilities (IOUs) and is overseeing deregulation in the state. Its responsibilities are to the customers; it assures safety and reasonable rates. It is also responsible for protecting utility customers from fraud.

- California State bondholders and IOU shareholders – As a result of the energy crisis, California bond ratings are on the decline, affecting the current bondholders' financial status and the state's ability to issue more bonds. In addition, PG&E's shareholders have lost millions of dollars due to the company's current financial standings.

- Competition, e.g. Southern California Edison – The other utilities often follow the lead of PG&E, as is the case with Edison's threat to file Chapter 11 Bankruptcy. PG&E is a leading utility distributor, and as a leader, it has a direct affect on wholesale prices.

- Federal Energy Regulator Commission (FERC) – The FERC regulates the following: the transmission and resale of natural gas in interstate commerce; the transmission of oil by pipeline in interstate commerce; the transmission and wholesale of electricity in interstate commerce. It also licenses and inspects private, municipal, and state hydroelectricity projects. It oversees related environmental matters. The FERC administers accounting and financial reporting regulations and the conduct of jurisdictional companies.[10]

- Governor Gray Davis's Administration – This administration took office in 1999 after Rep. Pete Wilson, the creator of AB 1890. Some say that Davis was dealt a bad hand from the start. However, most believe that he is not handling the crisis as effectively as he could. He has admitted that he could solve this problem in 30 seconds by raising prices, but for political reasons, this option isn't feasible.

- Independent System Operator (ISO) – The ISO assures safe and fair transfer of electricity from power plants to the IOUs. It manages the flow of electricity along the long-distance,

---

[10] http://www.caiso.com/powercentral

high-voltage power lines that increase the bulk of California's transmission system. Essentially, it safeguards the reliable delivery of electricity.

Conclusion

Throughout January 2001, PG&E issued several statements about the company's inability to meet their financial obligations and the increasing financial strain that all California utilities were enduring. In addition, PG&E asked consumers to conserve energy whenever possible. In each message, the company continued to stress the need for a stable supply of electricity through long-term contracts at affordable prices. They emphasized that utilities must be returned to financial health to avoid future outages. The company also issued several energy saving tips to their customers, offering simple methods to reduce power usage.[11] PG&E has stepped forward and taken an active public role, but has it come too late?

Questions

1.   Who are PG&E's primary stakeholders?

2.   How can PG&E best communicate with their stakeholders? What potential problems do you see with PG&E's communication structure?

3.   What advice would you give managers at PG&E about communicating their position and involvement in the current California energy crisis?

4.   How can PG&E regain financial stability?

5.   What implications does the energy crisis have on the rest of the U.S. economy?

---

[11] News release, http://www.pge.com/

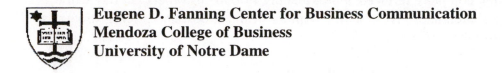
ValuJet
Disaster in the Everglades

On May 11, 1996, a ValuJet DC-9 with 110 people onboard, including passengers and crew, caught fire and crashed into the Florida Everglades. Everyone on board was killed. During the subsequent investigation, the National Transportation Safety Board (NTSB) found the Federal Aviation Administration (FAA), SabreTech – ValuJet's maintenance contractor – and the airline itself were all to blame for the incident. In a heartbeat, this relatively young, low-cost carrier was fighting for its life.

Background

ValuJet was an Atlanta-based airline that began service in 1993. Shortly after an Initial Public Offering of stock in June of 1994, ValuJet surged onto the market with explosive growth. With returns of better than 500 percent, ValuJet proved to be a profitable and attractive investment. According to *Air Watch,* a newsletter that tracks airline financial performance, ValuJet offered the strongest financial returns of any domestic airline. After strategically developing an image as a fun and friendly low-cost airline, ValuJet was beginning to establish itself as an excellent value, both for its customers and for its shareholders.

In 1995, the young company continued to grow at a phenomenal rate and managed to triple its profits, double the number of planes in its fleet, and add several new destinations. As part of its aggressive growth strategy, ValuJet increased the number of airframes from only two to more than fifty in just 24 months. The decline of Pan American World Airways and Eastern Airlines enabled ValuJet to minimize its costs by recruiting the furloughed pilots and flight attendants at below-market wage rates. With $128 million in cash reserves and minimal debt, ValuJet's strong financial position helped the company to become the number one publicly traded company in Georgia.[1]

Unlike other airlines, ValuJet targeted the cost-conscious consumer rather than frequent business travelers. As a result, ValuJet attracted millions of passengers and developed a strong

[1] Ho, Rodney, "The Crash of Flight 592," *Atlanta Journal and Constitution*, May 19, 1996.

market niche. The young company serviced approximately 17,000 customers per day while significantly increasing shareholder investment.[2] With its stringent cost and pricing strategies, ValuJet became an overnight success.

Cost Strategy

Although ValuJet was a young airline, the company did have the "oldest fleet in the business."[3] It purchased older planes for reasonable prices and made all necessary restorations and upgrades. The airline saved money in other areas as well. The company relied on outside contractors for virtually all maintenance. ValuJet also required its pilots to pay approximately $10,000 apiece for their own training. Furthermore, ValuJet paid their pilots *half* of what the other major airlines paid their pilots. A week before the fatal crash, an analyst at BT Securities Corporation wrote, "Growth has been so aggressive that, to date, costs have not been properly matched with revenue production."[4]

ValuJet's aggressive cost strategy may have caused a few problems. Although statistical data negates the notion that older planes are less safe than newer planes, ValuJet had experienced problems with the renovation of one of its older airframes. After purchasing the plane from a Turkish airline, ValuJet sent the plane to be restored in a Turkish repair facility. Instead of accomplishing the restoration correctly, serious corrosion was simply covered with paint. The plane later caught fire and seven people were injured, one of whom was severely burned.

According to FAA studies, ValuJet had a higher rate of minor accidents than almost all other discount airlines.[5] In June of 1995, a plane on the ground in Florida caught fire, with flames spreading to the fuselage. The passengers were evacuated. No one was injured, but the DC-9 was destroyed.[6] On January 12, 1996, another DC-9 slid into a snow bank at Dulles International Airport in Washington D.C. A few weeks later, on January 26, 1996, one of ValuJet's planes slid off of a runway in Atlanta, Georgia. On February 1, another DC-9 blew a tire when the plane landed in Nashville, Tennessee. And on February 28, 1996, a DC-9 went off the runway in Savannah, Georgia.[7]

ValuJet was praised by shareholders for holding down expenses and maintaining large profit margins. However, the percentage of seats that the airline filled fell steadily from January of 1996 until May of 1996. In May of that year, the "load" (or percent of seats filled) fell seventeen percentage points.[8] Because ValuJet appealed to the leisure traveler, the company was more susceptible to negative trends in the economy. Despite the marginal decline in its passenger load, ValuJet continued to entice customers with their low prices. While other airlines

---

[2] Mahaffey Center for Business Information, University of Notre Dame.

[3] Liscio, John, "The 15-Year Bull Market Began with the Patco Strike: Why the ValuJet Crash Could Signal the Party's End," *Barron's*, June 3, 1996.

[4] Ibid.

[5] Kazel, Robert, "ValuJet Insured for Crash Losses," *Business Insurance*, May 20, 1996.

[6] "Cost-Cutting Airlines' Top Priority Should be Passenger Safety," *Ft. Lauderdale Sun-Sentinel*, May 13, 1996.

[7] Burch, Audra and Ted Reed, "ValuJet was Under Federal Scrutiny," *Austin American-Statesman*, May 12, 1996.

[8] "Unsafe at Any Price," *Forbes*. Riva Atlas. Vol. 158. No. 6. September 6, 1996.

demanded a significantly higher rate for customers who needed to travel at the last minute, ValuJet offered the same service for its walk-up travelers at a charge of only $39.00.

The Crash

On May 11, 1996, five boxes of oxygen generators (each containing a total of 50-to-60 generators), along with several airplane tires, were loaded onto a ValuJet DC-9 in Miami, Florida. Oxygen generators are 8-by-4 inch stainless steel cylinders that hold chemicals used to produce oxygen for emergency masks in the passenger cabin. Because oxygen generators had caused fires in the past, airlines were *not* authorized to carry generators in their cargo area if the containers were full.[9] Since the generators were deliberately mislabeled as "empty," they were not equipped with safety caps and were improperly packaged. The boxes containing the generators were loaded onto the ValuJet plane without the required hazardous warning labels.

At some point after the generators were loaded, one or more of them was punctured, setting off a chain reaction that produced intense, searing heat in the cargo hold of the McDonald-Douglas DC-9. Within ten minutes after take-off, ValuJet Flight 592 crashed. Oxygen generators, like those in the cargo hold of that DC-9, are capable of producing heat up to 500 degrees Fahrenheit. Investigators later learned that the intense heat and flames caused the flight controls to fail.[10] Shortly after the plane left Miami in route to Atlanta, the crew experienced control problems, unaware that a fire had erupted in the cargo hold. Within just five minutes, the aircraft was enveloped by a raging onboard fire. The crew attempted to return to the Miami airport, but their efforts proved unsuccessful as the plane crashed into the Florida Everglades. The NTSB investigation suggests that the crew may have been incapacitated by heat and smoke. All 110 people aboard the plane were killed.

National Transportation Safety Board's Findings

After the crash, federal regulators forced the airline to stop flying until October of 1996 while they pursued a full investigation. The National Transportation Safety Board determined that the FAA had failed to follow a ten-year-old recommendation to require fire detection and suppression systems. If the FAA had followed the recommendation, the NTSB claims that ValuJet 592 would not have crashed. Furthermore, the frequency of the FAA's inspections was down 47 percent and ValuJet was being monitored by an unqualified FAA inspector by the name of David Harper.[11] According to the U.S. Transportation Department's Office of the Inspector General, Harper falsified his work experience and did not possess a sufficient amount of civilian aviation experience to properly oversee ValuJet's maintenance. During the two years that he was responsible for evaluating ValuJet, Harper had visited the airline's maintenance contractor on just one occasion for a total of three hours.

The NTSB found SabreTech, ValuJet's maintenance contractor, guilty of failing to properly "prepare, package, identify, and track" the hazardous oxygen generators that were

---

[9] Kazel, Robert, "ValuJet Insured for Crash Losses," *Business Insurance,* May 20, 1996.
[10] "ValuJet Reports: All to Blame," *The Washington Post*, August 20, 1997.
[11] Ibid.

placed in the cargo hold.[12] The maintenance contractor's mistake was identified as the "probable cause" of the crash. In an effort to clean out its hangar to impress a new potential customer (Continental Airlines), SabreTech allegedly lied about the empty state of the canisters in order to ensure that ValuJet would transport the generators to the airline's headquarters. ValuJet also alleged that shipping documents had been deliberately falsified by SabreTech when they determined that it would take too much time to dispose of them properly. When asked about their involvement in the situation, SabreTech's personnel pled the Fifth Amendment, protecting them from self-incrimination. At the time of the case, a criminal investigation was already pending against the maintenance company.

Although the NTSB found that the FAA failed to adequately monitor ValuJet and that SabreTech engaged in unethical practices, the board eventually ruled that the ultimate responsibility belonged to ValuJet. They said that ValuJet could contract out the work, but not the responsibility.

Reputation and Image

The *Atlanta Journal-Constitution* summarized the frustration experienced by the airline's senior team: "After most crashes clean-up can be done in a week or two, enabling the bad news to fade from the public's mind within a week. But in this case, the clean-up may take much longer, meaning ValuJet's name may be plastered in the media in a negative way for an extended period."[13]

Because ValuJet was a small start-up company, it was particularly susceptible to the fluctuations in demand for its services. Unlike other airlines, however, ValuJet had yet to establish a nationwide presence and was, therefore, unable to rely on its past performance as a means of influence over public perception. Because ValuJet had only serviced a small market, the nationwide attention that its crash generated served as the means by which many other potential customers were first introduced to the airline. As ValuJet attempted to grow into other markets, the image of the fatal crash would be strongly connected to the company.

ValuJet's president, Robert Priddy, repeatedly commented that the airline's safety record was "certifiably among the very best" in the industry. But, nine days before the crash, the FAA issued a report that singled out ValuJet as more accident-prone than nearly all its low-cost competitors. The FAA also disclosed that they conducted a seven-day investigation of the airline because of repeated safety problems and concerns regarding pilot training and maintenance procedures.[14]

The ValuJet crash set off a feverish debate about whether low-price airlines are more risky because they cut costs to reduce ticket prices.[15] David Hinson, an FAA administrator, argued that low-cost airlines are not necessarily more dangerous. The price of the ticket is totally

---

[12] Ibid.

[13] Ho, Rodney, "Rebuilding Faith Remains Major Test," *The Atlanta Journal-Constitution*.

[14] "Shareholders Sue ValuJet," CNN, May 30, 1996.

[15] "Fatal crash pushes ValueJet stock down 23%," *Daily Money*, Michael Brush, May 14, 1996.

irrelevant to the FAA's oversight of an airline. "Our business is making sure that all the airlines meet the same high safety standards."[16]

Image and reputation are closely linked to investors' attraction to a company. Within weeks, news of the fatal crash pushed ValuJet's stock down 23 percent. Despite the tragedy, many expected the well-run airline to recover. Many investors believed that if ValuJet could keep a clean record for a few weeks after the crash, while under the intense glare of the media, it would have the management and cash to pull it through over the long term.[17]

ValuJet Chairman and CEO, Lewis Jordan, said, "this airline will survive this crash and will prove to authorities that it is a reliable airline that does all it can to ensure the safety of its passengers." Jordan also said, "We will be working to restore the public confidence and I am 100 percent confident when all the facts are known that we will be able to do that very, very effectively." Industry analysts, he said, seemed to think that the flying public had forgiven other airlines in the past during troubled times and had been loyal to carriers that could provide the public with low-cost travel.[18]

Communication and Strategy

Jordan went on to say that he felt that the single, biggest factor in his mind concerning the media was a "rush to judgement." The reports were slanted and led the public to believe that the accident was the result of an aging aircraft, poor maintenance practices, insufficient training, and an inexperienced crew. Under such an intense spotlight, ValuJet executives knew they needed a central voice. They did not place a gag order on their employees, but they made them aware of the fact that what they said could be misunderstood or misconstrued . Everyone at ValuJet was aware that the press was going to be very aggressive and the company would receive bad press. ValuJet felt that some reporters were looking for anything negative to say about the company. Jordan felt that ValuJet had been very open and cooperative with the press, and he knew how important it would be to have the press on their side.[19]

As the company continued to face media scrutiny, their spokespersons did not help to ease the situation. A ValuJet executive left relatives of crash victims seething by repeatedly avoiding questions and blaming a contractor for putting oxygen-generating canisters aboard Flight 595 without safety caps. Investigators later said that the $1 caps could have prevented the fire. David Gentry, ValuJet's vice president for heavy maintenance, appeared rattled several times during nearly three hours of questioning at a hearing before the National Transportation Safety Board. He also clearly frustrated investigators by giving vague responses, requesting that questions be repeated two and three times and pointing the finger squarely at a maintenance company hired by the airline.[20] Gentry said that SabreTech should have put the $1 safety caps on the oxygen canisters before loading them into the jet's cargo hold. Bernard Loeb, the NTSB's

[16] Ibid.
[17] Ibid.
[18] Barrett, Katharine, "ValuJet Struggling to Overcome Woes," CNN, May 16, 1996.
[19] "Rebounding from Tragedy," *The Strategist*, June 6, 1997.
[20] "ValuJet Official Irks Crash Victims' Relatives," The Associated Press, Catherine Wilson, November 12, 1996.

safety aviation chief, was angry at Gentry's dismissal of responsibility and asked him, "Are you responsible for making sure that an airplane is air worthy, and therefore are you responsible for what your contractors do?" Gentry finally answered, "Yes."

Communication problems continued to surface for the company. Marcia Scott, a spokeswoman for ValuJet, said, "The bottom line is that the airline should be held blameless. We believe there's nothing any ValuJet employee could have done to have kept this terrible tragedy from happening." After an internal investigation, ValuJet cited SabreTech as the sole responsible party for the crash. The refusal of ValuJet to accept responsibility encouraged some in the media to attack them even more.[21]

Airtran Airlines and Future Strategies

In July of 1997, ValuJet attempted to reconstruct its image by merging with Airways Corporation, another low-fare airline.[22] "The combined company took AirTran's name to get away from the negatives associated with ValuJet's name."[23] Because the AirTran name bore no resemblance to ValuJet, the merger would offer ValuJet a chance to "re-invent" itself and shed its negative image. The new airline hoped to appeal to a broader audience base with the advent of its new business class and frequent flyer programs. However, the AirTran business model also hoped to maintain the affordable pricing strategy that made ValuJet a success.

Questions

1.   What communication strategy should ValuJet adopt in order to repair their tarnished image?

2.   Can ValuJet overcome this crash and continue to grow in the airline industry?

3.   What are the options available to ValuJet for the future?

4.   How should ValuJet have handled the crisis of the airplane crash?

5.   Who should ValuJet blame for the crash, and how should this be communicated to the public?

6.   How should ValuJet handle a crash in the future?

7.   What will ValuJet and AirTran have to do to succeed in this competitive industry, and how should future communications be handled?

---

[21] Ibid.

[22] "Business Loop-the name game," *Electrical World*, Vol. 212, No. 1, January 1, 1998.

[23] "Discount Airlines Flying in Turbulence. Two Are Bankrupt, Others Struggling," Christopher Carey, *St. Louis*

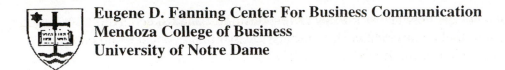

Eugene D. Fanning Center For Business Communication   99-04
Mendoza College of Business
University of Notre Dame

Northwest Airlines
and the Blizzard of '99

Toilets in the sleek, new Boeing 757s overflowed. Hysterical passengers vowed to blow open an emergency door and jump into the freezing darkness. Grown men wept and begged to be freed. The air stank. Babies screamed. Adults screamed, too.

Anyone who flies regularly has an airline horror story, but short of a crash or a hijacking, few trips are likely to compare to those taken by passengers booked into Detroit, Michigan on Northwest Airlines during the first few days of 1999.

During a New Year's weekend blizzard that produced 60 below-zero wind chills and snowdrifts more than a foot deep, Northwest Airlines stopped answering their telephones. They did not, however, stop landing flights at Detroit Metropolitan Airport. As a result, 34 of Northwest's airplanes landed in Detroit on January 3, 1999. Twenty-four of them were stranded on the tarmac, some of them tantalizingly close to the terminal building, for periods ranging from one hour to eight hours and 38 minutes.

One flight dispatcher later said that Northwest's operation center in Minneapolis, Minnesota, started to divert planes from Detroit as soon as it became apparent that no gates would be opening. But another dispatcher admitted that the "quality and quantity of information [needed to make decisions] was lacking." During an investigation of the incident in the weeks that followed, airline officials in Detroit say they repeatedly attempted to get the airline's operations center in Minneapolis to divert flights to another city or cancel them. At three different times, they say, Detroit schedulers made such requests, to little or no avail.

Throughout the ordeal, airline officials were faced with the task of communicating with multiple audiences and stakeholders, including passengers, the press, civic officials, and airline employees. Their choice of words, timing, message, and media would be closely followed by

---

This case was prepared by Research Assistants Alissa Dutmers, Lucy Littlejohn, and Cara Lorch under the direction of James S. O'Rourke, Concurrent Associate Professor of Management, as the basis for class discussion rather than to illustrate either effective or ineffective handling of an administrative situation.

everyone from network news anchors to stock analysts to plaintiff's bar lawyers. And all would have a direct effect on the company's reputation for professionalism and concern for passenger rights as well as safety.

A New Year's Weekend Fiasco

Friday, January 1, 1999. Early on New Year's Day, Northwest Airlines' meteorology department in Minneapolis, Minnesota, predicted that between 8 and 10 inches of snow would fall in Detroit, Michigan, on Saturday. In response, Northwest Airlines officials canceled 50 flight arrivals into Detroit Metropolitan Airport. In a typical day, more than 700 airplanes would land in Detroit.

Saturday, January 2, 1999. Snow began to fall in Detroit in the early morning hours on Saturday. By 1:30 that afternoon, Northwest's chief dispatcher suggested to the Strategic Operation Center (SOC) director and three Northwest planners "that we should shut down" Detroit Metro. Rather than shut down Detroit operations, the SOC director in Minneapolis decided simply to cancel more arrivals.

Around 3:00 p.m., two Northwest cockpit crews reported poor braking action on one of Detroit Metro's runways. Half-an-hour later, two Northwest managers left for the remote pad where planes are de-iced and got lost in white-out conditions. Airport escorts rescued them after a frantic one-hour search in a blinding snowstorm.

At 6:30 p.m., Northwest's control center manager in Detroit told the SOC to shut down operations at Detroit Metro until at least noon on Sunday. The SOC canceled "most" flights a half-hour later, with a few exceptions.

As evening came and the flight ramp grew dark, as many as eight mobile jet bridges used for passenger deboardings began to fail because they had not received winterizing lubrication. Furthermore, Northwest officials in the Detroit Metro tower could not see well enough to count the planes that were scheduled for takeoff and waiting to be de-iced. That hardly mattered, since the de-icing system was no longer functional and all outbound flights were canceled.

Sunday, January 3, 1999. At 2:00 a.m., the Detroit control center manager again requested that the Northwest Strategic Operations Center cancel all flights before noon. The manager also asked that all DC-9 flights be canceled until 4:00 p.m. Most arrivals before noon were canceled and only two planes arrived Sunday morning.

By the early morning hours, Detroit Metro's total snowfall measured 10.6 inches. High winds compounded the problem. Because of the snow, only 185 Northwest ramp personnel arrived for work, compared to 400 who would be at work on a normal day. By 11:00 a.m., more than 12 inches of snow blanketed the ground and luggage belt loaders could no longer move. Northwest's Detroit chief toured the ramp with his de-icing manager. After seeing that nothing was moving, the chief called Minneapolis and asked that all operations be shut down. The operations chief in Minneapolis says he does not remember any such call.

The first Detroit-bound flight on Sunday arrived at 11:16 a.m. and waited 28 minutes to taxi to its gate. The second plane arrived before noon and waited approximately 48 minutes for a gate. Within an hour and 45 minutes after the first arrival, however, eight more arrivals followed when it was agreed that only a few aircraft would land.

At 1:00 p.m., the SOC director decided that Detroit could not handle any more arrivals for at least two-and-a-half hours. He advised the airline's chief dispatcher that flights which were already taxiing toward the runway could proceed. Flights en route to Detroit were also allowed to continue. Between noon and 4:00 p.m., Northwest landed a total of 34 planes at Detroit Metro. Because departures were at a standstill, these planes were stranded without gates for periods ranging from one hour to eight hours and 38 minutes.

By mid-afternoon, Northwest officials in Detroit began drafting plans to go out to the planes and unload passengers. De-icing equipment was ordered to begin clearing ice from the exterior stairways. After an extended discussion about weather conditions on the ramp, however, airline officials decided not to unload passengers onto the airfield for safety reasons.

At 8:00 p.m., a pilot on one of the stranded planes reported that a passenger was having a heart attack. A medical crew was sent to deplane the passenger, causing all gates to be blocked for an extended time. The passenger, it turns out, was not having a heart attack and was left on the airplane. Just before 11:30 p.m., the last arriving plane was unloaded after sitting eight hours and 38 minutes on the runway.

Monday, January 4, 1999. Northwest Airlines decided not to operate any in-bound flights into Detroit Metro Airport before noon on Monday. However, the airline did attempt to operate as many outbound flights as possible to allow snow removal equipment access to tarmac areas. The airline also had to contend with angry passengers who lost luggage. Early Monday morning, a line of more than 300 passengers formed outside Northwest's baggage claim complaint office. By mid-afternoon, a Northwest representative told passengers in the baggage claim area that they should go home and return another day to look for their luggage. To make matters worse, about 25 percent of Northwest's employees could not make it into work on that day. The airline responded by sending four-wheel drive vehicles to pick up employees and bring them to work.

Four days had passed since the snowstorm began, and Northwest Airlines had yet to resume full operations in Detroit. By that point, however, some 5,000 suitcases were still separated from their owners and had piled up at airports across the country. Northwest brought in 30 employees from around the country to aid in the process of sorting and transporting luggage to its owners. It would be more than another two weeks, however, before some passengers were reunited with their luggage.

The Passengers' Stories

According to Bill Goldstein, a passenger on one of the many stranded flights, there was no food or water and toilets were full or overflowing. These two events had serious consequences for individuals trapped on an aircraft for nearly nine hours. Without food, children were extremely hard to deal with and were forced to share crackers. Parents with infants quickly ran out of formula and baby food. Without bathrooms, passengers were forced to urinate in paper cups.

The combination of a lack of food, inoperable bathrooms, and confined room to move resulted in passengers feeling as if they were in a hostage situation. In fact, many suffered panic attacks. One stranded passenger ranted and raved and told the flight crew that she could not stand it any longer. She then threatened to open the door and activate the emergency chute. She was immediately read her rights and told that the sheriff's department would be at the gate to arrest her if she did not calm down. That was not a rare event. When passengers attempted to stand or move about the airplane, they were immediately told that they must remain in their seats. One woman unbuckled her seatbelt and the stewardess threatened to have her arrested. Restrictions such as these were difficult for some, but nearly intolerable for others, including passengers with rheumatoid arthritis and for others recovering from surgery.

Passengers were not only deprived of food and restrooms, but also of information concerning their status on the runway. Most were unaware, for example, that when they stepped on the airplane, they surrendered their legal right to get off once the plane left the gate. One passenger, Robert Carita, was trapped on an aircraft for five hours. According to Carita, every hour the pilot announced that they would be on the runway for one more hour. On other planes, pilots showed movies to calm passengers. One pilot, prompted by frustration, used a passenger's cell phone to call Northwest Airlines President John Dasburg at home to convey the desperate nature of the situation. Unfortunately, even that measure did not alter the status of any of the aircraft on the tarmac at Detroit Metro.

Lawsuits

Timothy and Susan Koczara of Gross Pointe, Michigan, filed a lawsuit against Northwest for the treatment they received during their flight back from St. Martin's. After being stranded on an airplane at Detroit Metro for eight hours, they felt that they had received inadequate treatment. "We had no food, no water, nothing. It was liked being trapped on an elevator," said Timothy Koczara. Both wanted to get off the airplane, while Northwest's main concern was its passengers' safety. Larry Charfoos, a Detroit attorney, later filed the Koczara's lawsuit in Wayne County Circuit Court. The lawsuit sought class-action status against Northwest, the Detroit airport, and Wayne County, which owns the airport. The formal complaint alleged that passengers detained on the ground for hours were subject to "negligent and intentional infliction of emotional distress" and "false imprisonment."

Passenger Rights

Attorney Byron Siegel was also aboard one of the snow-bound Detroit airplanes. After approximately four hours on the tarmac, his "lawyer instincts" took over and he passed a legal pad around the plane. More than fifty people signed the paper, frustrated with the way Northwest was handling the situation. Siegel said, "It was time to do something as a matter of principle so that hopefully other people would not have this happen to them again." Siegel declared his hope that the class-action lawsuit filed in Wayne County Circuit Court might eventually change the regulations governing the rights of passengers. Currently, the people aboard an airplane have no legal right to be released from a plane on demand, no matter how long they have been held, no matter what circumstances.

The passengers' plight also inspired House Representative John Dingell (D-Michigan) to ask U.S. Department of Transportation Secretary Rodney Slater to evaluate whether Northwest Airlines and other carriers lacked "prudent preparedness."

Northwest Airlines' Dilemma

Placing Blame

Although Northwest Airlines and Detroit Metropolitan Airport blamed Mother Nature for the January blizzard crisis, each pointed the finger at the other. Northwest began blaming the airport's snow removal crews on Monday, January 4, claiming that other carriers' terminals were plowed before Northwest's. Robert Ball, Jr., Northwest's vice president of customer service in Detroit, asserted that Wayne County's snow crews did not plow Northwest's gates until about 5:30 a.m. Monday, more than twenty-four hours after twelve inches of snow fell.

David Katz, Detroit Metro's director of operations, and a contractor who helped plow the airport, defended the snow removal process, saying that work was not completed in one day because of the unusually heavy snowfall. Katz said, "We worked 24-hour shifts and there were very few no-shows." The contractor, Jack B. Anglin Inc., had 20 plows and 14 dump trucks operating around the clock to remove snow from the taxiways. Metro also had 30 county plows, truck mounted blowers, and dump trucks working 24 hours a day.

On the other hand, only half of Northwest's ground workers in Detroit arrived for work on the days of the blizzard. The shortage of Northwest workers slowed the movement of the airplanes in and out of the gates. The airline, however, insisted that it did the best that it could and blamed the city of Detroit for many of the problems, claiming that its policy of not plowing residential streets may have prevented some Northwest employees from traveling to work. See Attachment 1 for the responsibilities of Wayne County, Northwest Airlines, and the United States government at Detroit Metropolitan Airport.

Weather

Jon Austin, managing director of corporate communication for Northwest, said "this was a blizzard-of-the-decade kind of event. I think everybody was frustrated to find themselves in a situation out of their control . . . . But most people I talked to recognized that, try as we might, we don't control the weather." Northwest's senior vice president Richard Hirst added that the severity of the storm caught Northwest by surprise; professional weather forecasters, however, had been predicting a major snow storm days before the New Year's blizzard. Nevertheless, Northwest's operation center in Minneapolis felt they could handle the storm and allowed flights to land in Detroit through Sunday. By Sunday afternoon, the snow had stopped and all the planes had landed; yet, the gates were not accessible because the planes that should have left early Sunday morning were snowed in, broken down, or had no one to fly them.

The Turning Point Comes

By the afternoon of Thursday, January 7, 1999, Northwest Airlines operations had returned to normal at Detroit Metropolitan Airport. A lawsuit, however, had just been filed in Wayne County Circuit Court on behalf of the Koczaras. Their attorney, Larry Charfoos, was seeking class-action status for the lawsuit, allowing other disgruntled passengers to join. Although the county and the airport were named as co-defendants, Charfoos contended that Northwest is the party most at fault. Given the lawsuit, the potential investigation into passenger rights, and Northwest Airlines' response during the storm and the confusion that followed, the national media's interest in the passengers and their tales was beginning to grow.

Jon Austin, Northwest's managing director of corporate communication, had to determine how to proceed. With him in the Flight Operations Center at Detroit Metro were Andrea Fischer Newman, vice president for state and local affairs, and Ray Vecci, vice president for customer service.

Questions

1. What are the critical issues in this case?

2. What should Jon Austin's priorities be? Can you provide him with a brief list, rank-ordered by priority?

3. What should the company's strategy be as they try to dig out of the publicity and customer service nightmare they face?

4. With whom should they communicate? Which audiences are most important to them right now? Which audiences will become more important as time passes?

5. What's the message? What, precisely, should Mr. Austin say at this point?

6. What actions should Austin, Newman, and Vecci urge the company to take at this point?

7. Can the airline ever hope to recover from lost business, bad publicity, angry passengers, enraged lawmakers, and the damage to its corporate reputation?

Sources

Bradsher, Keith. "Plenty of Snow in Detroit, But Hardly a Plow in Sight," *The New York Times*, Tuesday, January 12, 1999.

Carey, Susan. "'I'm Opening a Door' 'No, No, Don't Do It!' 'How About a Valium?'" *The Wall Street Journal*, Wednesday, April 28, 1999.

Fricker, Daniel G. "Report Shows Airline Chaos in Storm. Northwest Paper Details January Snow Fiasco," *The Detroit Free Press*, Tuesday, February 9, 1999.

Fricker, Daniel G. "U.S.: Northwest Had No Plan. State Will Also Probe Airlines Snowstorm Response," *The Detroit Free Press*, Thursday, June 3, 1999.

Gallagher, John. "Northwest Still Holding Vouchers for Snowbound," *The Detroit Free Press*, Tuesday, February 9, 1999.

McDowell, Edwin. "Business Travel. Halcyon Days for Airlines, If Not for Many Passengers," *The New York Times*, Saturday, April 3, 1999.

Neal, Rubin. "Northwest's Apologist Andrea Fischer Newman Continues to Dig the Airline Out of a Public Relations Fiasco," *The Detroit Free Press*, Sunday, February 7, 1999.

ATTACHMENT 1
Allocation of Responsibilities

WAYNE COUNTY, MICHIGAN

- The airport is obligated to remove snow removal on 500 acres of concrete runways, taxiways, and areas around the gates.
- Restrooms in hallways are the county's responsibility.
- Baggage handling facility falls under airport authority.
- Security officers inside and outside the terminal are airport employees.
- Vendors, including airport parking and restaurants, fall under the control of the airport.

NORTHWEST AIRLINES

- Ground crews are responsible for bringing aircraft in and out of gates.
- The airline is responsible for clearing snow in the footprint of aircraft.
- Northwest Airlines is also responsible for maintaining Concourses C through G, including restrooms.
- The airline is responsible for passenger baggage.
- Security at checkpoints within the terminal is contracted by Northwest.

THE UNITED STATES FEDERAL GOVERNMENT

- The Federal Aviation Administration air traffic controllers have control of all aircraft on the ground when the aircraft is away from the gate area.

Source: Detroit / Wayne County Metropolitan Airport.

Attachment 2: Flight numbers and tarmac waiting time, Sunday, January 3, 1999.

A Bad Trip For Northwest Flight 1829

On Jan. 2, vacationers left St. Martin for Detroit. The flight was scheduled for five hours. The journey would drag on for more than 30 hours–the last seven spent pinned on the Detroit tarmac. For the 198 people trapped in the smothering plane, the ordeal would become an experiment in their capacity for patience–or panic.

Robert Patchett
First Officer

Nikki Ward
Flight Attendant

Barry Forbes
Flight Attendant

Christina Wade
Passenger

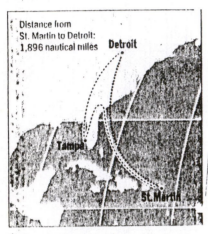

Distance from St. Martin to Detroit: 1,896 nautical miles

The flight plan: Northwest Flight 1829, St. Martin to Detroit. Scheduled air time: five hours. Actual route: Departed St. Martin 3:08 EST Saturday; arrived Tampa 8:03 EST after turning back over southern Georgia. Departed Tampa 12:27 p.m. EST Sunday; arrived Detroit 2:45 EST. Elapsed time: 23 hours and 37 minutes.

William Goldstein
Passenger

Leslie McCoy
Passenger

Eugene Pettis
Passenger

Sonya Friedman
Passenger

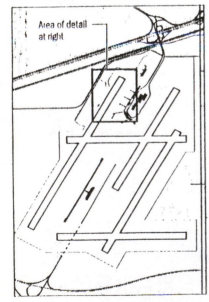

Area of detail at right

The airport: Detroit Metropolitan Wayne County Airport. The flight touches down at 2:45 p.m. The runways appear clear.

Sharon Friedman
Passenger

Scott Friedman
Passenger

A Bad Trip For Northwest Flight 1829 continued

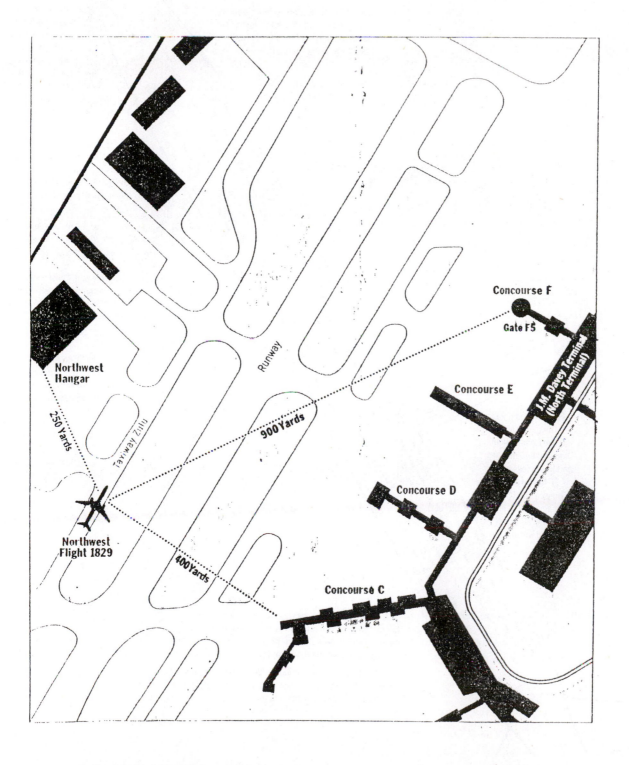

So near and yet so far: At 2:50, Flight 1829 parks on a little-used Zulu taxiway, not far from the gates, some of which are vacant, and even closer to a Northwest hangar. The plane moves only once in the next seven hours.

A Bad Trip For Northwest Flight 1829 continued

1. In the cockpit, Capts. Peter Stabler, Robert Patchett and Chuck Miller struggle to avert total anarchy and plead with Northwest officials to bring Flight 1829 in.

2. The first class galley, where flight attendant Nikki Ward encounters a heart patient who begs to be freed. Four hours into the flight, Ms. Ward notes things could be worse: "No one has to eat each other."

3. In Row 5, Sonya Friedman, a psychologist, and Barbara Ruskin chat about Mrs. Ruskin's fear of flying. Mrs. Ruskin is comforted-for a while.

4. Sharon Friedman, Sonya's daughter, breaks down in Row 7 after five hours on the tarmac. Later she worries about which of her two children to deprive of water.

5. In Row 14, Dr. Bill Goldstein irks others with his bickering over seats, but his audacity is welcomed in the end. At about 8 p.m., he begins hunting for Northwest CEO Dasburg.

6. Dr. Scott Friedman and his wife Amy, in Row 8, Seats E and D, disagree over the best course of action: Sit tight or jump?

7. More than five hours into the wait, Christina Wade, Row 9, Seat D, screams, "I'm jumping!" The windchill factor outside is more than 20 below. Capt. Stabler tries to calm her, but some passengers urge her on.

8. Honeymooners Doug Post and Dawn Chamberlain had endured roaches and foul smells at their St. Martin hotel. They couldn't have imagined that life in Row 20 would be worse.

9. In Row 23, Stephen London eyes a nearby hangar and can't fathom why the jet doesn't pull in and evacuate passengers. After five hours, he begins enlisting support for lawsuits.

10. From 32D, Leslie McCoy rebels against drink charges and-at around 8:30 -rages: "Get me off this f— plane!" Shortly thereafter, in 32 C, Eugene Pettis detects a sewage leak from the right rear lavatory behind Row 26.

11. Stationed in the rear galley, flight attendant Barry Forbes calls for movies 30 minutes into the wait and is astonished at the reaction. Hours later, he must stick his arm into a fetid lavatory waste tank.

Left rear lavatory

Illustration by K. Daniel Clark

Eugene D. Fanning Center for Business Communication   **01-04**
Mendoza College of Business
University of Notre Dame

Navistar Corporation and a Workplace Shooting

It was 10:12 a.m. on Monday, February 5, 2001, when Martin Reutimann, a 24-year-old engineer at Navistar International's Truck Engine Plant in Melrose Park, Illinois, heard someone yell, "There's a guy in the center aisle with a gun!" The gunman, a former plant employee, had driven his truck past a security post and forced his way into the facility by overpowering an unarmed female guard at gunpoint. Before taking his own life, the assailant used a Soviet assault rifle and a .38-caliber revolver to go on a 10 to 15 minute shooting rampage that would eventually leave four people dead and four others wounded.

Less than an hour earlier, the day had gotten off to a much more auspicious beginning. Greg Elliott, Navistar's Vice President of Communications, had concluded his weekly conference call with his staff. They had discussed how some new and exciting company initiatives would be handled. In particular, Elliot had been working very closely with Bob Carso of the Melrose Park location to prepare announcements for the launch of an all-new product and an upcoming joint venture with a major automobile manufacturer. When Elliot received a call from Carso later that the morning, he initially thought it was related to something that had been left out of the meeting. However, when he learned that Carso was calling about the shooting that had just taken place at the engine plant, Elliot knew that his team's efforts would have to be quickly redirected.

This case was prepared by Research Assistants J. Thorman and D. Wesner under the direction of James S. O'Rourke, Concurrent Associate Professor of Management, as the basis for class discussion rather than to illustrate either effective or ineffective handling of an administrative situation. Information was gathered from corporate as well as public sources.

The Shooter

William D. Baker, age 66, had been a 39-year veteran of Navistar International. Known as a steady employee, Baker worked as a tool room attendant and forklift operator at the Melrose Park facility, and was perceived by one former colleague as "an easy going guy." However, in September 1993, Baker had a run-in with the law and was placed on probation for criminal damage to property and reckless conduct. Around the same time, he became involved in an internal theft scheme at the plant that would last until the following spring. Baker was one of six cohorts, including four other company employees. They would steal new and used truck engines and components from the factory to sell across state borders. Specifically, stolen items were loaded into trucks by Baker and then driven off for sale or distribution at a small parts business owned by one of the conspirators. Once shipments left the state, they became the concern of federal authorities. In early 1994, the FBI successfully tracked and arrested the main participant in the ring. It was not long before Baker was also apprehended and subsequently fired from Navistar.

For the next six years, Baker's case remained in the appeals courts. In many ways, Baker felt as though he had been unjustly convicted of a crime in which he had played a relatively insignificant role. As stated by his attorney, Charles Piet, "He didn't feel it was fair given that his participation was very minor." In the meantime, Baker perpetuated more trouble with the law when he was found guilty in 1998 of criminal sexual assault involving a family member under the age of 17. Now, a registered sex offender serving four years of probation, Baker awaited the final outcome of his previous indictment. After it became apparent that his case would not be reversed, Baker was formally charged with his second felony in June 2000. The sentence, handed down in November, stipulated that Baker serve five months in federal prison, followed by five months of home confinement and two years of supervised probation. In addition, Baker was ordered to pay restitution to Navistar in the amount of $195,400 for the value of the stolen items. Interestingly, Baker was to report to prison and begin serving his sentence one day after he began his shooting spree.

Company Background

Chicago based Navistar International has been in business for more than one hundred years. Today, its largest subsidiary, International Truck and Engine Corporation is the second largest producer of heavy-duty trucks in the nation. Navistar was ranked number 202 on the latest Fortune 500 list of America's largest companies. Total revenues for 2000 exceeded $8.5 billion.

In addition to its heavy-duty truck line, the company produces mid-sized trucks, school buses, and diesel engines. Navistar also owns non-manufacturing businesses including a financial services and insurance subsidiary. Currently, more than 17,000 people are employed at the company's operations in the United States, Canada, Mexico, and Brazil. Navistar sells its products in more than 70 countries around the world.

Major customers include Ford Motor Company and other large automotive equipment manufacturers.

The Melrose Park truck engine plant is located on a seventy-acre site fifteen miles west of Navistar's downtown Chicago headquarters. The facility covers two million square feet and employs approximately 1,400 fulltime workers. The plant manufactures midrange diesel engines for Navistar trucks and diesel engines for school buses that are sold under the International brand. The plant also contains a diesel engine technology center.

Violence in the Workplace

The Navistar tragedy should serve as a reminder that workplace violence is a growing problem in the United States. According to the Bureau of Labor Statistics, murder is second only to highway accidents as the leading cause of death on the job. Other government reports indicate that homicide in the workplace is the fastest growing category of murder in the U.S. Every year, 1,000 people are killed on the job and 1.5 million are injured as a result of workplace violence.

The shooting at Navistar came just a few months after a similar tragedy had occurred at Edgewater Technology, a Boston based e-commerce consulting firm. Other such incidents have been reported at Xerox, Ford Motor Company, Daimler-Chrysler, and Merrill Lynch. According to Kathryn Hartrick, a partner in the Chicago law firm of Stickler and Nelson, workplace violence is becoming more widespread across a broader range of companies. Hartrick also says there are usually warning signs that precede an outbreak of violence in the workplace. The three key ingredients that most often contribute to work-related violence include:

- An employee who has a heightened potential for aggression. Potentially violent employees may have a substance abuse problem, experience mental illness, or harbor a long-standing perception of being treated unfairly by an employer.

- A workplace environment that can be a catalyst for an unstable or angry employee. High-pressured, fast-paced, low-paying workplaces can be high-risk environments for employees pre-disposed to violence.

- A triggering event experienced by a company employee, either on the job or at home. This could include the termination or layoff of an employee or a personal setback such as divorce or the break-up of a relationship.

The effects following a violent incident in the workplace can be devastating to a company. For survivors, witnesses, and friends of the victims, the trauma may be more than they can handle. Some employees refuse to return to the area where an incident occurred. Others request transfers, and some even change careers. Other problems include lower productivity, higher error margins, lawsuits, and difficulty in recruiting new employees.

After the Shooting Stopped

Greg Elliott had expected the next few weeks to be very busy and challenging for the company, even before he was faced with the issues surrounding the shooting. For some time, he had been working on the details of a joint venture between Navistar and Ford Motor Company. The two corporations were planning to make a public announcement regarding the partnership later that week. Shortly thereafter, Navistar intended to make another announcement about a new product the company was preparing to launch. Elliot had also been working with the Investor Relations Department to issue the company's quarterly earnings statement, which was scheduled to be released in the next few weeks. Finally, he had to begin concentrating on Navistar's annual stockholders meeting scheduled for the following month.

As news of the tragedy began to sink in, Elliot wondered how he would manage to keep the company's initiatives on track while simultaneously refocusing his efforts on the crisis Navistar now faced.

Questions

1.   What are the key communications issues for Navistar?

2.   Who are the major stakeholders that Elliott and his team must consider in formulating a communications strategy? How will the needs of such parties be identified, prioritized, and incorporated into the chosen strategy?

3.   With workplace violence on the rise in the United States, is it necessary for companies to have formal prevention programs in place? What might the role be of a corporate communications department in creating these initiatives?

4.   Is it important to have formal communications policies and procedures in place to respond to crisis situations? How might a company go about developing such guidelines?

5.   Does a company have a responsibility to monitor the behavior and mental stability of its associates? If so, to what extent?

Sources

Elliot, Greg, Vice President Corporate of Communications, Navistar International. Personal Interview, 16 April 2001.

France, Mike. "After the Shooting Stops," *Business Weekly,* 12 March 2001, p98-100.

Harris, Leon and Kris Habermehl. "Several Wounded in Illinois Shooting; One Confirmed Dead," *CNN: Breaking News*, Monday, 5 February 2001.

Webber, Tammy. "Ex-employee Kills Four and Commits Suicide at Illinois Engine Plant," *Associated Press Newswires*, Monday, 5 February 2001.

Webber, Tammy. "Gunman Kills Himself, Four Others at Navistar Plant," *Associated Press Newswires*, Monday, 5 February 2001.

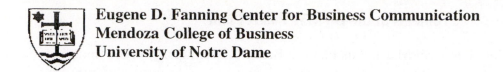
Sara Lee Corporation and the Listeriosis Scare of 1998

Background

Sara Lee Corporation was founded in 1939 by a Canadian entrepreneur named Nathan Cummings. Originally called C. D. Kenny Company, it began as a distributor of sugar, coffee, and tea in Baltimore, Maryland. The company grew through Cummings' implementation of new management methods.[1]

By 1942, Cummings renamed the corporation Sprague Warner-Kenny Corporation after a strategic purchase gave his company greater distribution access. Cummings relocated the company to Chicago and focused on aggressive growth for the next 50 years.

Cummings was an ambitious man who made a number of strategic acquisitions during the early years of the then-named Consolidated Grocers Corporation. In 1953, they changed their name once more to Consolidated Foods Corporation to reflect the company's more diversified holdings. In 1956, Cummings purchased the Kitchens of Sara Lee, which served to expand Consolidated Foods' reach into the frozen baked goods sector.

Through the early 1970s, Consolidated Foods continued to diversify. Additional food companies were acquired, including Bryan Foods, Hillshire Farm, and Rudy's Farm. Consolidated Foods also entered the direct sales, apparel, and personal care industries through acquisitions. By 1985, the $20 billion giant had changed its name to Sara Lee Corporation and was the producer of numerous brands ranging from Ball Park frankfurters to Hanes underwear.[2]

This case was prepared by Research Assistants Sabine Bonnet, Fernando Burciaga, and Kevin Fuller under the direction of James S. O'Rourke, Concurrent Associate Professor of Management, as the basis for class discussion rather than to illustrate either effective or ineffective handling of an administrative situation. Information was gathered from corporate as well as public sources.

---

[1] *Detroit Free Press Special Report*, http://www.freep.com.
[2] http://www.saralee.com.

Problems at the Bil Mar Foods Plant

Employees at Sara Lee's Bil Mar Foods Plant in Borculo, Michigan, worked under intense pressure. Shift after shift, they feverishly scrubbed, mopped, and sanitized to remove grease, dirt, and most importantly, bacteria from a plant the size of ten football fields. They scrambled to clean every nook and surface in the massive plant, but time pressures caused many employees to take shortcuts.

The management at Bil Mar Foods was also under pressure from Sara Lee's Chicago headquarters. Earlier that year, the United States Department of Agriculture (USDA) had shut the Bil Mar office down for health violations. They were previously cited for minor infractions, but by the spring of 1998, other, more serious violations began to appear. In some instances, inspectors discovered excrement-stained carcasses on the plant floor, as well as foreign objects in the food such as metal shavings, rust, and other debris.

The meat packing industry was undergoing a number of changes at the time. The inspection of processed foods in America's largest meat packing plants was being turned over to the corporations themselves, and inspectors were placed in a supervisory role. In the past, federal meat inspectors directly inspected all the food and had the final say as to whether the food was fit to be sold. Recently, however, the responsibility was given to the plant employees. The most federal inspectors could do was supervise the job performed by plant employees.

Inspector Mueller of the USDA was frustrated by his observations and concerned about the ramifications of improper inspections. Voicing his concerns, he said he did "not believe the plant employees should be able to contaminate product . . . and then just leave it [and hope] someone else will catch it . . . it should be either corrected or taken care of."

Saturday, July 4, 1998

The management at Bil Mar Foods had been plagued by a water condensation problem for months. Water would condense on the plant ceilings and then drip onto work surfaces within the plant. The condensation was dangerous because it carried bacteria, which thrives in a moist environment. Over the holiday weekend they decided to remove a failing refrigeration unit, which was the source of the majority of the condensation problems.

The project turned out to require the complete dismantling of the unit. The resulting dust spread throughout the plant as workers hauled the pieces of the cooler away. For the next six weeks, swab tests results were positive for cold-loving bacteria. The plant workers cleaned all the equipment thoroughly after every positive sample, but, as it was not required, further testing was never performed on the initial swab samples. Normally, these bacteria were relatively harmless. In this case, however, there was no way to know for sure.

What is Listeriosis?

Listeriosis is caused from a bacterium called Listeria monocytogenes. Unlike most other food-borne bacteria which grow only at room temperature, Listeria monocytogenes can also grow in cold, refrigerated environments. Several distinct strains of the bacterium have been discovered. The lethal strain in the Bil Mar Foods outbreak was called the "e-strain."

Listeriosis strikes the central nervous system and causes flu-like symptoms such as fever, nausea, and headache. Nearly one in four who become infected with the bacterium will die. It can strike anyone, but most healthy bodies are able to fight it off. Those most vulnerable to listeriosis are the elderly, newborns, and those with weakened immune systems. Pregnant women and their unborn children are especially susceptible. About 1,850 cases are reported in the United States each year. Many more cases probably go undiagnosed. Foods likely to harbor the bacterium include luncheon meats, hot dogs, and other ready-to-eat cooked meats.

Listeriosis Case

John and Helen Bodnar of Memphis, Tennessee, had been married for 52 years. One night in October 1998, Helen collapsed on the kitchen floor. That evening she had eaten Ball Park brand hot dogs produced by the Bil Mar plant in Michigan. John rushed her to the hospital where she was given a battery of tests for two days. Doctors could not find anything wrong with her, so she was sent home. Within 24 hours, Helen was back in the emergency room again, this time with a 104-degree temperature and an abdomen that was grotesquely bloated. She soon developed meningitis, a serious condition that can be caused by the listeria bacterium. By the time the diagnosis was made, Helen had lapsed into a coma. Before long, Mrs. Bodnar suffered heart failure and died.

Beginnings of an Outbreak

Donna Gibbs came across cases of salmonella and e. coli frequently in her job at the Tennessee Health Department. Within the course of a couple of weeks she had received reports of four cases of listeriosis in the state of Tennessee. She normally only saw two or three cases a year, so she immediately alerted Allen Craig, the state epidemiologist, who in turn alerted the U.S. Centers for Disease Control and Prevention (CDC) in Atlanta. The cases appeared unrelated because the victims involved were a two-week old infant and a 60 year-old-man. To compound the problem, the listeria bacterium has up to a 70-day incubation period. It wasn't until mid-November that cases from other states were reported and the CDC went on alert.

Two More Cases Reported, Linked to Sara Lee

Another case involved a young woman enrolled at Western Michigan University in Kalamazoo. One day in October, the woman had flu-like symptoms, and the next day her roommate found her delirious in their room. She was rushed to the local hospital and diagnosed with meningitis, a dangerous swelling of the lining of the brain and spinal cord that can cause coma and death. A spinal tap revealed that the listeria bacterium was causing the meningitis. During a routine follow-up by health officials, it was discovered that nearly every day the young woman would have a deli-turkey sandwich served at the university. The meat was supplied to the school by the Bil Mar Foods plant in nearby Borculo, Michigan.

Still another case involved a 56 year-old woman in Detroit who suffered from multiple myeloma, which causes bone marrow tumors. The condition had weakened her immune system to the point that she was no match for the listeria. She died just before Thanksgiving in 1998. Her family received the test results shortly after her death. Through genetic fingerprinting, the tests indicated that she had been infected by the listeria bacterium traced to the same Bil Mar plant in Michigan.

The Pieces Fall into Place

Dr. Paul Mead, epidemiologist for the CDC, had been closely following the cases of listeriosis outbreak throughout the Midwest and Northeastern United States. He and Dr. Eileen Dunne worked to put together the facts and come up with a definitive lead on where the listeria originated. They conducted genetic fingerprinting tests, which looked for a commonality across the listeriosis cases by tracking the unique genetic structure of each infection. Evidence was mounting against the Bil Mar Plant. However, the results were not conclusive, and it would take several days for them to come back.

Dunne decided to investigate further by traveling to the Bil Mar Plant in Borculo, Michigan. By then, a total of 37 cases had been reported across eight states. The commonalities among the cases were striking: all had eaten Sara Lee brand deli meats and hot dogs, and all were infected with the e-strain of Listeria monocytogenes. Dr. Dunne's efforts later uncovered 15 more cases that had not been reported to state health officials, nine of which were of the same origin.

Bil Mar Foods

Dr. Dunne examined the processes and tested extensively for bacteria throughout the Bil Mar Plant. The stress of the rigorous examination began to show on the plant managers, but the doctors needed a few more days to ensure the adequacy of the samples. Dr. Dunne was having a difficult time pinpointing the source of the outbreak. She noted that most of the plant was kept clean and that most infractions were small. When she was told of the removal of the faulty refrigeration unit, she quickly developed a theory. Dr. Dunne followed up by asking whether the plant had conducted advanced testing on the bacteria that they had swabbed immediately after the removal. At first, they said, "No."

A Call For Action

Dr. Michael Osterholm of the Minnesota State Health Department was an expert in epidemiology. He was aware of most outbreaks that occurred in the U.S., and his counsel was often sought by the CDC to help solve intractable problems. Officials at Sara Lee asked him to serve as a consultant in the listeriosis outbreak case.

After weighing the evidence that was presented, he came to the conclusion that the products from the Bil Mar Plant were most likely the main culprits in this case and that Sara Lee should initiate an immediate recall of all the products that came from that plant until the problem was resolved.

The Problem Escalates

Steven McMillan of Sara Lee had taken a long-needed vacation. As President and Chief Operating Officer, he had a reputation as a demanding executive. He had recently announced record sales to shareholders at the company's annual meeting. Before he left, however, an issue began simmering with the Bil Mar Foods processing plant in Michigan. Feeling concerned, McMillan called headquarters from the Caribbean island of St. Thomas to see if the issue had been resolved. He received troubling news of the situation at Bil Mar. Just a day after his vacation had begun, McMillan decided the unresolved issue was too pressing and would require his presence and full attention. He was on the plane out of St. Thomas the next day.

Meanwhile, at Sara Lee headquarters, executives hesitated to act because of the inconclusive evidence. They still had not received the definitive results from the tests conducted at the Bil Mar Plant. They were concerned about the costs involved in such a recall, and they worried about the effect that bad publicity would have on their brands and corporate identity.

Dr. Mead at the CDC was concerned about issuing a recall without the proof to back it up, but he was also worried that if he waited any longer, more lives would be at stake. Mead decided that it would be in the public's best interest for the CDC to issue a recall request. Here is an excerpt of the letter he sent to Sara Lee officers, dated December 21:

> Strong evidence suggests that Ball Park brand hot dogs produced on September 17, 1998, at the Bil Mar plant in Michigan were the vehicle for at least one case of human illness from *Listeria monocytogenes* (LM). The outbreak strain of LM was discovered in the placenta of a woman who had a pre-term delivery, and from an open package of hot dogs from this mother's refrigerator. The mother reports eating these hot dogs on October 5; pre-term delivery occurred on November 7, 1998.[3]

---

[3] CDC letter courtesy of the *Detroit Free Press*

Timeline of Events

July 4, 1998: A failing refrigeration unit is moved out of the Bil Mar Plant.

October 19, 1998: Helen Bodnar dies from listeriosis. First known reported victim.

October 1998: Donna Gibbs of the Tennessee health department documents four cases of listeriosis within a two week period.

October 20, 1998: Donna Gibbs mails her concern to the CDC in Atlanta. She receives no reply to this correspondence.

Mid-November 1998: CDC receives calls from other states:
- 4 cases in Tennessee;
- 35 in Ohio;
- 8 in Connecticut;
- 15 in New York (fingerprints are similar in each case).

December 11, 1998: Forty-one of the victims report eating hot dogs.

December 16, 1998: Inspection of the Bar Mil Plant.

December 19-20, 1998: Steven McMillan flies to St. Thomas and back.

December 21, 1998: Dr. Mead writes a memo requesting a recall.

Sara Lee Finally Acts

In the balance at this time were not only millions of dollars but more importantly, the health and lives of people who consumed their products. The corporate officers at Sara Lee estimated the costs associated with a recall would range from $50 to $80 million.

The senior managers at Sara Lee did not receive any clear message from the various government agencies. They initially decided to wait until definitive proof was available to determine if the Bil Mar plant was responsible for the outbreak. Neither the CEO nor the Chairman felt comfortable with the decision to wait: there were human lives at stake. The decision to launch the biggest recall in Sara Lee's history would concern many of Sara Lee's premier products including: *Ball Park, Bil Mar, Bryan Bunsize and Bryan 3-lb Club Pack hot dogs, Grill master, Hygrade, Mr. Turkey, Sara Lee deli meat, and Sara Lee Home Roast brands.*

Questions

1.   Suppose Steven McMillan asks for your help. What recommendations would you make in responding to this crisis?

2.   Should Sara Lee have waited for confirmation that the listeria bacteria originated at the Bil Mar Plant before acting?

3.   How do you apologize for the loss of human life? What is Sara Lee's responsibility to the families in this crisis?

4.   How could Sara Lee effectively communicate the recall? To whom should the communication be directed?

5.   How can Sara Lee reassure the public that other products are safe?

Sources

Taylor, Jeff. "Not so ready-to-eat food safety no longer taken for granted," *South Bend Tribune*, August 24, 1999. pp. A1, A6.

Taylor, Jeff, Alison Young, and Janet Fix, "Safeguarding meat quality Sara Lee struggles with course of action," *South Bend Tribune*, August 26, 1999. pp. A1, A10, A11.

http://www.freep.com

http://www.saralee.com

Christie's and Sotheby's
The Art World's Price Fixing Scandal

Some cite the old cliche, that Christie's executives are gentlemen trying to be businessmen, while Sotheby's are businessmen trying to be gentlemen. In light of recent events, however, it appears both may have been businessmen all along.[1]

On January 29, 2000, news emerged of a price-fixing scandal embroiling the world's two most venerable auction houses, Christie's International and Sotheby's Holdings Incorporated. The Antitrust Division of the U.S. Department of Justice began an investigation in 1997 of dealers and auction houses to look into allegations of market rigging, but had been unsuccessful in locating incriminating evidence. When Christie's came forward announcing it had uncovered information relevant to the antitrust investigation, however, and would deliver it to the Justice Department in exchange for immunity from prosecution, a scandal ensued.

Collusion in setting sales commissions would constitute an illegal practice in restraint of trade under the Sherman Antitrust Act. Penalties for violations can include substantial fines and imprisonment for as long as three years. Under the Amnesty program, only the first company to come forward with evidence of a crime can be considered for leniency. The program also requires that the company, in this instance Christie's, must give prosecutors evidence they would not have otherwise have uncovered against Sotheby's that would likely result in a "sustainable conviction."[2]

Since this news was unveiled on January 29, 2000, hardly a day passed without an article bearing the name of either Christie's or Sotheby's in the most prominent newspapers in the

---

This case was prepared by Research Assistants Jeremy Griffin, Susan Nemeth, and Joey Flemming under the direction of James S. O'Rourke, Concurrent Associate Professor of Management, as the basis for class discussion rather than to illustrate either effective or ineffective handling of an administrative situation. Information was gathered from corporate as well as public sources.

---

[1] Reputation of the art auction houses takes a hammering. *World News: The Americas*, February 8, 2000.
[2] Sotheby's Acts Quickly to Resolve Inquiry. *The Wall Street Journal*, February 25, 2000.

world. Headlines read, "Christie's admits fixing commissions: Auction house tells the U.S. Justice Department that it made a deal with Sotheby's," "Sotheby's plunges on fears of antitrust inquiry," and "Reputation of the art auction houses takes a hammering." One law firm filed a class action lawsuit against Christie's and Sotheby's on February 2, 2000, on behalf of all persons who sold items through either company during the period March 1995 through present. Numerous civil lawsuits emerged from angry buyers and sellers who contended that the auction houses inflated their fees as a result of illegal price fixing.

The disclosure was highly embarrassing for companies that stake their livelihoods on their image. One art scene veteran stated, "This is absolutely shocking. It's going to reinforce the idea that you can't trust the art world, that they're selling something with no intrinsic value and then pumping up the price of it."

The High-end Art Auction Business

Tracing their roots to the late eighteenth century, the impetus of the high-end art auction houses has always been on maintaining strong reputations in order to attract buyers and sellers of valuable pieces of art for sale. The goods offered at major auction houses vary from Rembrandt and Picasso paintings to antique furniture to the personal effects of deceased celebrities. Sotheby's and Christie's control 97 percent of the high-end art auction market.

The auction house earns a commission from both buyers and sellers by charging a stated percentage of the sales price of each item sold. For instance, prior to recent changes, both Sotheby's and Christie's charged buyers 15 percent of sale price up to $50,000 and 10 percent on sales prices exceeding $50,000. Both charged sellers on a sliding scale with a commission percentage that moved inversely with sale price – that is, more expensive items were charged a lower commission percentage. Prior to the adoption of this price structure, the houses had struggled to remain profitable because both offered deep discounts to sellers.

Sotheby's Holding, Inc.

The founder of Sotheby's, Samuel Baker, held his first sale of "polite literature books" in 1744. By 1998, international auction sales were just under $2 billion. As with Christie's, its notable expertise and superlative customer service have helped create Sotheby's exceptional reputation.

Alfred Taubman acquired Sotheby's in 1983 and began transforming the once insular upper-class institution into a service-obsessed marketing machine (See Exhibit 1). Since his takeover, both sales and profits steadily increased. A large part of the success has been attributed to Chief Executive Diana Brooks, considered the most powerful woman in the art world and virtually indistinguishable from the auction house. She became the face of Sotheby's.

As the inquiry widened, on February 21, 2000, both Taubman and Brooks stepped down from their respective positions. In a letter to shareholders, Diana Brooks wrote "My decision is a very difficult one, but I have taken it in the best interests of the company and of my colleagues." Although at one time they were amiable colleagues, the relationship between Taubman and

Brooks was reported as being somewhat strained. It was rumored that Taubman and Brooks had been advised to communicate only through their lawyers.

At a party toward the end of February, attended by Alfred Taubman, a Fifth Avenue collector made the comment "I'm impressed Al has the courage to show his face. In his position, I'd be home, not answering the phone."[3] By that time, as information continued to emerge on the possible conclusive evidence of price fixing, Sotheby's was either unavailable or declined comment.

Christie's International

In 1766, James Christie opened his London auction house and launched the world's first fine art auctioneers. Continuing as a privately held company, it has grown into an international business with sales held in 15 major cities around the world. Its name came to exemplify a place of extraordinary art and international glamour. Its two most important assets fueled its success: renowned expertise and exemplary customer service.

Christopher Davidge, the Christie's former chief executive, is said to have supplied the incriminating evidence. Davidge departed the firm after 34 years of service in an announcement on Christmas Eve 1999, via a curt internal e-mail sent to the company's 2,200 employees worldwide. The evidence in question was said to be a document that outlines a telephone conversation that took place in the mid-nineties between Sir Anthony Tennant (Christie's chairman from 1993 to 1996) and Alfred Taubman (Sotheby's Chairman), during which the two men debated the commissions charged by the two firms. The question arises as to whether Christie's disclosure to the Justice Department was honorable in light of their findings, or calculated as a brilliant, albeit cutthroat, attempt to destroy its longtime rival, Sotheby's.

Antitrust Laws

Antitrust laws are those designed to preserve the free enterprise of the open marketplace by making illegal certain private conspiracies and combinations formed to minimize competition. These include illegal agreements among competing firms to avoid competitive pricing by charging identical prices or by raising or lowering prices at the same time. Section 45 of the Competition Act prohibits price-fixing and other forms of horizontal agreements among rivals by imposing criminal sanctions on parties to arrangements which "unduly lessen competition." [4] Adjusting rates to match those of a competitor is not by itself a violation of antitrust laws unless the companies collude to fix prices.

Events leading up to price-fixing allegations

During the art market recession of the early 1990s, competition between Sotheby's and Christie's grew fierce and the practice of eliminating the seller's commission in order to win business spiraled into a pattern of increasingly extravagant inducements. Tempted over boardroom banquets and gourmet dinners given by prominent socialites and paid by Christie's

---

[3] Mason, Christopher, "Price-Fixe," *New York Magazine*, March 20, 2000.
[4] "Rethinking Price-Fixing Law," *McGill Law Journal*, 1993.

and Sotheby's to increase business, prospective sellers were enticed with offers of free cataloging, insurance, shipping, or world tours of their collections, all at the auction houses' expense. Income declined sharply as commissions were cut, effectively wiping out profits and putting pressure on the auction houses to improve financial performance.

In early 1992, Sotheby's announced a buyer's premium commission strategy that was adopted by Christie's within six weeks. On March 10, 1995, Christie's announced the introduction of a nonnegotiable sliding scale of seller's commissions, ranging from two to ten percent, based on the value of each consignment. Five weeks later, on April 14, Sotheby's matched Christie's scheme precisely.

Perhaps close competition between Sotheby's and Christie's would result in similar prices as they sell the same specialized goods, cater to the same clientele, and draw on the same small pool of workers. Perhaps, however, it was indeed contrived. In either case, both Christie's and Sotheby's faced a major challenge in regaining confidence from their customers. Although these two auction houses together controlled 97 percent of the world's fine-art auction business, that market share could be somewhat tenuous. In the past, there were few alternatives for persons wishing to buy or sell if the customer wished for a prestigious, reputable establishment. With emerging technology allowing fine art buyers and sellers to complete the same types of transactions through a growing variety of sources and at a lower cost, however, both Christie's and Sotheby's must get through this discrediting situation if they wish to remain viable competition.

Exhibit 1: Principal Actors in the Price-Fixing Scandal.

Sotheby's:

Alfred Taubman	Chairman, resigned February 21, 2000.
Diana (Dede) Brooks	Chief Executive, resigned February 21, 2000.
Michael Sovern	New Chairman.
William Ruprecht	New Chief Executive.

Christie's:

Sir Anthony Tennant	Chairman from 1993 – 1996.
Christopher Davidge	Chief Executive, resigned December 25, 1999.
Francois Pinault	Current Owner and President.

Other:

John Greene	Leading the Department of Justice investigation.
Herbert Black	Major art collector and Christie's customer, first to bring a lawsuit against the companies.

Questions

1.   Identify the audiences Christie's and Sotheby's must reach to properly regain their images.

2.   What are the critical issues in this case?

3.   What should be the approach to addressing illegal actions on the part of these companies?

4.   What are the elements of the messages?

5.   Who should deliver the message? What role does credibility play in this situation?

6.   What channels would be most appropriate to deliver the message?

7.   Would it be important for Christie's and Sotheby's to separate themselves from each other? Or would solidarity be beneficial?

8.   Due to the nature of the business, how can the auction houses regain the confidence of their clientele?

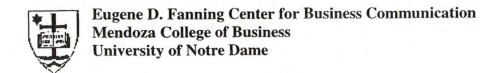

United Airlines
Customer Service in the Summer of 2000

"We'll never fly United again!"
Mary Lin Haddock, Summer 2000 United Passenger [1]

"She's just, like, useless. And I just feel like taking her out back and beating the living hell out of her..." says an angry customer about an airport gate agent.
Unidentified woman, interviewed by *Dateline NBC*

By almost any measure of client satisfaction, 2000 was a disastrous year for the airline industry. While complaints of lost luggage and poor service reached new heights, record amounts of delays and cancellations were the greatest cause of customer dissatisfaction. A whopping 25 percent of all flights were delayed or cancelled in 2000, affecting 119 million passengers.[2] United has received an overwhelming majority of the complaints, and disgruntled customers are demanding answers and action from the world's largest airline.

Flight delays and cancellations during the summer 2000 travel season were particularly harmful to United's image as a well-run and highly regarded airline. The airline behemoth canceled over 100 flights every day during the week of July 21, 2000.[3] Nearly 43 flights were canceled at San Francisco Airport alone on August 7, 2000.[4] In the most recent Airline Quality

---

This case was prepared by Research Assistants J. Gallagher, K. O'Neill, and M. Putney under the direction of James S. O'Rourke, Concurrent Associate Professor of Management, as the basis for class discussion rather than to illustrate either effective or ineffective handling of an administrative situation. Information was gathered from corporate as well as public sources.

---

[1] "Passengers Frustrated With United; 43 flights canceled yesterday at SFO," *The San Francisco Chronicle,* August 8, 2000, Final; Peninsula edition: A15.
[2] www.airlines.org
[3] "United Airlines Canceling More Than 100 Flights Every Day," *World News Now*, ABC News, July 21, 2000.
[4] "Passengers Frustrated With United; 43 flights canceled yesterday at SFO," *The San Francisco Chronicle* August 8, 2000, Final; Peninsula edition: A15.

Rating (AQR) Survey, United ranked last in on-time arrivals with 61.4 percent. United had the second largest decline in overall AQR score, and customer complaints doubled from 1999. Overall, United canceled two percent of all its flights between May and September of 2000. Summer cancellations alone cost the company an estimated $50 million in revenue.[5]

The lost revenue has affected United's balance sheet more negatively than its peers in the airline industry. For example, in fiscal year 2000 United's return on equity was 4.15 percent compared to an industry average of 17.12 percent, and its return on assets was 1.21 percent compared to a 5.99 percent average for its competitors. In addition to its fiscal woes, this period has caused immeasurable damage to United's formerly well respected brand, while alienating many of its loyal and valuable repeat customers. Investors also appear to be steadily losing confidence in United. From mid-summer 2000 until April 2001, United's stock price plummeted from approximately $60 per share to roughly $30 per share as investors eliminated over $1 billion from the firm's market capitalization. (Exhibit 1)

Although almost a year has passed since last summer's fiasco, the customers are still complaining, the government is demanding answers, and the media is finding this topic to be excellent fodder for their ratings. In the summer of 2001, United Airlines celebrates its 75th anniversary in the midst of yet another labor dispute. This time it is not the mechanics or pilots, but rather the flight attendant's union. Larry De Shon, Vice President of Customer Satisfaction at United, now faces the upcoming busy summer travel season. Is United prepared to meet customer expectations or will they fall short again, providing the news media with even more embarrassing material?

The Air Transportation Industry

Commercial airlines began as an aerial mail service. Eventually, the idea of air travel caught on. Due to limited capacity and government regulations that determined where and when planes would fly, only the upper class could afford the comfort and ease of air travel. However, in 1978, the government decided to deregulate the air transportation industry. After the initial shake out, the surviving firms established a hub and spoke system across the country by establishing control over a large number of gates at major airports. The deregulation brought prices down and increased the volume of air travelers in the United States.

To handle all the traffic, air traffic controllers (with slide rules in hand) set up a ground based navigation system that basically divided the air above the United States into 3.5 million square miles. Certain routes were established between airports, similar to the highways on the ground. The air traffic controllers' salaries are paid for by cargo taxes, fuel taxes, and other taxes included on a typical airline ticket.

The Federal Aviation Administration (FAA) is the government branch that monitors the safety of air travel. The aerial highways were designed by the air traffic controllers using radar, which is not as accurate as today's satellite systems. As a result, the FAA requires that planes be separated by at least five miles horizontally and 1,000 feet vertically. Because of the hub system that airlines have established, the majority of flights across the United States end up at one of the

---

[5] Ibid.

28 biggest airports. Therefore, this network of one-lane "skyways" is prone to congestion even under normal conditions. In fact, the 20,000 scheduled flights per day consistently jam this system.[6]

These airports are the arenas where the customers board their planes and enter this aerial highway system. For years, the airports have tried to expand their capacity but have faced strong opposition from the surrounding communities. No one wants to have his or her home at the end of an airport runway. As a result, only three new runways have opened at the 28 largest airports between 1995 and 1999, according to the Transportation Department.[7] This lack of expansion, coupled with a growing customer base, has severely stressed the system. The Load Factor, which is the number of passengers traveling in relation to the amount of potential passengers, reached a historical peak in 2000. Industry sources estimate that 650 million people will fly in 2001, and they expect that number to rise to one billion by 2009.[8]

Many economists insist that the FAA should set a fee-based system for air traffic control services instead of the flat rate on cargo, fuel, and tickets. If airlines were charged for these services on a fee-based system that included higher prices during peak hours, they would have the incentive to reduce congestion. Even if these fees were passed on to customers, demand would become more evenly distributed throughout the schedule, ultimately reducing congestion.

Since 1993, Congress has requested that the FAA assign a cost to each of the services air traffic controllers provide the airlines. However, the FAA still has not responded. In 1996, Congress ordered the FAA to determine the fees. The FAA reports that the study will be completed at the end of 2002. Many also suggest that the FAA be thrown out completely, privatizing the air traffic control services like those in Germany, Canada, and New Zealand.

The sentiment for privatization of the air traffic control services looks even more attractive when people consider the many failed attempts by the FAA to modernize the technology that tracks the aerial highways. The FAA started working on a more efficient air traffic control system in 1981. This was in response to President Reagan firing 11,000 controllers after they went on strike. The new system was supposed to take 10 years and $12 billion dollars to develop. However, the project never replaced the antiquated radar system and was eventually scaled back dramatically, wasting an estimated $2.8 billion. The project continues today with a budget of $40 billion through 2004 and no real end in sight. The only notable change over the years has been the upgrade of monitors to color radar screens and a new mainframe system. A switch to a Global Positioning System was supposed to occur in 1998. It is currently available on a limited basis only and is not expected to be fully operational until 2002. Few believe that it will significantly reduce in the number of delays.

The final major player in the air transportation industry is Mother Nature. Although, weather accounts for approximately 75 percent of all airline delays, airlines continue to schedule flights based on optimal weather conditions. Weather can further reduce the aerial highway

[6] "Gridlock in the Skies," *The New York Times*, September 5, 2000, Tuesday, Late Edition – Final: A1.
[7] Ibid.
[8] Swoboda, Frank. "Airlines Discuss Service Problems," *The Washington Post*, November 16, 2000, Final Edition: E11.

system capacity. A storm can force air traffic controllers to space planes out further or even close the "skyways" off altogether. This adds extremely long delays at the airports to already unrealistic flight schedules.

As detailed above, the air transportation industry has been burdened with problems that reduce air traffic capacity. Nonetheless, airlines continue to schedule flights as if the system could handle customer demands. Because the system is already pushed beyond its limits, any unexpected, or arguably expected, weather problems or labor disputes result in the system crippling air travel across the country.

History of United Airlines

Walter Varney created Varney Air Lines, the predecessor to United, on April 6, 1926 as the nation's first permanently scheduled airmail service. Over time the airmail companies began transporting people, but these services were expensive and reserved for only movie stars and industry leaders. Ironically, a 1946 *Fortune Magazine* article noted, "Few airline executives came near to guessing correctly the depth of the packed-down public demand for air travel."[9] To paraphrase the rock band BTO, "they hadn't seen nothing yet."

When the industry was deregulated, United survived the shakeout and flourished as a member of the new mass-market transportation service. As more and more customers sought airlines for their travel needs, they began to demand service to all corners of the world. United met this demand by setting up the Star Alliance, a partnership of 14 global airlines, which expanded United's service to 815 destinations in more than 130 countries.[10]

In 1994, the UAL board, the parent of United Airlines, approved the Employee Stock Ownership Plan, which created the largest employee-owned corporation in the world. Stephen Wolf, who had gone from union member to CEO of United, had been unable to win the support of the union and was immediately forced out.[11] During the past five years, employee-owned United has achieved record profits, earned an investment-grade credit rating on its debt, and established more efficient routes with the help of the IBM supercomputer known as "Deep Blue."

United Airlines' Problems in 2000

United's problems in 2000 were the result of internal and external forces. Between labor disputes, weather problems, and the general inadequacy of the airline infrastructure, United Airlines struggled to meet even the most basic customer expectations.

United's labor troubles began in April 2000, when pilots refused to work overtime until a new contract was approved. United's maintenance workers contract also expired. As a result,

---

[9] http://www.united.com/site/primary
[10] "Where News and History Meet, " *Hemispheres Magazine,* March 2001: p 13-14.
[11] "Histories of United, Stephen Wolf Intertwined," *Denver Rocky Mountain News*, May 28, 2000, Business; Ed. Final: 1G.

many mechanics refused to work overtime, nearly doubling the number of grounded planes.[12] Both pilots and maintenance workers engaged in work slowdowns during the summer of 2000. Eventually, United reached an agreement that provided the pilots with a 24 percent raise designed to provide pilots with competitive wages.[13] They had taken a wage cut in 1994 in order to take part in the Employee Ownership plan. As a result, United's pilots considered themselves underpaid compared to their counterparts at other airlines, and they demanded a significant raise to restore industry equality.

In May 2000, United Airlines hoped to bolster its presence in the Northeast through a merger with US Airways, whose service was concentrated in the region. Combined, the airlines would have a sizable market share in many cities. The idea of a merger riled some employees. "I am deeply disappointed that the company would enter into a transaction of this magnitude without reaching full agreement with the United pilot group on all issues, " said Cat. Rick Dubinsky, chairman of the UAL Master Executive Council. [14]

By July, the situation had became worse. Statistics tracking United's performance during the summer underscored passengers' frustration. In July 2000, only 41 percent of United's flights arrived on time.[15] Through July 2000, delays were up 14 percent over the first seven months of the previous year on top of a five-year, 58 percent increase in delays. Not surprisingly, complaints to the Department of Transportation were up 60 percent in the first half of the year. [16]

During August 2000, on time arrivals had fallen to 38 percent.[17] On one August day, there was no mention of the labor dispute when explaining the delays and cancellations in United's San Francisco terminal. Instead, they blamed the situation on runway restrictions caused by fog and low clouds.[18] On August 21, 2000, Transportation Secretary Rodney E. Slater summoned airline executives, union leaders, and FAA officials to discuss solutions to the crisis.[19] "We had a very tough summer," said Mark Anderson, United senior director of affairs.[20]

By the end of 2000, performance was beginning to improve. On time arrivals increased to 71.8 percent by October 2000[21] and on time arrival percentage for the twelve-month period ending January 31, 2001 was 61.8 percent.[22] Other measures indicated that while United Airlines had room for improvement, their performance was fair in the beginning of 2001

---

[12] *The San Francisco Chronicle*, August 8, 2000, p 1.

[13] Swoboda, Frank. "Airlines Discuss Service Problems," *The Washington Post,* November 16, 2000, Final Edition: E11.

[14] *Denver Rocky Mountain News,* May 28, 2000, p 4.

[15] Ramstack, Tom. "United Airlines Compliments Enactment of Customer Service Plan," *KRTBN Knight-Ridder Tribune Business News: The Washington Times,* November 16, 2000.

[16] "Commentary: Airport Hell," *Business Week Online*, September 4, 2000.

[17] "Divided at United: A Talk with Two Top Execs," *Business Week Online*, August 25, 2000.

[18] *The San Francisco Chronicle*, August 8, 2000, p 1.

[19] "Commentary: Airport Hell," *Business Week Online*, September 4, 2000.

[20] Ramstack, Tom. "United Airlines Compliments Enactment of Customer Service Plan." *KRTBN Knight-Ridder Tribune Business News: The Washington Times,* November 16, 2000.

[21] Ibid.

[22] U.S. Department of Transportation, "Air Travel Consumer Report," March 2001.

compared to their peers. However, this improvement was too late to help stem the estimated $200 million in lost earnings from the disruptions.[23]

United's Response

Although their performance was improving, one of United's biggest challenges was convincing customers to give them another chance. Customer frustration with the airlines was at an all time high as evident by the increase in customer complaints to the Department of Transportation.

United Airlines instituted a 12-point customer service plan in response to the Department of Transportation inspector general's preliminary report in June 2000, which cited the areas in which airlines needed to improve. Elements of the plan include notifying passengers when flights would be delayed or cancelled, seeking to return lost baggage within 24 hours, and offering the lowest fare to a customer through their reservation system. United Airlines officials report improvements in customer service due in part to their 12-point plan. However, as these improvements come, Congress threatens to intervene unless airline delays, cancellations, and customer complaints are reduced.

In addition to the 12-point customer service plan, United enacted other measures to meet customer needs. They have released mobile chariots; battery powered ticketing machines, that can be transported within an airport to assist in booking flights or speed check-in. United also has new technology for tracking lost baggage, a toll-free telephone line for reporting service problems, improved flight and passenger scheduling software, a flight paging system that informs passengers of flight delays or changes as they occur, and more training for customer service representatives.

Finally, United Airlines has been reaching out to their customers to admit they made mistakes and to begin rebuilding customer trust and loyalty. In early fall 2000, United CEO, James Goodwin, appeared in a television commercial apologizing for the problems customer encountered in the first half of 2000. He promised improvement. Direct mailing targeted United Airline frequent fliers in an attempt to communicate the initiatives that United was implementing to solve the problems passengers experienced. In addition, United terminals have been inundated with brochures covering topics ranging from online features to customer service comment cards. Would this all be enough and was United Airlines prepared to follow-up on these promises?

" A lot of the bad things that happen to airline passengers are not the airlines' fault. A lot of the bad things that happen to airline passengers are the airlines' fault."
Andy Rooney, *60 Minutes* (April 2, 2001)

---

[23] "Divided at United: A Talk with Two Top Execs," *Business Week Online*, August 25, 2000.

Questions

1. What are the most critical issues facing Larry De Shon, Vice President for Customer Satisfaction, and John Kiker, Vice President for Corporate Communication?

2. Which audience groups seem most important in the summer of 2000? What are the most effective means to reach each of them?

3. Should Mr. Kiker devise separate messages for each audience? In other words, should he be saying different things to employees, shareholders, customers, regulators, and others?

4. In a highly competitive industry such as commercial air transportation, how can De Shon and Kiker build any form of enduring customer loyalty? Should all customers receive exactly the same message and same level of attention from the company?

5. In what ways should corporate advertising, internal communication, investor relations, and other communications be integrated and coordinated?

6. Is it a wise idea for Mr. De Shon to roll out all 12 elements of his 12-Point Customer Service Plan at once? Won't a skeptical traveling public expect high levels of performance right away?

7. What's the role of the Chief Executive Officer in all of this? How visible should Mr. Goodwin be during this period?

Exhibit 1 - United Stock Price History

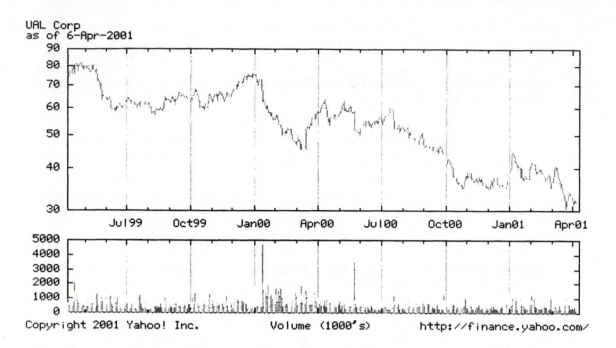

Reproduced with the permission of Yahoo! Inc. © 2000 by Yahoo! Inc. YAHOO! and the YAHOO! logo are trademarks of Yahoo! Inc.

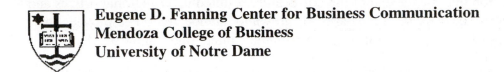
State Farm Insurance Company

One of Peggy Frey's most valued possessions is her 1988 black Ford Mustang 5.0 convertible. When the front of the car was damaged by an errant pickup truck, the Tampa homemaker expected State Farm Mutual Automobile Insurance Company to restore it with genuine Ford parts. Instead, the auto insurer approved generic replacements (non-OEM parts), which hardly fit together. Now, when Ms. Frey slams the hood, the Mustang headlights comically pop out.

In Ms. Frey's opinion, the repair job was so shoddy that she believes the value of her Mustang has dropped by at least $2,000. That may not sound like much money, but as many as 4.7 million other policyholders have the same complaint as Ms. Frey. Their claims led to a lawsuit in which six plaintiffs claimed State Farm misrepresented the quality of generic replacement car parts.

How State Farm Started

State Farm was founded in 1922 by George J. Mecherle (pronounced Ma-herl), a retired farmer who had taken a job selling insurance after his failing health prevented him from farming any longer. He was successful as a salesman, but he did not feel the rates or the business practices of the company suited the needs of farmers. Mecherle believed that farmers should pay less for insurance because they drove less and had fewer losses than folks living in cities.

When he suggested a better way to sell insurance, his employer laughed and said, "If you think you've got such a good idea, why don't you start your own company?" Using this idea, he started State Farm, a mutual automobile insurance company owned by its policyholders.

By 1928, the decision was made to decentralize. Employees from the Bloomington, Illinois office established the company's first branch office in Berkeley, California. This office provided support for agents and brought service closer to the customer. The Berkeley office was the beginning of a tradition that, by the end of the 20th century resulted in 27 regional offices and more than 1,000 claim service centers. State Farm has grown to include 76,500 employees and more than 16,000 agents servicing 66.2 million policies in the United States and Canada.

In just over 75 years, State Farm has grown from a small auto insurer into one of the world's largest financial institutions. Despite its growth, the company's original philosophy of insurance coverage at a fair price coupled with fair claim settlement has remained.

Today, State Farm insures one of every five cars in the United States and is the largest insurer in the country with $24.4 billion in assets. The company is a mutual, which means that it is owned by its policyholders. State Farm does not answer to shareholders. Any dividends are paid out to policyholders. State Farm's reputation and earnings all benefit the policyholders. Because of this structure, drop in share price or angry shareholders are not at issue. The possible effects of the lawsuit are policy cancellations and increased premiums for the policyholders.

The Use of Non-OEM Parts

Non-OEM (Original Equipment Manufacturer) parts are external body parts such as door panels, hoods, fenders and the like, modeled on parts from the automakers and manufactured and sold at lower cost. State Farm has worked to improve quality in the non-OEM industry by contributing to the formation of the Certified Automotive Parts Association (CAPA). CAPA is designed to scrutinize and certify, where its standards are met, non-OEM parts for use in the repair industry. CAPA's goal is to provide quality auto parts and eliminate the monopoly of the auto manufacturers: "For years, the car companies have had a monopoly on the millions of parts used by consumers to repair car accidents each year . . . The consumer is being taken advantage of by car companies who are free to charge whatever they want for a product that continues to drive up the cost of crash repair."

State Farm only uses non-OEM parts which are not integral to the mechanics of the vehicle and which have been certified by CAPA. Many body shop owners say that non-OEM parts fit poorly, look shabby, and do not provide the same safety margins as parts manufactured by Ford, General Motors, or other auto manufacturers. State Farm regularly uses non-OEM parts in repairs of cars that have been involved in collisions.

State Farm learned years ago that many body shops were using non-OEM parts without State Farm's or State Farm policyholders' knowledge. Moreover, some of the shops charged State Farm and its policyholders OEM prices for such repairs. State Farm, along with other insurers, determined that having a viable non-OEM parts industry could benefit consumers by lowering the price of auto repairs.

At least forty other companies have policies requiring use of non-OEM parts, including Allstate, Geico, Nationwide, USAA, Progressive, Metropolitan, and Farmers Group of Insurance Companies. These companies are also involved in lawsuits, but the State Farm case is the only suit that has gone to trial.

In fact, many states recommend and at least one requires auto insurers to use non-OEM parts when possible. Insurers maintain that the policy favoring non-OEM parts benefits the customers by keeping premiums low. State Farm shows that it saved its customers $54.7 million in 1987 and $233.6 million in 1997.

The Lawsuit

Six plaintiffs filed suit against State Farm, accusing the company of breaching its contracts with its policyholders when the company specified the use of non-OEM parts in the repair of vehicles damaged in crashes. The suit was given class action status, and about six million current and former State Farm policyholders joined the suit. These six million policyholders were from 48 states and had been insured between July 1987 and February 1998. All of them had auto insurance claims in which non-OEM parts were installed or specified in estimates for their vehicles during the repair process. Not all of the plaintiffs, however, had actually had a non-OEM part installed on their automobiles. Specifically, the lawsuit charged that:

- State Farm breached its insurance contract by specifying non-OEM parts on estimates for repairs to policyholders' vehicles.

- State Farm knew that non-OEM parts would never return a vehicle to its pre-crash condition and the company's failure to advise policyholders of this knowledge constituted a violation of the Illinois Consumer Fraud Act.

- Non-OEM parts are incapable of returning a vehicle to its pre-loss condition, so State Farm should cease referring to the parts as "quality" parts. Although none of the plaintiffs claimed physical harm, their attorneys argued that the use of non-OEM parts raises a safety issue because they are not crash-tested and because modern vehicles are designed to react in certain ways in collisions. Their claim was that because competitive crash parts are designed through "reverse engineering" (a process that involves measuring and then copying the original parts), they will not perform in the same manner as OEM parts, and that, they say, is a safety problem.

Plaintiffs relied on a number of documents from State Farm and CAPA to argue that State Farm had known for years that non-OEM parts are inferior to OEM parts. The most damaging among these documents were several internal memos found which cite a highly placed State Farm executive stating that non-OEM parts are inferior to OEM parts. State Farm defends itself saying that portions of the memos were taken out of context. The full body of the document reveals that the authors were pointing out problems found with certain non-OEM parts, which needed to be addressed. Company spokesman Edward Domansky says that the memo demonstrated State Farm's concern for its policyholders and dedication to quality.

State Farm's Defense

According to State Farm, use of non-OEM parts by a professional repair shop will return a vehicle to its pre-loss condition. In insurance policies reviewed and approved by state insurance offices, State Farm's policyholders are fully informed of the proposed use of non-OEM parts when they are specified. During the trial, State Farm presented copies of auto repair estimates that fully disclosed the proposed use of non-OEM parts, a copy of a State Farm brochure that spelled out possible use of non-OEM parts, and the State Farm guarantee that stands behind them. State Farm also showed that no state law bans the use of non-OEM parts and in fact, some encourage or even require their use. In a survey of 1,400 claims with estimates specifying non-OEM parts, only 0.59 percent of State Farm policyholders complained about repairs made using those parts.

Like a Good Neighbor

State Farm's mission statement says, "We are people who make it our business to be like a good neighbor; who built a premier company by selling and keeping promises . . ." From the time of filing in February, 1998 the media across the country reported regularly on new developments in the case. With the trial date not set until February 1999, State Farm had to figure out how to retain its good neighbor image.

Questions

1.   What is at stake for State Farm?

2.   How can they retain the "good neighbor" image amidst the legal battles?

3.   What are the possible effects the lawsuit will have on retaining and attracting clients?

4.   What are the critical issues surrounding the alleged use of non-OEM parts and how should State Farm respond to those allegations?

5.   What is the strategy for responding to the public's awareness of the lawsuit and the issues surrounding it?

Sources

The Associated Press, "Damage Award in State Farm Case Grows to Nearly $1.2 Billion," *The St. Louis Post-Dispatch*, October 9, 1999.

The Associated Press, "State Farm Auto Parts Goes to Jury," *St. Louis Post-Dispatch*, September 30, 1999.

Certified Auto Parts Association website: http://www.capacertified.org

Conrad, Dennis, "Insurance Company in Battle to Retain Good Image," *Associated Press Newswires*, October 10, 1999.

Felsenthal, Edward, "Supreme Court Declines to Review Class-Action Suit Against Insurer," *The Wall Street Journal*, October 6, 1998.

France, Mike and Andrew Osterland, "State Farm: What's Happening to the Good Neighbor? Judges and Juries have found the insurer guilty of serious misconduct," *Business Week*, November 8, 1999.

Gallagher, Jim, "State Farm Stops the Use of Aftermarket Parts Action Comes as a Result of Suit; Judgement is Being Appealed," *St. Louis Post-Dispatch*, October 8, 1999.

Lohse, Deborah, "Policyholders at State Farm Win Parts Case," *The Wall Street Journal*, October 5, 1999.

Pearson, Michael, "$456 mil. Verdict vs. State Farm," *Chicago Sun-Times*, October 4, 1999.

Pearson, Michael, "At least seven other insurers being sued over imitation repair parts," *Associated Press Newswires*, August 24, 1999.

Pearson, Michael, "Documents prove State Farm knew parts were inferior, consultant says," *Associate Press Newswires*, August 17, 1999.

Pearson, Michael, "Trial set in State Farm inferior repair parts case," *Associated Press Newswires*, August 9, 1999.

PR Newswire, "Trial Date Set in Nationwide Class Action Against State Farm," February 27, 1998.

State Farm corporate website: http://www.statefarm.com

PART VI

Financial Services

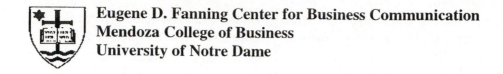
Long Term Capital Management

Nestled in posh Greenwich, Connecticut, a collection of powerful Wall Street bankers, two Nobel Laureates, and dozens of PhDs operated a hedge fund that was cloaked in secrecy. Even the fund's ultra-rich investors knew nothing more than their monthly return. And why should they care? The returns had been staggering since its inception in 1994, with a pinnacle of 42.8% in 1995. Those who secretly feared this success was too good to be true began to see signs that they might be right in June 1998, when the value of the $3 billion dollar fund fell 10.1%.

Despite the heavy losses, Long Term Capital continued its information blackout with investors, a tacit agreement upon investing. The fund's continued hemorrhaging through August sent shock waves all the way to Wall Street and Washington, D.C., because of its potential to trigger a catastrophic collapse that would rock the foundations of global financial markets.

The seriousness of this emergency would soon be defined by its confluence of interests. In addition to the fund's investors and marquee partners, the cast of characters that would become rapidly involved in this financial drama would be fitting of a novel found in an airport bookstore: Warren Buffet, Alan Greenspan, Robert Rubin, members of Congress, and the heads of 13 major Investment and Commercial banks on Wall Street.

Hedge Funds

Long Term Capital (LTC), like all hedge funds, had tremendous flexibility to operate autonomously due to virtually no SEC regulation. This luxury allowed LTC to operate secretly and eventually take on absurd amounts of financial risk through leveraging. Typically, hedge funds are contracted with investors for a one percent management fee and a performance bonus, commonly a 25 percent share of profits. LTC, however, commanded a two percent management fee based upon its high-priced talent.

This case was prepared by Research Assistants F.J. Fee and Michael C. Meyer under the direction of James S. O'Rourke, Concurrent Associate Professor of Management, as the basis for class discussion rather than to illustrate either effective or ineffective handling of an administrative situation. Information was gathered from corporate as well as public sources.

LTC specialized in bond arbitrage, a trading strategy that uses mathematical formulas to capitalize on small price discrepancies among securities, in order to exploit mispricing of certain types of bonds. In particular, LTC racked up huge gains in the mortgage-backed securities markets. The line separating arbitrage from being considered either a science or high-stakes betting is thin and gray.

Long Term Capital's Pitch

LTC's intellectual capital and trading operation, the sophistication of which rivaled the major investment banks, presented a compelling reason for ultra-rich investors to take a stake in the fund. The investment track record during the 1980s of LTC's leader, John Meriwether, along with his successful Wall Street partners in the firm, spoke for itself within the U.S. For international investors who were unfamiliar with Meriwether's reputation, Nobel Laureates Myron S. Scholes and Robert C. Merton, Harvard Business School professor William Krasker and former Federal Reserve Vice Chairman David Mullins provided the reputation and capital to many investors. The argument was deceptively simple: success is virtually guaranteed given the firm's extraordinary talent. The 40 percent returns then sealed the deal.

The Eye of the Storm

John Meriwether was one of Wall Street's brightest stars during the 1980s. He pioneered arbitrage trading at Salomon Brothers by launching one of Wall Street's first bond arbitrage groups. The performance of his group, often contributing two-thirds of the firm's profits, propelled him to Vice-Chairman. Meriwether's departure from the Wall Street scene was as explosive as his rise to prominence when he was forced to resign in the wake of a 1991 trading scandal.

Recently, Meriwether's former group, which is now a part of Traveler Group's Salomon Smith Barney Inc., was disbanded in order to lower the firm's risk profile.

The Crisis

LTC's problem was as simple as its appeal: they guessed wrong. Tremendous losses due to the downturn in the mortgage-backed securities market were amplified by the tremendous leverage exercised by LTC. Specifically, LTC used derivative instruments such as swap agreements to hedge investments and take their bets. Derivatives derive their value from underlying securities or other assets, and can be a low cost way to make leveraged bets. Some speculated that LTC had more than US$1 trillion at risk. LTC was in a precarious position because of the difficulties associated with unwinding thousands of bond, stock, and currency arrangements that add stress to the financial system in a crisis situation.

August 1998 brought disaster to financial markets, both in the U.S. and abroad because of Russia's loan defaults and currency devaluation, as well as the tenuous global economic condition resulting from the slumps in Asia and Latin America. LTC's random unwinding of bets in response to this global financial crisis began to create havoc for dealers. Clearing partners became increasingly nervous about LTC's ability to meet its obligations, pressure that intensified the stress on the firm. Considering the problems that a struggling LTC was having on financial markets, a failed LTC would be a devastating blow.

Bailout

The Federal Reserve Bank was created in 1913 to help the U.S. Government maintain financial stability. The primary job of the Fed's trading operation is to follow the Chairman's desired market interest rate by buying and selling government securities. Similarly, if the Treasury Secretary wishes to prop up the value of a foreign currency, the Fed will intervene in the market by buying and selling dollars to achieve the desired rate. In August of 1998, because financial markets were experiencing shocks due to Russia's debt default and currency devaluation, investors were beginning to shun risky investments, even in the U.S. This fundamental shift in global risk tolerance acted to destabilize financial markets. The Fed monitored rumors about firms in trouble, and LTC's name became increasingly frequent throughout August.

Peter Fisher, the second-ranking official at the New York Federal Reserve Bank, was stunned by the acute trouble that the secretive and unregulated hedge fund was in when he was called to an emergency review of LTC's books on the evening of Sunday, September 20. Upon review, Fisher realized that much of the bond market turmoil was greatly exacerbated by LTC's dumping investments in order to raise cash – a situation that underscored how harmful the firm's collapse could potentially be for the markets. This crisis led Fisher and New York Fed President, William McDonough, to undertake an emergency rescue plan for LTC. After consulting with Fed Chairman, Alan Greenspan, and Treasury Secretary, Robert Rubin, they summoned the biggest names on Wall Street to the imposing headquarters of the New York Federal Reserve Bank in order to orchestrate a bailout.

The Consortium

Greenspan, Rubin, McDonough, and Fisher all agreed that a collapse of LTC would be chaotic for the markets and, therefore, a collective industry bailout was in the "public interest." McDonough made sure that the heads of the Banks understood the government's interest in seeing their actions align with that "public interest." The consortium included members such as Goldman, Sachs & Co.; Merrill Lynch & Co.; Morgan Stanley Dean Witter & Co.; J.P. Morgan & Co.; and Chase Manhattan Corp. The bailout gave the consortium's 13 Wall Street Investment Banks and Commercial Banks a 90 percent stake in the fund for a $3.65 billion investment, leaving the LTC partnership with only a 10 percent stake valued at $405 million. Within the consortium, resentment for Goldman, the only private Investment Bank in the bailout group, simmered due to Goldman's attempt to play several options.

A Competing Offer

Billionaire investor Warren Buffet, American International Group, and Goldman Sachs offered to buy LTC for $250 million with the requirement of Meriwether's ouster. The buyout group, led by Buffet's $3 billion, would put up a total of $3.75 billion for full ownership. The fund's original investors would have received only five percent of the approximately $4.6 billion their stakes were worth at the beginning of the year from this deal. Not coincidentally, Buffet had disclosed in a special shareholder meeting earlier in the month that Berkshire Hathaway, of Omaha, Nebraska, was sitting on $9 billion in cash and despite its tradition of a buy and hold value investing strategy, was prepared to capitalize on certain risky "alternative" investment opportunities. Buffet would be the financial "brawn" while Goldman, Sachs & Co. would act as the "brains" by managing the portfolio in addition to making a $300 million contribution.

Ironically, Warren Buffet was familiar with Meriwether's abilities and trading strategies from the late 1980s, when Buffet took over as chairman of Solomon Brothers after the Treasury-bond-rigging scandal of 1991 that lead to Meriwether's resignation. Certainly a power play existed for Meriwether to maintain control of LTC, and his own reputation, rather than have a repeat of his 1991 disgrace. The Fed's orchestrated bailout gave Meriwether the necessary leverage to accomplish this. Meriwether rejected Buffet's offer by objecting to the low price and by claiming difficulty in obtaining approval from the fund's investors on such short notice.

In addition to Buffet, a Saudi Arabian prince, one of the world's richest investors with a net worth over $10 billion, was also approached by Goldman Sachs with an offer of considerable upside potential.

Criticism

Critics complained that pulling the Wall Street Consortium together to form a bailout gave Meriwether the option to rebuff Warren Buffet's bid. Buffet's bid would not only have wiped out Meriwether and his partners' ownership, it would also be more consistent with free market theory to allow markets, not the government, to guide outcomes. Critics included the investing public, politicians, and even members of the consortium who claimed in hindsight that they would have put more pressure on Meriwether to accept Buffet's bid, had they known about it. Meriwether, accustomed to operating under intense pressure throughout his career, capitalized on the confusion created by the urgency of the crisis. He operated with a distinct informational advantage, a competitive edge that allowed him to protect his reputation and prevent his ouster.

Feeding Frenzy

In early October, the Federal Reserve Chairman testified for four and a half hours to Congress regarding the Fed's role in brokering the LTC bailout. In his testimony, Greenspan suggested that the hedge fund's collapse could have "triggered the seizing up of markets. . . and could have potentially impaired the economies of many nations, including our own." Unfortunately for LTC, Greenspan received little support from either side of Congress. Representative Mike Castle (R., Del.) stated, "I have a problem that we're sort of letting this go on. I don't want to just have this hearing and then all of a sudden have other problems." The Congressional panel's chairman, Iowa Republican Jim Leach, even suggested that the consortium that took over Long Term Capital had violated antitrust laws. In his concluding remarks, Greenspan said that more regulation of the hedge fund industry would not work, and would probably result in the hedge funds moving their operations overseas. He further stated that, "Today's relatively unfettered financial system brings benefits, and we do not have the choice of accepting the benefits without accepting the costs." Shunning economic theory, some politicians' objections were based on the sincere belief that ultra-rich investors should not be protected at the expense of "common investors." Less principled politicians, however, attempted to enhance their political reputation by using this high profile situation to grandstand for the "benefit of the people."

Decisions

The Director of Investor Relations for Merrill Lynch & Co. prepared for an emergency staff meeting to address the concerns of his Relationship Managers who were being besieged by irate shareholders. Shareholders were demanding an immediate explanation of why ultra-rich speculators in a private hedge fund were bailed out at their expense. Often at their best when forced to perform on the brink of disaster, Merrill's IR Chief began to craft a persuasive communications strategy for his managers.

Meanwhile, several thoughts raced through John Meriwether's head as he glanced over Greenwich Avenue during a fleeting moment between emergency calls. "How can I regain control of this battered fund?" "How can I protect my reputation?" "Where did I go wrong?"

Timeline

August 17, 1998: Russia devalues the ruble and declares debt moratorium.

September 2, 1998: Long Term Capital tells investors they've lost 52% between January and August, seeks capital injection. Partners at LTC call New York Federal Reserve Bank President McDonough "to notify him of difficulties."

September 18, 1998: McDonough calls senior Wall Street officials; LTC asks to brief Federal Reserve Officials on plans to raise capital.

September 20, 1998: New York Federal Reserve Bank Officials and the U.S. Treasury team meet LTC partners in Greenwich early morning.

September 22, 1998:
Early morning, N.Y. Fed's Fisher meets with Goldman Sachs, Merrill Lynch, J.P. Morgan. Late afternoon, Goldman, Merrill, Morgan, and UBS meet with Federal Reserve officials. At 8:30 p.m., 13 Wall Street firms meet with New York Federal Reserve on broader-based rescue.

September 23, 1998:

McDonough after returning at midnight from London, convenes creditor meeting at 9:30 a.m.

McDonough delays planned meeting with Wall Street firms to see if investor group will buy LTC portfolio.

At 12:30 p.m., McDonough learns offer has fallen through.

At 1:00 p.m., banks, securities firms meet for five hours to discuss rescue plan: 14 agree to kick in $3.5 billion.

Source: WALL STREET JOURNAL. EASTERN EDITION [STAFF PRODUCED COPY ONLY]. Copyright 1998 by DOW JONES & CO INC. Reproduced with permission of DOW JONES & CO INC in the format of Textbook via Copyright Clearance Center.

Questions

1.   How would an effective communication strategy have helped LTC through the crisis? Why is communication crucial in this situation?

2.   What factors, other than communication, did LTC need to consider in this crisis?

3.   How could LTC communicate their position on the issues with their investors? What obstacles stand in the way of being truthful and direct in this scenario?

4.   Do you agree with John Merriwether's actions? Explain what you would have done differently.

5.   Suppose you are Merrill Lynch's IR Director. Describe what you would have your managers explain to the shareholders about the situation.

Sources

Lewis, Michael, *Liar's Poker*, Penguin Group Publishing, New York, New York, 1989.

Lewis, Michael, "How the Eggheads Cracked," *New York Times Magazine*, January 24, 1999.

Morris, Kenneth M. and Alan M. Siegel, *The Wall Street Journal Guide to Understanding Money & Investing*, Simon & Schuster, New York, New York, 1993.

Lipin, Steven, "Long-Term Capital Pressured by Underlying Bets," *The Wall Street Journal*, Dow Jones & Company, Inc., September 28, 1998.

Pacelle, Mitchell and Zuckerman, Gregory, "Long Term Capital Has Its First Loss Last Month," *The Wall Street Journal*, Dow Jones & Company, Inc., July 20, 1998.

Raghavan, Anita and Mitchell Pacelle, "Key Figures Set to Leave Hedge Fund,"
    The Wall Street Journal, Dow Jones & Company, Inc., February 3, 1999.

Schlesinger, Jacob M., "Long-Term Capital Bailout," *The Wall Street Journal,*
    Dow Jones & Company, Inc., November 2, 1999.

Schlesinger, Jacob M. and Michael Schroeder, "Greenspan Defends Long-Term
    Capital Plan," *The Wall Street Journal* , Dow Jones & Company, Inc., October 2, p. 1.

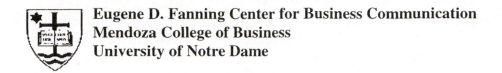
Quality Dining and Bruegger's Bagels

When David Findlay, the CFO of Quality Dining, placed the phone in its cradle, he felt as though someone had kicked him in the stomach. He had just finished telling an inquisitive MBA student that talking about Bruegger's Bagels was like discussing the death of a close friend.

The difficulty began in February 1996 when Quality Dining, a Mishawaka, Indiana, company that operates 145 fast-food and casual dining restaurants in twenty states, decided to buy Bruegger's Bagels for $142 million in stock. At the time, the acquisition was viewed as an important and favorable development because the bagel industry was growing very fast.

According to the National Restaurant Association, U.S. bagel consumption had risen 169% between 1984-1996. Daniel Fitzpatrick, CEO of Quality Dining, wanted to capitalize on the expanding market by purchasing Bruegger's Bagels, the largest operator of bagel-based restaurants in the United States.

Investors lauded the move and pushed Quality Dining's stock to a 52-week high of $39.50 when news of the impending purchase was made public.

Daniel Fitzpatrick and the History of Quality Dining

Daniel Fitzpatrick's first exposure to the restaurant business began in 1970 in Toledo, Ohio, at the age of fourteen. It was then that he realized what hard work entailed. His father, Timothy Fitzpatrick, had just suffered a stroke that left him unable to work or support his family. Consequently, Dan's mother had to raise six children on her own. During that difficult time, she told Dan that the family had three options, ". . . starve, steal, or go to work."

This case was prepared by Research Assistants Ted Mager, Vincent Pedone, and James O'Connor under the direction of James S. O'Rourke, Concurrent Associate Professor of Management, as the basis for class discussion rather than to illustrate either effective or ineffective handling of an administrative situation. Information was gathered from corporate as well as public sources.

Young Dan lied about his age to secure a job as a bus boy in a local Italian restaurant where his brothers worked. Several years later, as a high school student, Fitzpatrick worked for his brother at a Burger Chef restaurant. After graduating from high school early, he decided to stay home and attend the University of Toledo, where he eventually earned a business administration degree in three years. To support himself while in school, he continued to work in the burger business, not at Burger Chef, but at an up-and-coming rival, Burger King.

In 1977, Burger King decided to transfer Dan to Kalamazoo, to assume responsibility as the Director of Operations for several restaurants in southwestern Michigan. Shortly after the move, he and his brother, John Fitzpatrick, formed Burger Services Inc. and decided to buy two floundering Burger King restaurants in suburban Detroit.

After turning around the struggling restaurants in the Detroit area, Fitzpatrick looked for other acquisition opportunities. In 1981, he found the opportunity he was looking for when three Burger King restaurants in Mishawaka, Indiana, became available. The next year, Fitzpatrick left his brother in Detroit and relocated to Mishawaka to take over the day-to-day operations of the three Burger King restaurants.

In 1982, Daniel and his brother established the strategic direction of the company. "We wanted to become a major player in the restaurant business." This is exactly what they did. From 1983 to 1991, the company opened a Burger King every 85 days. In 1994, the company went public and changed its name from Burger Services to Quality Dining.

During 1994 and 1995 Quality Dining continued to expand. During that period, they acquired 19 *Chili's Grill and Bars*, 5 *Spageddies Italian Kitchens*, and 42 *Grady's American Grills*. This brought a Quality Dining presence to 20 states with $106 million in sales in 1995, a 64% increase from 1994. Such positive results did not go without notice. In early 1996, a leading financial analyst for Merrill Lynch listed Quality Dining among three "great young growth companies."

On February 22, 1996, Quality Dining announced a proposed merger with Bruegger's Bagels Corporation of Burlington, Vermont. Critics questioned the acquisition and wondered if Quality Dining had ". . . put too much on its plate." These concerns were two-fold. First, analysts felt that Quality Dining might be expanding too quickly. Secondly, some industry observers noted that Quality Dining was entering a business realm with which they were unfamiliar. Historically, the company ran restaurants as a franchisee. With the acquisition of Bruegger's, Quality Dining would take on the role of franchiser. Fitzpatrick commented on this concern, saying "We are going to stub our toe, but we've got 10,000 people working in this company and more coming in the advent of the merger. We've got a plan, and we're going to execute the heck out of it."

The History of Bruegger's Bagels

In 1983, Nordahl Brue and Michael Dressell founded the franchise bagel concept when they opened Bruegger's Bagels. Up until that point, bagels were considered mostly an ethnic food and were uncommon outside of New York. At that time, fewer then one-third of Americans had ever tasted a bagel.

Brue and Dressell pioneered a new concept by expanding the product line of traditional bagel bakeries to include specialty cream cheeses, custom-made sandwiches, soups and premium coffee.

Before launching their venture, however, Brue and Dressell set out to find the perfect bagel recipe. They worked with a professional bagel baker from New York City for two-and-a-half years to perfect their recipe and baking process. Their pursuit of the perfect bagel was overwhelmingly successful. Bruegger's expanded rapidly and, by 1996, operated 275 restaurants.

The Bagel Business

According to estimates from restaurant analysts, bagel sales reached $3 billion in the U.S. in 1996. However, many bagel stores where still independently owned and operated. Manhattan Bagel Company and Einstein/Noah Bagels (a subsidiary of Boston Chicken) were the only two with significant market presence. Therefore, the minor penetration of the national bagel concept created an opportunity for high growth.

In response to the tremendous growth expected from the acquisition of Bruegger's, Fitzpatrick said, "I would like to think we'll be in every market in the country in the not so distant future, in another couple of years. We think Bruegger's will become to the bagel business what Starbuck's has become to coffee. This will be a huge, huge business."

The Bruegger's Purchase

In the period leading up to the acquisition of Bruegger's, Quality Dining enjoyed healthy growth and a solid corporate reputation. In fact, *Forbes* recently ranked Quality Dining the 6th best small company in America based on its financial results. The stock price reflected this image, and eventually hit an all-time high of $39.50 shortly after the merger occurred.

Following the merger, it became evident that the synergies assumed to exist between the two companies were non-existent. By attempting to expand Bruegger's too rapidly, Quality Dining's profits vanished quickly, and the stock price plummeted to $1.94 a share on January 25, 1999.

Quality Dining executives have traced the Bruegger's failure back to other factors as well, starting with an inability to respond to customer demands. Fat-free cream cheese, stronger coffee, and bagel chips were industry innovations provided by the competition that Bruegger's was late to offer. Furthermore, clashes between Quality Dining's management and Bruegger's management contributed to the failed acquisition. After seeing their stock lose more than sixty percent of its value, Bruegger's founders, Nordahl Brue and Michael Dressler, lost their patience. "Management has proved itself incapable of managing and growing these various businesses in a successful manner. In general, the company lacks strategic direction," Dressler and Brue said in filings with the U.S. Securities and Exchange Commission. The two, who own 25 percent of Quality Dining stock, pushed for a sale of various business units, with the intent of getting their bagel shops back.

In March 1997, Brue and Dressel planned to pursue an auction of Quality's various restaurant components including Bruegger's, Burger King, Grady's American Grill, Chili's and other owned and franchised restaurant operations. Fitzpatrick responded to Brue and Dressel's plans by stating, "Quality Dining is not for sale, and there will not be an auction of the company. Brue and Dressel are on Quality's board to participate in constructively managing the company's affairs. The company expects that they will do so."

In response to the proposed takeover, Quality Dining's Board of Directors approved a "poison pill" plan. The company stated publicly that "the plan is designed to ensure that the company's shareholders receive fair treatment in the event of an unsolicited attempt to acquire the company."

Unfortunately, the steep decline in the stock price convinced the board that divestiture of the Bruegger's division was the only prudent step left to them. Fitzpatrick said, "We have worked hard to create value for shareholders through the strategic expansion of the Bruegger's brand; however, the value of the Bruegger's brand to Quality Dining has deteriorated since our decision to purchase the company." In the Spring of 1997, the company announced a $203 million charge to earnings including $185 million for the reduction of Bruegger's as an asset and $18 million for store closings and severance payments.

The damage did not end there. On May 14, 1998, the firm of Milberg Weiss Bershard Hayes and Lerach filed a class action lawsuit on behalf of all persons who bought Quality Dining stock between June 7, 1996 and May 13, 1997. The suit, which did not specify an exact dollar figure, claimed that Quality Dining presented false and misleading comments regarding stock price as a result of the Bruegger's acquisition, thus greatly exaggerating the price.

Negative media coverage compounded Quality Dining's problems. *The Wall Street Journal* described the purchase as, "one of the most immediately disastrous acquisitions in American business." Additional disparaging stories ran in respected publications, including *The New York Times, Forbes,* and *Business Week*, for several weeks.

Quality Dining had no choice but to sell back Bruegger's to its founders for one-third of what they initially paid and took a $185 million charge over the failed deal.

Exhibit

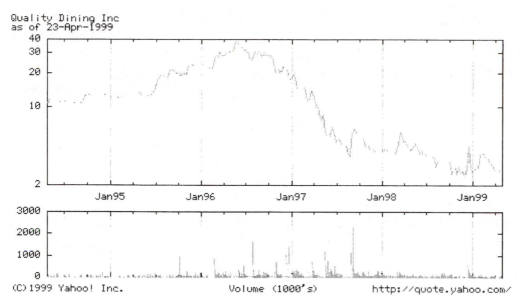

Quality Dining Inc
as of 23-Apr-1999

(C) 1999 Yahoo! Inc.   Volume (1000's)   http://quote.yahoo.com/

Reproduced with the permission of Yahoo! Inc. © 2000 by Yahoo! Inc. YAHOO! and the YAHOO! logo are trademarks of Yahoo! Inc.

Questions

1. How can Quality Dining salvage their reputation?

2. Can you suggest a list of priorities that Dan Fitzpatrick will need to address?

3. Who should handle the communication with the public? With stakeholders? With the media?

4. Would an outside consulting firm be useful in this situation? How?

5. Can Quality Dining ever hope to be a successful franchiser in the future? If so, what steps will need to be taken to avoid making the same mistakes?

6. How can Quality Dining regain the confidence of investors after the stock lost 95% of its value?

7. How should the company handle the negative press?

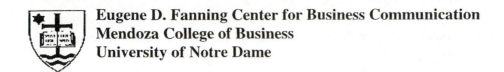
Bank of New York:
A Money Laundering Scandal

Scandal at One Wall Street

A troubled Thomas A. Renyi, Chief Executive Officer of the Bank of New York (BNY) selected his words carefully as he penned his communication to all bank employees. He stated, "We will do what ever is needed to prevent illegal or improper activities that involve the bank. Period." This just days after employees had to relive the embarrassment of recent events when the August 21, 1999, edition of *The New York Times* ran the headline, "Feds Raid Bank of New York in Money Laundering Probe."

On the morning of Friday, August 20, 1999, the hallowed halls of the Wall Street office of the Bank of New York were forever changed as Federal investigators halted business activity to conduct a search and seizure of bank files. A key BNY employee had been indicted on "illegal money transfer" charges and the federal investigators were making their move against her and, potentially, the bank itself. According to investigators, the bank could be involved in the biggest money laundering case ever. What events could have transpired to place New York's oldest, and one of the world's most respected, financial institutions in such a compromising position? And, could the bank's 200-year history withstand an assault on its reputation?

History of the Bank of New York

In 1784, the prominent citizens of New York retained the services of local attorney Alexander Hamilton to write the constitution for the newly formed Bank of New York. The bank has the distinction of being the first in New York and one of the oldest banks in the world. Many historical milestones are credited to the institution including making the first loan to the Federal Government and being the first corporate stock to be traded on the New York Stock Exchange. The bank also helped establish much of the American infrastructure by investing in such projects as the construction of the Erie Canal, the New York subway, and nearly every U.S. railroad and utility throughout the 1800s.

This case was prepared by Research Assistants Marcus Fields and Michael Swain under the direction of James S. O'Rourke, Concurrent Associate Professor of Management, as the basis for class discussion rather than to illustrate either effective or ineffective handling of an administrative situation. Information was gathered from corporate as well as public sources.

The Bank of New York grew during the middle of the Twentieth Century by merging with such noteworthy institutions as The New York Life Insurance & Trust, The Fifth Avenue Bank, and the Empire Trust Company. The bank began its global expansion in 1966 by opening a branch office in London, England. Today BNY has branch offices in key locations around the world including Brussels, Paris, Hong Kong, Tokyo, Cairo, Istanbul, and Moscow.

On January 13, 1998, Thomas A. Renyi was named CEO of the $61 billion institution. J. Carter Bacot, the outgoing CEO said that, "Tom Renyi's proven abilities, his depth of experience and knowledge of our businesses, combined with his strong leadership skills make him the right person to ensure the future success of our Company."[1] Under the stewardship of Mr. Renyi, the bank now boasts $5.7 billion in annual revenue, $1.2 billion in annual profit, and market capitalization of $30.3 billion. The bank is recognized as a leader in the banking industry, and a historical marker in the U.S. economy. The prospect of being accused of money laundering threatens to weaken one of the most revered financial institutions in the world.

Taken to the Cleaners

Money laundering is the process by which criminals conceal the origin of their income by moving it through a network of bank accounts and dummy corporations and blending it in with normal commerce. The term "money laundering" is said to originate from Mafia ownership of legitimate laundromats in the United States to disguise money earned from extortion, prostitution, gambling, and bootleg liquor. The laundering process consists of three distinct phases where the launderer places, layers, then integrates illegal funds to conceal their true origins.

Placement. Money generated from illegal transactions, usually in the form of cash. Criminals try to wash the illegal origins away by placing the cash with financial institutions or the retail economy. The aim is to avoid detection by gaining distance from the source, and providing the opportunity to transfer into other assets such as travelers cheques or money orders.

Layering. Layering provides greater distance between the cash and its source by creating a complex web of financial transactions aimed at concealing any audit trail. Typically this web is created by moving money in and out of offshore bank accounts held by shell companies via wire transfer, or by completing complex stock, commodity, and futures transactions. Given that millions of electronic transactions and billions of dollars are transferred daily, these vehicles greatly reduce the chance of detection because of high volume and the ability to conduct them with near anonymity.

Integration. The final stage of the process is when the illegal cash is cleansed and returned to the launderer's mainstream economy as legal wealth. Some launderers use shell companies in countries with guaranteed secrecy rights to make anonymous loans to themselves. Some countries, such as Russia, allow banks to be established quickly and cheaply. In this case

---

[1] Leyden, Paul J. "Thomas A. Renyi Named Chairman of the Bank of New York Co., Inc.," BNY *Press Release,* January 13, 1998.

launderers can simply transfer money from their bank to a legitimate bank to withdraw their cleansed money.

Case Background

The Bank of New York is caught in the middle of what could be a major communications crisis with global implications. The allegations surrounding the Bank of New York were brought forth in mid-August and involve four major players:

The Bank of New York (BNY)

The Bank of New York is presently being investigated for the suspicious movement of seven to ten billion dollars in what U.S. Federal law enforcement agencies say is money from Russia's organized crime organizations. The bank issued a statement saying, "The Bank of New York has been cooperating with the office of the United States Attorney for the Southern District of New York in a confidential investigation of the use of the bank's facilities to transfer funds from Russia to other countries."[2] They added, "There are no allegations of wrongdoing by the bank . . . and that no customer or bank funds had been lost."[3] BNY would not comment any further than what has been officially released to the media. Public relations representative Cary J. Giacalone commented, "There are no written statements that we (BNY) can provide at this time" and as of November 9, 1999, "The Bank cannot make any other comments at this time as the investigation is still ongoing."[4]

United States Federal Government

American and European officials have been investigating the infiltration of Russian organized crime syndicates into the financial markets of Europe and the United States for some time. Since the collapse of the Russian financial system, the exchange of money outside of the country had accelerated in a suspicious manner. With the assistance of British authorities, the Federal Bureau of Investigation was alerted of alleged money laundering activities involving BNY. For more than a year, investigators indicate that BNY had financial dealings with Mr. Semyon Yukovich Mogilevich, a major figure in Russian organized crime. The Central Intelligence Agency and European intelligence had been monitoring Mr. Mogilevich's activities ever since he placed a contract on the life of *New York Times* foreign affairs columnist Thomas L. Friedman in 1995. Suspected money laundering operations tied to companies controlled by Mr. Mogilevich were uncovered last summer as a product of these investigations.

BNY was linked to Mr. Mogilevich through a company called Benex International that had financial dealings with BNY's Eastern European operations. Benex International opened its account with BNY last year and money transfers began occurring at an alarming rate. Banks are required to file "suspicious activity reports" whenever unusual activity occurs in an account. The United States Treasury, along with other banking regulators, was responsible for monitoring this report. The bank filed only one report and only after Federal authorities began their money

---

[2] Bonner, Raymond. "Activities at Bank Raises Suspicions of Russia Mob Tie," *The New York Times,* August 19, 1999, pp. A1, A6.

[3] Ibid.

[4] Personal communication with Michael D. Swain, November 9, 1999.

laundering investigation. The Federal government did take action and froze the Benex International account, which contained $34 million, but quickly released it in hopes of determining where the money was originating and terminating.

Federal subpoenas issued to BNY produced 3,500 pages of transactions involving Benex International. Federal investigators are refusing to comment any further on Benex, reveal what information they have, or talk about its location or its activities. Additionally, the Federal Reserve Bank of New York and the New York State Banking Department have declined to comment on whether or not they will open their own investigation into BNY.

On September 21 and 22, the United States House of Representatives Committee on Banking and Financial Services held two hearings on Russian money laundering and BNY's alleged involvement. Chairman James A. Leach presided over the hearing and requested the presence of banking officials and businessmen from all over the world. Three key BNY executives were also invited to appear: Chairman and CEO Thomas Renyi accepted and provided testimony; Natasha Kagalovsky, former head of BNY's eastern European division, and Lucy Edwards, formerly with BNY's London office declined the invitation.

Natasha Gurfinkel Kagalovsky

Once heralded for transforming BNY into the bank of choice for Eastern Europe's mushrooming western-style banks, forty-five year old Natasha Kagalovsky is presently caught up in a financial scandal that may tarnish her career forever. Acting as senior vice president for BNY's Eastern European Division, she was one of two executives suspended on August 18, 1999, for their involvement in alleged money laundering activities. Under the intense scrutiny of Federal Investigators and feeling abandoned by BNY, she resigned on October 12 from her $900,000 a year position declaring, "Not once during the investigation, with all the media it has had, has the bank seen fit to publicly or privately defend me and let it be known that there is not one negative thing to say about me."[5]

Born in Russia, Ms. Kagalovsky emmigrated from there to the United States in 1979 and eventually earned a master's degree from Princeton University. She joined BNY shortly after graduating and quickly rose within the corporate ranks. In the early 1990s, she was promoted to lead business liaison for eastern European operations and the former Soviet Union. Under Ms. Kagalovsky's stewardship, BNY started providing correspondent banking services to allow European banks to open U.S. accounts and to transfer dollars around the world. At its peak, BNY had as many as 300 correspondent relationships in the countries of the former Soviet Union, including the lion's share of the region's most powerful financial institutions. "Natasha had a near monopoly . . . there was an envy felt toward her,"[6] said George Skouras, who set up Citibank's representative office in Moscow.

---

[5] O'Brien, Timothy L. "Bank of New York Executive Resigns in Laundering Inquiry," *The New York Times*, October 13, 1999, p. A6.

[6] Davis, Ann. "Borrowing Trouble: Natasha Kagalovsky Rose Fast, Fell Hard at Bank of New York," *The Wall Street Journal*, November 23, 1999, pp. A1, A14.

Ms. Kagalovsky's husband, Konstantin Kagalovsky, a former Russian banker is also under investigation. It is believed he helped develop the network of offshore shell companies allegedly linked to the money laundering scheme. Investigators are also curious about two $300,000 money transfers made between the couple's Citibank and Channel Island bank accounts this past August. Although Ms. Kagalovsky has not been formerly charged with any wrongdoing by any law-enforcement agency, she remains under the scrutiny of investigators because of her supervisory role over Lucy Edwards, a key figure in the government's investigations.

Lucy Edwards

On October 6, a Federal grand jury indictment was unsealed in Manhattan charging Lucy Edwards, a former BNY vice president from the London office; her husband Peter Berlin, a Russian businessman; and Russian business associate Aleksey Volkov with conspiracy to run an unlicensed money transfer business through three companies. The indictment represented the first criminal charges resulting from the multi-billion dollar BNY money laundering investigation, though it does not mention BNY or money laundering. It does confirm, however, reports that accounts held in the name of Benex International Company and Becs International L.L.C. moved nearly $7 billion through BNY over the past three-and-a-half years. The indictment also identifies Torfinex Corporation, which is owned by defendant Aleksey Volkov, as the illegal money transmitter. Additionally, Ms. Edwards allegedly used her foreign banking connections to feed clients into the underground money-transfer system that bypassed Russian tax and customs authorities. Federal Bureau of Investigation officials describe the indictment as the first product of one the most important investigations being conducted by the agency.

As press inquiries regarding the Federal investigation continued to arise, Ms. Edwards was suspended from BNY on August 18, 1999, along with Ms. Kagalovsky. Shortly thereafter, Ms. Edwards was released from BNY for what the bank called "gross misconduct." The attorney representing Ms. Edwards and her husband stated "they did nothing wrong" and declined further comment.

Making the Case

Though money laundering is one the largest criminal industries in the world, few cases are ever brought to trial because criminals are so successful at concealing their audit trail. It is even more difficult to indict an institution such as BNY because of the complexity and inherent distance of the agency relationship between the institution and the employee. Before the Federal government expends resources to conduct a complex money laundering audit, it must determine that the case meets criteria that warrant the investment. Those criteria include the:

- Rank of bank employee(s) at the center of the crisis.
- Amount laundered.
- Repetitiveness of laundering transactions.
- Top management's knowledge of benefits accrued to bank from the laundering activities.

The government must prove specific occurrences of unlawful activity on the part of BNY to levy charges of money laundering. Obstacles facing U.S. Federal prosecutors include lack of a discernable audit trail of suspected transactions and unfavorable extradition agreements between the U.S. and Russia that do not allow foreign violators to be brought before the American justice system. Prosecutors must also prove the BNY senior management team was aware of, and authorized, the allegedly illegal activities of Ms. Edwards if it hopes to pursue litigation against the bank. To date, such links have not yet been verified. In short, Bank of New York does not seem to be in imminent danger of being criminally indicted on money laundering charges. Even so, the financial world waits anxiously for BNY's next move in this landmark case. Does the lack of a strong legal case signal the end of BNY's current dilemma? What should the bank do?

Questions

1. What are the critical issues facing the Bank of New York?

2. Should the bank continue its policy of media silence?

3. Will Thomas Renyi's defensive stance be viewed as a blatant denial of the accusations facing New York's oldest bank? Are there legal reasons for not discussing the case?

4. Should the bank have supported Ms. Kagalovsky and Ms. Edwards during their investigations?

5. What should the bank include as part of their communication strategy in the aftermath of the allegations?

PART VII

Community Relations

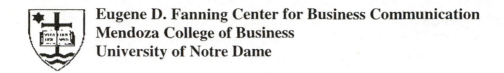
Chicago Transit Authority

Friday, July 11, 1997

Maria Toscano sat at her desk and stared out the window on a hot afternoon in the middle of July. The manager of public relations for the Chicago Transit Authority (CTA) had just received some disturbing information in a phone call from her boss, Noel Gaffney.

Noel Gaffney, vice president of corporate communications, called to tell her that the board of the Chicago Transit Authority had voted last night to approve a measure that would decrease service on several of the bus and train routes that served many Chicago area residents. The vote to approve the measure had come after weeks of often-hostile public debate over the CTA's proposed plan. Struggling under a large budget deficit, the board ultimately felt that it had no choice but to end service on many of its least profitable routes.

Maria could hear in Noel's voice that she was not done with all of the news. "Maria," she said, "there's something else . . . ." Noel went on to tell her that at a morning meeting with senior level officers, David Mosena, President of the Chicago Transit Authority, had just announced his intention to resign and take a job at the Museum of Science and Industry. David's resignation would mark the third departure of a CTA president since 1990. Noel also said that rumors were already floating around that the board was considering Frank Kruesi, an associate of Mayor Richard Daley, to take over David Mosena's job.

Maria's head was swimming with questions. She considered how these developments would affect the CTA, an organization that was struggling to maintain an image that was already tarnished in public opinion.

History of the Chicago Transit Authority

Public transportation in the city of Chicago originated with horse-drawn carriages in 1859. The loop, which was first opened in 1897, connected four separate rail systems

This case was prepared by Research Assistants John Northcut and Kevin Tucker under the direction of James S. O'Rourke, Concurrent Associate Professor of Management, as the basis for class discussion rather than to illustrate either effective or ineffective handling of an administrative situation. Information was gathered from corporate as well as public sources.

branching through different parts of the city. The horse drawn carriages gave way to San Francisco-style cable cars in 1882, and the cable cars, in turn, gave way to electric powered streetcars in 1906. The streetcar companies served the bustling, growing city's transportation needs well, and in 1914, five of the largest streetcar organizations merged into one entity. This company was called Chicago Surface Lines. With its 1,100 miles of track, it was the world's largest and most heavily used streetcar system of its time. In 1924, the four railways that merged into the loop became known as the Chicago Rapid Transit Company. The first use of buses for mass transportation in Chicago came in 1917 with the advent of the Chicago Motor Bus Company, which was succeeded by the Chicago Motor Coach Company in 1922.

The Illinois General Assembly created the CTA, which would become an independent agency of the government, with the passing of the Metropolitan Transit Authority Act of 1945. In a voter referendum passed on June 4, 1945, the City of Chicago approved an ordinance granting the CTA the exclusive right to own and operate a unified local transportation system. Public transportation had become consolidated, and with the birth of the CTA, all of Chicago's subways, buses, and elevated trains were to be managed under one umbrella. As the years passed and public transportation helped to carry the major urban centers into new eras of growth, the CTA gained an increasingly powerful role in the daily lives of the citizens of Chicago.

Rising Costs, Shrinking Revenues

The CTA generated revenues from riders fares, which at the time of this case were set at $1.50 per ride (either train or bus), with the option to purchase a transfer (to allow for second and third trips inside of a two-hour time-frame) for an additional $.30. In addition to this fee generation, the CTA relied heavily on subsidies in order to meet its operating expenses. These were derived from two primary sources: federal subsidies and funds allocated from the city sales tax revenues.

From 1979 to 1995, while the population of Chicago continued to increase, ridership on the CTA decreased approximately 33 percent. A negative public image of inefficiency, unreliability, and concerns about crime and a general lack of safety accounted for much of the loss. The CTA had been considering various marketing programs to reverse the negative image and increase ridership, but nothing substantial had been implemented. In addition to the declines in service usage, federal subsidies and budget deficits were under fire in Washington, and funds for the CTA were on the chopping block. Various projections indicated that funding from the federal government, which accounted for $41.5 million of CTA's budget in 1991, would be reduced to zero by 1999.

As a result of growing financial setbacks, CTA management, which had run budget deficits for most of the 1990s, was faced with public and political scrutiny regarding inefficiency and the inability to grow and maintain a sound system of public transportation. Year after year, the CTA struggled to get out of the red and into the black.

In an effort to revive the financially beleaguered agency, management prepared a proposal to change the structure of services offered in the city. The proposal amounted to a downsizing of available service, including the changing of times and withdrawal of late night service on various routes, as well as the outright elimination of a number of bus routes. The routes to be eliminated had been chosen based upon an "average number of riders per hour" statistic. The CTA found that buses should operate at a minimum of 12 riders per hour in order to break even. Some routes operating in the city had as little as seven riders per hour.

By applying the break-even rationale to the existing service routes, CTA management found that the majority of the routes that would be eliminated were in some of the cities lowest income, minority neighborhoods. The proposed cuts would affect an estimated one percent of the current ridership. While the new proposal would save an estimated $25 million by containing costs, the cuts were a matter of concern. Social and political backlash seemed inevitable to the management. The communications team at the CTA would not truly know the extent of this until the public forum committee meeting, which was held on June 30, 1997.

Trouble at the Thompson Center

As a stipulation of its operating agreement with the City of Chicago, the CTA was required to hold an annual public forum allowing the community to voice its concerns. In addition, any time that changes to existing service were proposed, such as fare increases or service cuts, the CTA was required to announce the proposal under review in advance and then schedule an open forum with the public regarding the changes.

On June 31, 1997, the CTA held such a public forum at the James R. Thompson center. About 1,000 people attended. The meeting was utter pandemonium and the "crowd booed every word out of CTA Board President Valerie Jarrett's mouth, including those she delivered when inviting people standing in the back to sit in vacated seats." It was apparent from the meeting that there were strong feelings against the proposed cuts. Residents voiced concerns that their jobs, health, and safety were being compromised by the CTA. Additionally, residents made it clear that they were concerned about how the cuts were targeting predominantly low-income minority neighborhoods.

In the days that followed, these sentiments were also reflected in the press. In articles, commentaries, and editorials with titles such as "From the Back of the Bus to No Bus at All," the CTA was being vilified for its proposal to eliminate the bus routes. Among concerns were the loss of main lines of travel to hospitals and jobs, as well as the potential that service cuts would force citizens to walk through unsafe neighborhoods.

Case Dilemma

As Maria Toscano sat at her desk, she stared at the CTA mission statement that was tacked up on her wall. The top paragraph read, "We deliver quality, affordable transit services that link people, jobs, and communities." She realized that the impending service cuts were going to have a major impact on the people of Chicago. The situation may have become such that people viewed public transportation as a right, and she was expecting that curtailing service would create a large backlash from the public. After all, the CTA had been formed to meet and serve the needs of the citizens of Chicago.

Regardless of what had brought them to their current situation, Maria knew that it would be up to her to communicate the service cuts to the public. The cuts had to be made to save the organization, but how could she make the public believe that these actions were in their long-term interest? How should she speak to them and when? And, were there other parties beyond the ridership that she needed to address?

Maria was also worried about the signal that David Mosena's departure would send to the public. This compounded the situation, as the CTA would have to have a credible public spokesperson to address the media. Mosena's departure might give the public the impression that the organization did not have any leadership. Was it dangerous to develop a communication strategy only to have it potentially changed when a new president was selected?

Questions

1. What are the critical issues facing Ms. Toscano and the CTA?

2. How should Maria Toscano communicate the CTA's position to the public? Should holding another public forum be considered? Should she contact local media to arrange to speak with them, or should she prepare press releases? Should the CTA wait to see how the media handles the information before contacting them?

3. What message should the CTA try to convey to the ridership and specifically to the people of the neighborhoods where routes are slated to be cut? Are there any other audiences whom the CTA should be considering? What kind of research should Maria Toscano do to help her create the most effective public relations message?

4. What effect does the departure of CTA president David Mosena have on the situation?

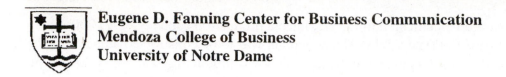
AM General Corporation and the Hummer Plant Expansion

FOR IMMEDIATE RELEASE - January 11, 2000
AM GENERAL TO BUILD SECOND HUMMER MANUFACTURING
FACILITY AT CURRENT MISHAWAKA SITE

ALLIANCE WITH GM TO ADD UP TO 1500 NEW JOBS TO AREA EMPLOYMENT
South Bend, Ind. (January 10, 2000) --- AM General Corporation announced today that the South Bend/Mishawaka based company will build a second facility at its current McKinley Highway plant in Mishawaka, Ind., for production of additional commercial Hummers, a result of its new alliance with General Motors (GM).
Source: Corporate Press Release, AM General Corporation, January 11, 2000, p. 1.

The Situation

Amid great excitement and fanfare, General Motors (GM) confirmed what had been rumored for seven months: GM was about to enter into an agreement with AM General to market its civilian version of the HMMWV (Humvee), the Hummer H1 (H1). The Humvee is a military vehicle that gained fame for its use during the 1991 Persian Gulf War and was popularized for civilian use by actor Arnold Schwarzenegger. While GM would bring its considerable marketing prowess to this brand, AM General would be responsible for the manufacture of the vehicle. When this announcement was made on January 9, 2000, there was speculation that a new facility would have to be constructed in order to accommodate the increased production levels and improved technology requirements. Speculation turned to reality on January 10, 2000, when officials from the State of Indiana, St. Joseph County, and AM General outlined a plan to construct a $200 million facility that would produce a brand new SUV, the Hummer H2 (H2).

This case was prepared by Research Assistants Tony Silveus, Jay Sarzen, and Michael Strilchuk under the direction of James S. O'Rourke, Concurrent Associate Professor of Management, as the basis for class discussion rather than to illustrate either effective or ineffective handling of an administrative situation. Information was gathered from corporate as well as public sources.

The new plant would be dedicated to the H2, have a production capacity of 40,000 vehicles per year, and create 1,500 new jobs. The new plant was to be constructed adjacent to the existing AM General facility in Mishawaka, Indiana, which was producing 3,000 – 5,000 H1s per year and employed roughly 600 people. As a result of this plan, fifty-one property owners and their families, some of whom who had lived most of their lives in their present homes, were about to be forced from them by this corporate expansion. These homes were located on the most optimal, as well as the most feasible, parcel of land.[1] Once the deal was sealed to construct the plant and bring jobs to the region, St. Joseph County offered to acquire the necessary property since the cost of the land was not within AM General's budget. Moreover, the County would reap benefits as a result of this acquisition, the plant construction, and the addition of new jobs to the region.[2]

When property owners are forced from their homes due to corporate expansion, there is a likelihood of negative feelings and perceptions about the company that is expanding. Realizing that negative perceptions could turn into a public relations nightmare, Craig MacNab, the director of public relations for AM General, pondered what his strategy would be for moving forward with this project.

A Brief History of AM General

The origins of AM General can be traced to 1903, when the Standard Wheel Company of Terre Haute, Indiana, expanded its bicycle operation to include the Overland Automotive Division to manufacture motor vehicles, and the Overland "Runabout" was introduced. In 1908, John North Willys purchased the Overland Automotive Company, which by then was located in Indianapolis, Indiana. As Runabout sales grew, production was moved in 1908 to the newly purchased Pope-Toledo automobile manufacturing plant in Toledo, Ohio. In 1912, the Willys-Overland Company was formed, and by 1940, Willys-Overland Motors, Inc., had entered the field of tactical truck development with the design and manufacture of a prototype for America's first four-wheel drive, quarter-ton, utility truck. In 1963, Willys Motors was renamed the Kaiser Jeep Corporation and, in 1964, began producing its trucks and jeeps in South Bend, Indiana. In 1970, American Motors Corporation purchased the Kaiser Jeep Corporation from Kaiser Industries and renamed the division AM General. In the ensuing years, AM General became known as a primary provider of several types of military vehicles for the United States Army.

In 1979, AM General was awarded an Army contract to develop a Hummer vehicle for the Armed Forces. This vehicle became the cornerstone of the company, which changed hands over the next several years before finally being purchased by the Renco Group, a New York City based holding company.[3]

By 1998, AM General had revenues of $393 million. However, much of that revenue was generated by a government contract that called for AM General to re-build two and a half-ton

---

[1] Interview with Craig Mac Nab, 4/20/00.

[2] Update Document, Project Future, January, 2000.

[3] AM General Website, www.amgmil.com

military trucks that had been worn out by the various divisions of the Armed Forces.   During 1998, the re-build contract was not renewed, leading to a reported net loss of $10.2 million in 1999. Since AM General's production level for the H1 was not high enough to generate sufficient revenues, the company's future prospects looked uncertain. However, even with an uncertain financial outlook for the company, the Hummer retained a high level of brand equity. Furthermore, the actual H1 was believed to be the most capable off-road vehicle in the industry.

While these events were swirling around AM General, General Motors was seeking to expand its automobile portfolio. GM recognized AM General's position in the marketplace as well as the value of the Hummer brand and approached AM General about bringing the Hummer brand under GM's wing.

The Litany of the Agreement

A long litany of events dating back to June of 1999 precipitated the potential relocation of local property owners. It was during this month that a memorandum of understanding was signed between Detroit-based General Motors and South Bend-based AM General. This memorandum stated that GM and AM General were to explore the possibility of GM marketing and distributing the civilian version of the Hummer but contained little detail of the agreement, though all details were available in AM General's 1999 10K.[4] This agreement would allow GM to acquire the exclusive ownership of the Hummer brand while AM General would retain the manufacturing rights for both the military and civilian versions of the Hummer. The agreement had no effect on AM General's military obligations, as the company would retain the right to market and distribute the Humvee to the military. At the time, it was believed by both GM and AM General that there would be no need to expand the existing facility to accommodate the demand for the vehicle. However, for those with a different perspective, it was believed that a plant expansion, or at the very least, a new plant, was imminent.

While plant construction would be an important issue in the near future, there was no way that this project would move forward without two key conditions to cement the agreement between GM and AM General. These conditions were: 1) a firm deal between the local UAW chapter and AM General and 2) prevention of public dissemination of information regarding the deal.[5]

The creation of a new union contract involved direct negotiations between AM General and its local UAW chapter. Craig MacNab of AM General communicated directly with the union that this deal was financially less attractive than the one offered by GM to its unions. However, after MacNab explained the future benefits of the new labor contract (such as securing retirement for many workers and providing new jobs for their families and friends) and its importance in the deal with GM, its union agreed to a ten year labor contract. The new contract

---

[4] South Bend Tribune/ Knight-Ridder News, 6/30/99.
[5] Interview with Craig Mac Nab, 4/20/00.

was made possible by AM General's willingness to share all information with its workers and its history of good union relations. Throughout these negotiations, AM General told their workers everything and ensured their support of the new facility. While this contract was not as lucrative as GM's contract with its union, AM General workers accepted it because they believed that having a job was better than no job at all.

Equally important to the union contract was the need to maintain silence regarding the GM/AM General association. General Motors wanted this silence so they could announce the deal on their own terms and in their own way. Over one thousand people knew of this secret, and leaks inevitably occurred. Even so, little was learned regarding the development of the H2 prototype outside of AM General. The union remained silent, knowing that future jobs depended on the deal. Furthermore, local media did not probe into the leaks as AM General made it clear that publication of any rumors could doom the new plant's construction. Later, AM General informed both the South Bend Tribune and WNDU that they should cover the January 9 auto show in Detroit, rewarding the media for their cooperation.

By the time the agreement was finalized on December 21, 1999, and after the unofficial announcement on January 9, there was speculation that a new plant would be constructed. This speculation was so intense that a dollar amount of $200 million for construction and possibly 1,400 – 1,500 new jobs was suggested. At this point, however, nothing more was said about the plant's location or if people would have to be relocated. Despite a lack of information, there was a positive consensus for the new plant. Civic leaders hailed the expansion as a great opportunity for the people of the South Bend region to produce a highly visible automobile within the GM portfolio. The local UAW was fully on board and residents of the area were also excited about the prospects of working on this type of vehicle.

All the speculation became real on January 10, 2000, when Indiana Governor Frank O'Bannon and Lieutenant Governor Joseph Kernan joined AM General and GM officials at a press conference in South Bend's Century Center to announce the company's plans, which called for an investment of over $200 million.[6] Representatives from the UAW, Saint Joseph County, the City of Mishawaka, and Project Future, all of whom were instrumental in the company's expansion efforts, joined in the announcement. The production of the H2 line would require construction of a new plant that would be located immediately west of the existing facility. Because the first H2 was scheduled to come off the line in two years, GM set a deadline for the construction of the new facility to begin May 1, 2000. As a result, the acquisition of neighboring properties became an immediate concern, and 51 property owners would have to relocate.

---

[6] Associated Press Newswire. 1/11/00.

Questions

1. How should AM General handle the public's reaction to the news of the plant expansion?

2. What is a fair way of dealing with plant expansion and relocation of the community?

3. How should AM General tell local residents that they will have to find new homes?

4. Is the plant expansion a positive situation for the community?

5. What is AM General's responsibility to the community during and after expansion?

6. What actions will James Armour and AM General need to take to ensure that all stakeholders are satisfied with the expansion plans?

PART VIII

International Corporate Issues

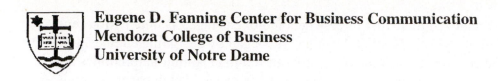
Daimler-Benz Corporation and the Mercedes A-Class

October 21, 1997

On a beautiful afternoon in October 1997, Dr. Klaus Mangold, Director of the Services division at Daimler-Benz received a disturbing phone call from Sweden: "Wir haben ein gröbes Problem hier; der Klasse A Versuch ist miblungen!" ("We have a problem here; the test on the A-Class failed!")

Robert Collin, a journalist for the Swedish automobile magazine *Tecknikens Vaerld,* attempted to execute a so-called "moose avoidance test" when the Mercedes A-Class automobile flipped over. This test is usually used in Scandinavian countries to avoid wandering animals and other unforeseen obstacles. A fully-laden car undergoes a double lane-change at 60 km/h (about 37 mph). The driver swerves to avoid a "moose" and then swerves back into his lane to avoid oncoming traffic. The test caused the tire sidewall to collapse until the wheel flange touched the ground, causing the vehicle to flip. The three passengers were slightly injured.

Dr. Mangold quickly realized how damaging this could be for the A-Class, especially after the money spent in the design and marketing of the car and following the good publicity it received. He knew the news would spread around the world quickly. He could already imagine the headlines "Mercedes, known for its reputation of safety, fails test in Sweden on its new A-Class model." As he stood up and looked out the window, he began to formulate a crisis management plan to save the A-Class' life.

Daimler-Benz

Benz & Co. was founded in 1883, by Karl Benz, with businessman Max Kaspar Rose and commercial agent Friedrich Wilhlem Esslinger. They started by producing motor bicycles,

This case was prepared by Research Assistants Benoit Guerin and Caroline Verot under the direction of James S. O'Rourke, Concurrent Associate Professor of Management, as the basis for class discussion rather than to illustrate either effective or ineffective handling of an administrative situation. Information was gathered from corporate as well as public sources.

and in 1886, they commercialized their first three-wheel motor carriage. Daimler-Motoren-Gesellschaft was founded in 1892 by Gottlieb Daimler. He began by designing engines. In 1900, Emil Jellinek established a company in Monaco in order to sell the Daimler automobiles but asked for exclusive rights. The company holds the name of Mercedes, which became a registered trade mark in 1902. In 1924, Benz & Co. and Daimler-Motoren-Gesellschaft joined in a "community of interest" and merged two years later.

Today, Daimler-Benz consists of 23 business units grouped into four divisions: Passenger Cars, Commercial Vehicles, Aerospace, and Services. The motor vehicle business is the major activity of the group with a turnover of DM 77.6 billion in 1997. In 1997, the Passenger Cars division had the best production, sales, and turnover figures in the 110-year history of the company: the three-star brand sold over 715,000 cars worldwide, an increase of 11 percent for a turnover of DM 53 billion. Juergen Hubbert is currently the Daimler-Benz AG management board member responsible for the Mercedes automobile subsidiary.

Reputation and Brand Image

Mercedes has been known for producing very conservative automobiles with classic design and high technology. Surveys show that the first attribute people remember when asked about the name Mercedes is quality (56 percent), followed by safety, price, and comfort. Other attributes that come to consumers' minds are luxury and value.

According to the *Financial Times*, the Mercedes three pointed star is "the quintessential prestige symbol – one of the world's most recognizable and respected." Lydia Aydon, the news editor of *Auto Express*, says Mercedes enjoys "a reputation for safety and knowing exactly what they do; a Germanic idea of everything being absolutely perfect and without problem." Consumers perceive Mercedes owners as well-educated, wealthy people of mature age.

History of the A-Class

Daimler-Benz made the decision to develop and produce a small, compact automobile in 1995. The company spent about $1.65 billion in the design of its newest product line, the Mercedes A-Class. The car was to strike the consumer as being unique among Mercedes products: it was the smallest car ever produced by the German car maker, just under 12 feet long and weighing only 2,200 pounds.

According to Daimler-Benz designers, this new car will revolutionize the perception of compact cars. The design will make it one of the safest compact cars on the road, especially on the narrow roads of European and Asian cities, its initial markets.

A Redefinition of the Compact Car

The design of the A-Class is all new. It creates a "two-story" car, with the fuel tank, axles, battery, and exhaust in the "basement," mounted under the floor of the body. The occupants sit above the car's drive train, about six inches higher than in a normal automobile, which makes the passengers safer in a crash. Another design feature is that an S-shaped engine and gearbox are made to sit at an angle beneath the front passengers, again to save space.

The engine design also increases safety in an accident because the engine is pushed down and back, instead of through the front firewall and back into the passenger compartment where legs can be broken. The design works so well that inside there is only 4mm less length than in the Mercedes C-Class, which is 941mm longer on the outside than the A-Class.

The Introduction of the A-Class

The A-Class was introduced for two main reasons:

· Growth in the overall market for luxury cars was slow and studies showed that it was likely to stay that way for the next few years;

· Baby boomers, rebelling against the kind of upper middle-class lifestyles their parents led, were looking for smaller, more compact and practical cars.

The A-Class was designed to target several markets that Mercedes had not previously targeted. It hoped to capture the young, urban professional market of singles in their thirties and two-person households. It was also positioned as a second car for those who are already Mercedes owners. Finally, the company wanted to appeal to consumers at an earlier age and build a strong sense of loyalty among them, so that when these consumers would become wealthier they would remain loyal to the Mercedes brand and trade up to the more luxurious models.

Knowing that potential consumers were all "new" to the Mercedes brand, and, therefore more difficult to convince, the company drafted a five-year strategy. They launched the A-Class marketing and advertising campaigns a year prior to the vehicle's launch. Mercedes' research showed that the average buyer contemplates a new car purchase a year in advance. They conducted an "A-Motion" Tour around Europe to create awareness of the new product. The campaign emphasized the car's affordability with strong emotional overtones.

The Public's Reaction

Before it even went on sale, Mercedes received positive feedback and comments about their new car. Most automobile magazines praised the design and the way it organized the space inside the car. For *Auto Revista*, "never before has a car this small on the outside been this large on the inside; while its exterior size suggests a sub-compact, the A-Class will offer its occupants the roominess and comfort of a mid-size car." According to *The Times*, "the feel is being at the wheel of something much bigger; inside it is all Mercedes . . . the robust feeling of a secure and quality build."

The majority of survey respondents gave positive feedback about the German company's new car, further confirming that the launch of the A-Class was the right decision. Most thought it would be beneficial for Mercedes to incorporate and use its well-established brand name in the subcompact market segment. In another survey, 56 percent of the respondents answered that with the introduction of the A-Class, their image of Mercedes had changed to a company that is trying to accommodate a wider array of the market, and "not only the rich." The words "affordability" and "practicality" were mentioned more often.

The survey results were confirmed in the number of orders the firm received even prior to the launch, initially planned for October of 1997. Mercedes booked 100,000 orders and announced an eight-month waiting list for the car. The company expected annual sales to rise to 200,000 by 1999.

Importance of the Introduction

With the introduction of the A-Class, Mercedes would be entering a totally new segment of the automobile market. The product addresses the high fuel costs and crowded conditions of many European and Asian cities, with a strong market potential for developing countries as well. The "Baby Benz" was expected to become the company's best-selling model in the next few years.

Moreover, Mercedes was planning the launch of an even smaller subcompact car with Swiss watchmaker SMH (better known as Swatch). The Smart Car was based on a similar design to the A-Class. Mercedes would have to succeed in launching a safe and reliable A-Class in order to secure sales of the Smart Car and to give it a positive reputation before its commercialization. There were some concerns in public opinion and among automobile reporters that the problems the company faced regarding the testing of the A-Class also existed in its other models. Many believed that the Smart Car's introduction would be delayed and that Mercedes would have to take a closer look at their designs.

As Mangold returned to his desk, he knew the struggle would be difficult, especially with a new product category. But, he also knew his team was well prepared. He picked up the phone and rang the Director of Corporate Communication to coordinate the strategy.

Questions

1.   Suppose you are the Director of Corporate Communication, what strategy would you suggest for dealing with the failed safety test?

2.   What are the critical issues facing Mercedes?

3.   How should they respond to the news of the safety test?

4.   Who are the important audiences for Mangold's team to address? Are different strategies and communication efforts needed for different audiences?

5.   What should be said at this point, and to whom?

6.   What, if any, peremptory measures could Mangold use to counter any confusion surrounding the news of the failed safety test. What communication strategy could be put in place?

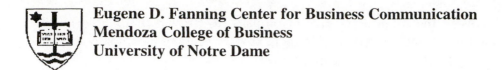
BP Colombia

It was a quiet night in London on August 8, 1997. The weather seemed perfect for that time of the year, and many people were strolling the night away at Trafalgar Square. That was not the case, however, for Sir John Browne, CEO of British Petroleum (BP), and his senior management team as they gathered at the BP Headquarters at Finsbury Circus. They had just finished viewing the television program, "Oil & Terror," that presented a year-long investigation of BP's operations in Colombia.

The program alleged that BP was responsible for severe environmental damage and human rights violations. This program was the apex of a series of newspaper articles accusing BP of training Colombian police officers and financing the Colombian Army to protect BP's operations in the Casanare region of Colombia. Additionally, the program made specific allegations that BP passed photographs and videos of local protesters to the Colombian Army, which led to rapes, killings, disappearances, torture, and beatings of local *"campesinos"*[1] by the Army and the paramilitary.[2] As Sir John Browne pondered what BP's next steps should be, he knew this would be a long night.

Company Background

British Petroleum's origins date back to 1901, when a wealthy Englishman named William Knox D'Arcy obtained a concession from the Shah of Persia to explore for and exploit the oil resources of that country. In May 1908, D'Arcy and his associates struck oil in commercial quantities in southwest Persia. It was the first commercial oil discovery in the Middle East, signaling the emergence of that region as an oil producing area.

This case was prepared by Research Assistants Ramon Delgado, Albano Garcia, Tina Villalobos, and Amanda Steedley under the direction of James S. O'Rourke, Concurrent Associate Professor of Management, as the basis for class discussion rather than to illustrate either effective or ineffective handling of an administrative situation. Information was gathered from corporate as well as public sources.

---

[1] "Campesino" refers to the peasant farmer.
[2] Paramilitary refers to the mercenary forces that serve the ultra-right movement in Colombia.

Following the discovery, the Anglo-Persian Oil Company (as BP was first known) was formed in 1909 to develop the oil field in Persia. For the next sixty years, the company focused on Persia and the surrounding Gulf states in its search for oil.

In the quest to find new sources of oil and gas, BP explorers began to examine regions of the world that for political or technical reasons remained relatively unexplored. Colombia, the republics of the former Soviet Union, and the deep waters of the Gulf of Mexico emerged as new possibilities for development.

In all its operations, BP maintained its policy of striving to be an industry leader in health, safety and environmental standards. By 1997, BP was not only one of the largest oil companies but also one of the largest companies in the world, with more than 70,000 employees and operations in more than 100 countries. Its key businesses are oil and gas exploration and production; the refining, marketing, and supply of petroleum products; and the manufacturing and marketing of chemicals.

Table 1: British Petroleum Financial Performance, 1995-1997

	1995	1996	1997
Oil Production (millions barrels)	2.8	2.9	2.9
Net Income	$3.7 billion	$7.4 billion	$5.6 billion

Colombia

The Republic of Colombia is considered one of Latin America's most prosperous economies. It has a population of almost 40 million people, making it the third largest country in South America. Ecuador and Peru border Colombia to the south, Brazil and Venezuela to the east and Panama to the northwest. Colombia also has an extensive coastline along the Pacific Ocean and the Caribbean Sea. All these factors, in addition to being close to North America with coasts on the Atlantic and Pacific oceans, give it a significant geographic advantage for trading purposes.

Colombia has many natural resources including agricultural land, water for irrigation, energy resources (oil, natural gas, and coal), and mineral resources such as nickel, gold, and emeralds. Many experts believe these assets explain Colombia's good record of economic development and social improvements over the last 30 years. The oil and mining industries represent one of the fastest growing sectors of the economy. Coffee exporting is among Columbia's other important economic activities.

For the last 20 years, however, the country has faced serious problems associated with drug trafficking and terrorism. The growth of the illegal drug industry in Colombia over the past two decades has had serious economic, political, and social effects. Colombia accounts, by some estimates, for nearly 75 percent of the world's supply of cocaine. The highly organized criminal groups that dominate the drug industry have accumulated enormous wealth and gained access to political and business spheres.

Political History

Between 1978 and 1982, the government focused on ending the limited, but persistent, insurgency that sought to undermine Colombia's traditional democratic system. This insurgency was supported by Fidel Castro's regime in Cuba and by the Soviet Union.

In 1984, President Belisario Betancur negotiated a cease-fire that included the release of many guerrillas imprisoned during the effort to overpower the insurgents. The cease-fire proved to be unsuccessful when Democratic Alliance/M-19 (AD/M-19) guerrillas resumed fighting in 1985. Other guerrilla groups continued fighting and exploited the peace offer with the intention to pressure the government to release imprisoned guerillas.

Although the government and the Revolutionary Armed Forces of Colombia (FARC), the largest guerrilla group, renewed their truce in March 1986, AD/M-19 and other guerrilla groups persisted with violence throughout the country when Betancur left office.

As foreign support for the guerrillas dwindled in the late 1990s, Colombia's next two presidents, Barco and Gaviria, managed to demobilize two large guerrilla groups (AD/M-19) through negotiation, political changes, and successful military operations. The two largest guerrilla groups, FARC and ELN, however, were not affected and did not join in the negotiations.

Sustaining the Colombian Guerrilla

With the end of Cuban and Soviet aid, the guerrillas had to find other resources. Like mobsters in 1920's Chicago, FARC and ELN discovered that it was possible to "sell protection" to people doing business in rural areas of Colombia.

FARC specialized in "taxing,"selling protection and enforcing contracts among producers of cocaine and the planters of the coca leaf, which is one of the raw materials of cocaine. Under this new Narco-Guerrilla alliance, FARC protected the *campesinos* who cultivated the coca leaf and also protected the drug refiners from the Colombian police and Army. In tribute for these services, the guerrillas received a fee that amounted to several million dollars per year. The guerrillas used the revenues to finance their operations and distribute money among the *campesinos*. As a result, the guerrilla's presence became more visible in impoverished circles, thus gaining more members and making them the "Robin Hood" of the 20th century. On the other hand, ELN specialized in selling protection to gold prospectors (large and small), oil project contractors, road contractors, and public infrastructure builders. The guerrillas also began to demand ranson funds by kidnaping executive employees of international companies and extorting funds with threats of kidnaping.

In Colombia, many of the oil pipelines run near or through small agricultural towns in rural areas. The oil companies paid high salaries and reparation for damages to these communities in order to avoid bad publicity. The guerrilla groups realized that the oil companies hired local labor for repairs and clean-up projects around pipelines when they broke. Recognizing an opportunity, the guerrillas started to organize the communities for a new business: pipeline destruction. Their plan was to contact community leaders, convince them to collaborate, and schedule pipe-blowing operations. The guerrillas collected a fee for the community "affected" by the damage from a destroyed pipeline. Therefore, the only *campesinos* who could participate in the clean-up and repair were those loyal to the guerrilla groups.

BP in Colombia

BP first invested in the exploration of crude oil in the Casanare region of Colombia in 1986. In 1988, the company discovered the Cusiana oil field located 250 miles east of Bogota, Colombia. In 1993, BP found the Cupiagua and Piedemonte oil fields also in the Casanare region. All three oil fields amounted to two billion barrels of reserves, making it one of the largest onshore oil fields in the world.

BP developed the oil fields under license of the Colombian government in a joint venture with the state-owned company Ecopetrol (50 percent), Total and Triton (31 percent) and BP (19 percent). Oil production began in 1994 and was expected to rise to 500,000 barrels per day by the year 2000. The production of this oil field would represent almost 50 percent of the country's total oil production. BP employed approximately 1,000 people from the region directly and more than 4,000 on a contract basis. Spending more than $10 million a year, BP funded diverse social programs in the region, influencing small business development, health, and education. In addition to their public commitment to environmental regulations and high company standards, BP spent some $30 million on environmental protection.

The revenues produced by the oil field development in Casanare benefitted many segments of the population, causing the area to boom economically. There were high expectations for BP to provide social support services above and beyond those offered by the Colombian government. Some *campesinos*, however, complained that the unmonitored economic growth brought negative effects such as increased crime and prostitution. Fortune seekers took advantage of the situation and started to complain in order to gain a personal profit.

From the beginning of its operations in Colombia, BP's executives received threats of kidnaping from the guerrilla groups. In response to this unfamiliar threat, BP solicited the collaboration of the government. In 1993, BP signed a protection contract with the Colombian Defense Ministry which included $54 to $60 million dollars to protect the firm's installations. This payment was made in the form of a special "war-tax," created by the Colombian government to legitimize the transfer of funds from BP.

Previous Allegations of Human Rights Violations: BP's First Response

Within the first year of BP's operations, some of the *campesinos* of Casanare started to complain. They alleged that the region's ecosystem had suffered severe damage at the hands of BP and asked for compensation. Allegations included blinded cows, dead fish, polluted rivers, illness amongst the local citizens, and even earthquakes. BP ignored the allegations hoping that only fortune seekers were complaining and the accusations would disappear over time.

On August 22, 1996, *The New York Times* reported that British Petroleum had signed a three-year protection contract with the Colombian Defense Ministry valued between US$54 and $60 million. The money, the article said, would pay for a new battalion of 650 soldiers. The following day, in a news release, BP Colombia denounced the article, calling it "extremely offensive." The press release stated: "BP categorically denies that it is forming an army of mercenaries exclusively for its protection . . . . There exists between BP and the Ministry of Defense, the Army, and the Colombian Police, some cooperation accords that were designed from the initial stages of the development project. The accords, however, don't amount to special protection."

Soon after, BP's spokesman, Alvaro Pardo, acknowledged that there was a three-year deal with the Defense Ministry. Both Pardo and Colombian General Harold Bedoya said that there were no plans to create a battalion to guard BP properties and that this was not an attempt to privatize the military. They maintained that the money was given to the Colombian military for "non-lethal aid" such as food, clothing, accommodations and transport. "These are accords between the Government, Ecopetrol (State-Owned Oil Company), and the companies that contribute funds for the security." Alejandro Martinez, the Colombian Oil Association President, also supported BP by saying said that "Oil companies are required to pay the government 'war-tax' which cost the whole industry an estimated $250 million in 1996." The people in some villages of Casanare, fearing no actions would be taken by either the local government or BP on their behalf, started to protest in front of BP's installations, provoking several contractors to strike. On September 16, 1996, the protests escalated to violence and the mayor of the area lost control of the situation. When an anti-riot police squad confronted the mob, the results were disastrous. Several *campesinos* were injured and one press photographer was killed.

The series of events attracted the interest of the international press. Several U.K. newspapers, including *The Financial Times, The Guardian,* and *The Observer* began to follow the story and publish articles that were damaging to BP's reputation.

The story reached new heights when Richard Howitt, an English politician from Essex South, decided to get involved. He demanded that the U.K.'s Prime Minister, Tony Blair, launch an immediate investigation into BP's conduct. "No amount of money can compensate for BP's systematic collusion with the Colombian military and the assassins who shadow [the] local activists who dare to speak out against the oil giants," Howitt said.

Communications Inside BP

BP's first communication strategy consisted of releasing as much information as possible to the press. The idea was to be open and available to the press in order to quell the rumors and allegations. In order to do this, the Office of Corporate Communications in London continuously asked the Colombian communications office for figures and updates on the situations. Their intention was to gather all the facts and release them to the public.

The BP Colombia public affairs office was overwhelmed with requests and spent more time dealing with requests from London than actually managing the situation. Meanwhile, the management of BP Colombia dealt with the issue by following the Crisis Management handbook and treating the allegations like an oil spill. BP Colombia management had very little knowledge or experience handling human rights issues.

The number of press articles attacking BP increased and become more aggressive. Also, the TV channels started to announce special programs with information on the situation. Journalists used every new piece of information that they obtained against BP.

A series of articles also appeared on the Internet published by non-government organizations. BP did not anticipate the degree to which Internet exposure would make the issues in Colombia a global problem, not just a local one.

There was also an ongoing internal debate as to who should handle the problem. The corporate communications office at headquarters claimed it was a London issue while BP Colombia claimed that it should be handled locally. The situation was out of control and seemed to be getting worse.

Questions

1. What are the priorities in responding to and handling the allegations of human rights violations? Environmental protection violations?

2. Who should handle the communication with the media and the public?

3. How would you propose BP Colombia and London work together to remedy the situation?

4. What corporate policies should be put in place to avoid this kind of situation again in the future?

5. What impact does this situation have on international business communication for BP as well as other companies?

6. What were BP's mistakes in this situation?

Xerox Corporation and International Accounting Practices

Executive Challenges Xerox's Books

On February 6, 2001, Paul Allaire, the chief executive officer of Xerox, and his management team were faced with yet another monumental challenge. Since the beginning of 2000, a crisis has erupted from every angle possible. Investor confidence is poor after two years of shrinking earnings and dwindling market share. Due to this poor financial performance coupled with large debts that are due soon, creditor confidence is also at an all time low. Management restructuring and recent announcements of large layoffs have strained relations with employees as well. While attempting to manage these relationships effectively, Xerox officials must now confront a new dilemma that could ruin Xerox's credibility with all three groups. After weathering so many storms over the past two years, is the team capable of surviving this one?

On February 6, 2001, *The Wall Street Journal* published an article detailing accounting irregularities in Xerox's Mexico division.[1] The article also outlined the story of James Bingham, Xerox's former assistant treasurer who had filed a wrongful termination suit against the company. Although Xerox described the cause of these irregularities as "perpetrated by a group of rogue accountants," Bingham identified the root cause of the problem to be Xerox's top executives, mainly the Chief Financial Officer, Barry Romeril. If these allegations are true, Xerox's task to restore the confidence of its constituents will become virtually impossible.

This case was prepared by Research Assistants Mike McGuire and Rohena Shaw under the direction of James S. O'Rourke, Concurrent Associate Professor of Management, as the basis for class discussion rather than to illustrate either effective or ineffective handling of an administrative situation. Information was gathered from corporate as well as public sources.

---

[1] Bandler, James and John Hechinger, "Executive Challenges Xerox's Books, Was Fired," *The Wall Street Journal*, February 6, 2001, p. C1.

Xerox Background

In 1906, the Haloid Company was created to make and sell photographic paper. To expand the business, Haloid purchased Rectigraph, a photocopier company, in 1935. Shortly after, Haloid issued its first public offering in 1936. Meanwhile, the Battelle Memorial Institute and Carl Carlson invented the process known as electrophotography. Haloid eventually purchased this process from the Battelle Memorial Institute and introduced the process of xerography in 1948 with the first Model A copier. The importance of the machine was not realized until 1959, when then Haloid Xerox introduced the Xerox 914 copier. This initial office copier eventually became the top-selling industrial product of all time. Haloid Xerox officially changed their name in 1961.[2]

From this point on, Xerox enjoyed the benefits of its dominance in the copier industry but failed in many other attempts to grow and expand.[3] Through the 1960s and 1970s, Xerox expanded through acquisitions of document related companies, such as publishing and computer companies and Western Union in 1979. Eventually, all acquisitions resulted in sub-par performance and were sold. To stimulate innovation, Xerox developed the Palo Alto Research Center in 1970. Although this world-renowned facility has been credited with the invention of the personal computer, laser printing, and Ethernet, Xerox has consistently been unable to capitalize on these innovations.

In 1974, the Federal Trade Commission dealt a fatal blow to Xerox's future prosperity. After an investigation of the industry, the FTC believed Xerox to be too monopolistic and forced the company to license its technology. With the introduction of many low cost Japanese competitors, Xerox's U.S. market share plummeted from 95 percent to 13 percent in 1982. Xerox CEO David Kearns rejuvenated the company with Japanese-style manufacturing, allowing the company to regain some of the lost market share and stabilize by 1990.

Paul Allaire, former president of Xerox, assumed the position of CEO in 1990. Allaire's first order of business was assembling an executive team from outside the company. Allaire's most significant recruit was Barry Romeril, former finance director at British Telecommunications.[4] The second part of Allaire's strategy was to refocus the company for the Digital Age. This included divesting the income-consuming financial services division and introducing the first digital copier, the Document Center. However, by 1997, Allaire began to search for his replacement. With Xerox's inability to completely realize the potential of the Digital Age, Allaire believed that an outside agent of change would be most beneficial to the company. Allaire eventually recruited Richard Thoman, former IBM Chief Financial Officer to the position of Chief Operating Officer in 1997 and CEO in April 1999.

---

[2] www.dwjnr.com

[3] Bianco, Anthony and Pamela Moore, "Downfall: The Inside Story of the Management Fiasco at Xerox," *Business Week*, March 5, 2001, p. 82-92.

[4] Ibid.

"There is no accounting standard that we can't beat."[5]

The above attitude was said to be the mantra of several Xerox executives in Mexico who believed that the corporate culture earnings estimates were more important than generally accepted accounting principles. Assistant treasurer James Bingham brought these and other financial practices to the attention of Chief Financial Officer Barry Romeril and other senior executives. In a presentation to the group, he explained that the situation in Mexico was brought about by several actions. Each action was initiated at the corporate level to help developing markets sustain profitability. Xerox fired Bingham claiming he had demonstrated "disruptive and insubordinate behavior."[6]

The situation began on June 26, 2000, when the Securities and Exchange Commission began an investigation regarding Xerox's financial troubles. This was ten days after the company itself had claimed difficulties in Mexico with unpaid bills. During the second and third quarters, these concerns would surface in the financial statements when Xerox would first incur a $78 million charge and then a $41 million charge due to delinquent accounts in Mexico. In an effort to reassure investors, the company launched an internal investigation that found the problems to be the results of "rogue executives" who had acted together in booking false revenue and hiding bad debt.

"Bingham concluded that there was a 'high likelihood' that Xerox in recent years has issued 'misleading financial statements and public disclosures.'"[7]

Bingham, on the other hand, had alleged that the creative practices were not limited to Mexico, but were also used in several other markets including Brazil, Argentina, Canada, Europe, and the United States. When the Mexico scandal was brought to the attention of headquarters, Bingham decided that he would try to get to the root of the problem. He found that the once profitable Mexican division of Xerox, with pretax profits of $128 million in 1999, was engaging in practices inconsistent with accounting standards. According to former employees, these numbers were inaccurate because of four reporting irregularities:[8]

- Inclusion of service and supplies revenues as sales revenue: Xerox offered customers options to lease equipment, allowing the customer to pay the company monthly over a certain period. With these transactions, a company is allowed to recognize revenue for the equipment, not the services and supplies that are also included in customer payments.

- Interest rate assumptions concerning future lease values were unrealistically low: Traditionally, when estimating the current value of future dollar amounts, companies discount the future value with a current market rate. A low discount

---

[5] Bandler, James and John Hechinger, "Executive Challenges Xerox's Books, Was Fired," *The Wall Street Journal*, February 6, 2001, p. C1.
[6] Ibid.
[7] Ibid.
[8] Ibid.

rate leads to a higher value, in turn allowing the company to realize greater profit than if the lease value were low.

- Reserves set aside for future profit boosting: Generally, reserves are used for expenses related to an acquisition. Instead, the company used this money for expenses related to continuing operations in an effort to smooth earnings.

- Revenues booked from sales of future revenue rights: Xerox allowed their customers an option of renting, as opposed to buying or leasing, equipment. Instead of recognizing the revenue as they were paid, Xerox would sell the cash inflow to the bank, personally guaranteeing the transaction amounts. The sum received from the bank as trade for the claim was then recognized as revenue— instead of as a loan, under which it would be more likely to qualify. This practice alone boosted income $247 million.

Bingham claimed that these practices might have raised Xerox revenue as much as $1.2 billion over the five-year period, in which the company reported $8.7 billion pretax profit. Mexican executives agreed that the above procedures were used and approved by those at corporate headquarters.[9]

Management Fiasco

In 1999, when Allaire stepped down from his office as Chief Executive Officer, Rick Thoman had been adequately groomed to step into the position. Thoman had been with Xerox for two years as Chief Operating Officer before he was recruited from his position of CFO at IBM in 1997. With a trail of success from previous jobs, Thoman was well liked and considered to be the change agent that the company would need to propel it into the future.

Unfortunately, Thoman was unable to fit into the company's political climate. He was removed 13 months later by Allaire, the Chairman of the Board at the time. While at Xerox, Thoman unsuccessfully sought to remove Romeril, Vice Chairman of the Board and Allaire's close friend, whom he felt was better suited elsewhere. Romeril had presided over the Mexico problem, witnessed stock value drop substantially, and watched the downgrade of company debt to junk bond status. He could also be blamed for the loss of nearly $1 billion, about 13 percent of the company's net worth, because of foreign currency losses in Brazil.[10] This loss could have been avoided had Romeril taken the advice of others to hedge the currency. Instead he stood by the pegging price of $80 million, steeping to secure their equity in such an unstable economy.[11] Amidst these events, Xerox reported its first loss in a quarter since 1984.

---

[9] Bandler, James and John Hechinger, "Former Xerox Officials in Mexico Assert Headquarters Ignored Fiscal Warnings," *The Wall Street Journal*, February 7, 2001, p. A4.
[10] Bianco, Anthony and Pamela Moore, "Downfall: The Inside Story of the Management Fiasco at Xerox," *Business Week*, March 5, 2001, p. 82-92.
[11] Bandler, James and John Hechinger, "Angry Investors Focus on Xerox's Romeril," *The Wall Street Journal*, February 22, 2001, p. C10.

Although analysts and investors alike have questioned the CFO's competence, CEO Allaire has asserted that Romeril is both competent and capable. The decrease in stock price has not been solely the fault of the CFO, but also the fault of others on the management team. Some have agreed that, although Romeril may have failed to notice the accounting irregularities, the board of directors failed to recognize the problem in a timely manner. This failure can be attributed, in large part, to the composition of the board. One-third of the members are insiders, while another third own less than 15,000 shares.[12]

Securities & Exchange Commission Steps In

As a result of losses, several lawsuits have been filed on behalf of shareholders who acquired stock between February 15, 1998, and February 6, 2001. The suit charges that because of Xerox's violation of federal securities law and accounting practices, investors lost hundreds of millions of dollars when Xerox shares went from a high of $124 per share to a low of $4.43 per share.[13] Further, the Securities and Exchange Commission announced in February 2001 that it would launch an investigation of Xerox's Mexican and other foreign branches, despite the company's internal efforts to investigate and remedy the situation.[14]

Questions

1. What issues should CEO Allaire address first?

2. What message should be sent to the various groups affected by the accounting problems? What is the most effective medium?

3. How does Xerox regain the confidence of investors? Employees? Creditors?

4. What alternatives are available to Xerox in terms of salvaging their reputation?

5. Who is the best person to present the company's stance to the various stakeholders? When would be the most appropriate time to send the message? How should the new message be communicated?

---

[12] Lavelle, Louis, "Shhh! You'll Wake The Board," *Business Week*, March 5, 2001, p. 92.
[13] The Law Office of Mark McNair, "The Law Office of Mark McNair Filed Class Action Lawsuit Against Xerox Corporation," *PR Newswire*, February 22, 2001.
[14] Roman, Monica, "Mexico Gets Muddier for Xerox," *Business Week*, February 19, 2001, p. 46.

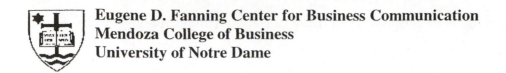
Coca-Cola and the European Contamination Crisis

Doug Ivester, CEO of Coca-Cola, thanked James Burke for his time and returned the phone to the handset. On June 18, 1999, four weeks after the first report was filed in Europe citing adverse health effects suffered following the consumption of Coca-Cola products, Ivester sought to reformulate his communication strategy. Ivester called Burke, the former CEO of Johnson & Johnson who successfully managed the Tylenol scare in the 1980s, to discuss how Coke could regain its reputation and credibility. He hoped it was not too late to mend Coke's relationship with European consumers.

Key Facts in the Crisis Coca-Cola Faced in Europe

During May and June of 1999, hundreds of consumers in Europe became ill after consuming Coca-Cola products. In the biggest recall in Coca-Cola history, Coke products, including *Coke*, *Coke Light*, *Fanta,* and *Sprite,* were pulled off the shelves in Belgium, France, Luxembourg, the Netherlands, and Germany. Following is a time-line of the specific events that took place from mid-May through the end of June, 1999:

> **May 12**: A bar in Belgium reports to the Belgian Health Ministry and to Coca-Cola that four people who drank Coke products have become ill. Samples of Coke from the same batch are sent for analysis at a government-licensed laboratory in Belgium. Results prove inconclusive and no poison is found. The incident is not widely reported and no public safety warnings are issued.

> **June 8**: School children in Bornem, Belgium reportedly experience dizziness, nausea, and other symptoms after drinking Coke. Forty-two people are hospitalized during the next 24 hours.

This case was prepared Research Assistants Hanna Smith and Anne Feighan under the direction of James S. O'Rourke, Concurrent Associate Professor of Management, as the basis for class discussion rather than to illustrate either effective or ineffective handling of an administrative situation.

June 10: Eight children are hospitalized in Bruges, Belgium after drinking Coke and Fanta.

June 11: The German Health Ministry summons Coca-Cola officials for a meeting regarding the reported illnesses. Thirteen children are hospitalized in Harelbeke, Belgium.

June 12-14: The Belgian government establishes a telephone hotline for health complaints about Coca-Cola products and receives more than 200 calls.

June 14: Forty-two children are taken to a hospital in Lochristi. The Belgian government orders all Coca-Cola products off the market and halts production at bottling plants in Antwerp and Ghent.

June 15: Eight children are reported sick in Kortrijk, Belgium. Luxembourg bans Coca-Cola products. Health authorities in France close a bottling plant in Dunkirk. The Netherlands bans all Coca-Cola products shipped through Belgium. At the same time, Coca-Cola Enterprises (CCE) holds a press conference in Brussels to provide an explanation for the cause of the illnesses.

June 16: Germany bans Coca-Cola products produced at the Dunkirk plant. Coca-Cola issues its first apology to European consumers in the form of a written release under Doug Ivester's name. German officials empty store shelves of Coke products.

June 17: The ban on products is eased in Belgium with the exception of thousands of Coca-Cola vending machines.

June 18: M. Douglas Ivester, chairman and CEO of Coca-Cola, arrives in Belgium to oversee management of the crisis.

Coinciding with the negative responses from the Belgian and French governments, Coca-Cola's sales and reputation suffer well beyond these borders. Following the product bans issued by these two governments, the Netherlands and Luxembourg restrict sales of certain Coca-Cola products until possible health risks are fully identified. There are also reports that Saudi Arabia and Germany have banned imports of all Coca-Cola beverages produced in Belgium and that the Spanish government had stopped a shipment of Belgian-bottled Coca-Cola and other brands for fear of contamination.

Even the health minister of the Central African Republic takes a stand on the issue, saying citizens of that country shouldn't drink Coke "until further notice" because of the health questions. Sweden's *Svenska Dagbladet* runs a headline on June 16 claiming, "200 Poisoned by Coca-Cola." An Italian newspaper's front page headline reports "Alarm Across Europe for

Coca-Cola Products." *Wall Street Journal* reporters James Hagerty and Amy Barrett describe the rapid proliferation of news of the crisis across international borders:

> "It amounted to a harsh lesson for Coke in the perils of global marketing in the electronic age. No one has been better than Coke at creating an enticing image and sending it flashing around the world. Now Coke is learning that an image can come unraveled in an instant."

The Source of the Problem

The outbreaks appeared to be caused by two sources, contaminated carbon dioxide and fungicide sprayed on wooden pallets used to transport the product. The contaminated carbon dioxide found its way into the product at a bottler in Belgium. The company was unable to determine whether the carbon dioxide was already contaminated when the bottler received it or whether contamination occurred later, at the bottling facility. In an interview with the *Wall Street Journal*, Anton Amon, Coca-Cola's chief scientist, said that, "contrary to Coke procedure, the plant wasn't receiving certificates of analysis from the supplier of the gas, Aga Gas AB of Sweden. This certificate vouches for the purity of the CO_2." A CCE spokesman confirmed this statement and acknowledged that the company did not test the CO_2 batch at the Antwerp plant. In either case, key quality control procedures were not followed.

At the Coca-Cola bottling facility in Dunkirk, France, the plant received wooden pallets that had been sprayed with a fungicide that left a medicinal odor on a number of cans. Jennifer McCollum, a spokeswoman for Coca-Cola, described the substance as p-chloro-m-cresol or PCMC, "a chemical commonly found in wood preservatives and cleaning fluids." The Environmental Chemicals Data and Information Network (ECDIN) states that PCMC can be absorbed through the skin and cause redness, burning sensation, pain and skin burns. If inhaled, the chemical can cause symptoms such as cough, sore throat, shortness of breath, headache, dizziness, nausea, vomiting, unconsciousness, and may cause effects on the central nervous system, liver, and kidneys. These more severe conditions are said to require large doses or chronic exposure to the chemical.

Coca-Cola said that the substance was sprayed on approximately 800 pallets used to transport cans produced in Dunkirk to Belgium. The supplier of the pallets was said to be Dutch. The company, however, declined to name the company, stating only that it was not one of their regular suppliers. The foul odor is believed to have caused numerous symptoms, including headaches and nausea, after drinking the product.

Dr. Hugo Botinck, medical director at St. Joseph's Clinic in Belgium and one of the first physicians to see these patients, stated in an interview that affected persons were treated for, "headaches, dizziness, nausea, and muscular vibration." He added that, "some of them were vomiting, but there was no fever."

Company Profile

The Coca-Cola Company is the global leader in the soft-drink industry, with world headquarters located in Atlanta, Georgia. Coca-Cola and its subsidiaries employ nearly 30,000 people worldwide. Syrups, concentrates, and beverage bases for Coca-Cola, the company's flagship brand, and more than 160 other soft-drink brands are manufactured and sold by Coca-Cola and its subsidiaries in nearly 200 countries around the world. Approximately 70 percent of volume sales and 80 percent of profit come from outside the United States. The European market provides 26 percent of the company's US$18 billion in revenues. Coca-Cola owns a 49 percent share of the European soft drink market, compared to Pepsi-Co's five percent.

Coca-Cola's Corporate Mission Statement

We exist to create value for our share owners on a long-term basis by building a business that enhances The Coca-Cola Company's trademarks. This also is our ultimate commitment.

As the world's largest beverage company, we refresh that world. We do this by developing superior soft drinks, both carbonated and non-carbonated, and profitable nonalcoholic beverage systems that create value for our Company, our bottling partners, our customers, our share owners, and the communities in which we do business.

In creating value, we succeed or fail based on our ability to perform as worthy stewards of several key assets:

1. Coca-Cola, the world's most recognized trademark, and other highly valuable trademarks.

2. The world's most effective and pervasive distribution system.

3. Satisfied customers, to whom we earn a good profit selling our products.

4. Our people, who are ultimately responsible for building this enterprise.

5. Our abundant resources, which must be intelligently allocated.

6. Our strong global leadership in the beverage industry in particular and in the business world in general.

Additionally, Coca-Cola has a stated commitment to social responsibility through philanthropy and good citizenship. The company's reputation for good corporate citizenship results from charitable donations, employee volunteerism, technical assistance, and other demonstrations of support in thousands of communities worldwide. The Coca-Cola Foundation, the company's philanthropic arm, contributed more than $100 million to education during the

1990s, supporting mentoring programs and scholarships at more than 400 schools, colleges, and associations around the world. On a local level, Coca-Cola offices and bottlers around the world support community activities. From supporting the arts in Russia to building schools in rural areas of China and the Philippines to funding a class for entrepreneurs at the University of Zimbabwe, The Coca-Cola Company is an active corporate citizen.

The company states that honesty and integrity have always been cornerstone values of The Coca-Cola Company. Coca-Cola feels that all company representatives have a responsibility to act according to the highest standards of ethical conduct in every situation.

Coca-Cola Management

From 1984 to 1997, Robert Goizueta ran Coca-Cola like a ship in calm waters. In his 13 years at the helm of Coke as CEO, Goizueta transformed Coke from an Atlanta cola company to an international brand phenomenon. Analysts and employees alike viewed Goizueta like a "god." In 1997, Doug Ivester succeeded Roberto Goizueta as CEO of Coke following Goizueta's death from lung cancer. Ivester, an employee of the company since 1979, had previously been Goizueta's right hand financial engineer and later his chief operating officer. On the face of it, the transition appeared seamless.

Doug Ivester has often been described as a very "rational" man with a "bulldog" leadership style. James Chestnut, Coca-Cola's chief financial officer, says Ivester is a "terribly rational" manager. He states, "Doug believes everything should go through a logical sequence. He's fixed on where he wants the company to be." Ivester's recent focus had been on two potential acquisitions to increase Coca-Cola's presence in Europe: Orangina in France and Cadbury Schweppes. The tactics Ivestor pursued to acquire Orangina and Schweppes, however, have been met with much criticism, especially by Europeans.

A July article appearing in *Fortune* magazine summarized the conventional wisdom this way: "the way Coke went about the acquisitions – arrogantly, urgently, intensely – absolutely reflects Ivester's personality. And it's not working." Other analysts who have followed Coca-Cola for years believe that if Goizueta were still running the company, controversy surrounding the recall in Europe would not be festering as it was under Ivester.

Bottling and International Distribution

One of Coke's greatest strengths lies in its ability to conduct business on a global scale while maintaining a "multilocal" approach. At the heart of this approach is the bottler system. Bottling companies are, with only a few exceptions, locally owned and operated by independent business people, native to the nations in which they are located, who are contractually authorized to sell products of The Coca-Cola Company. These facilities package and sell the company's soft drinks within certain territorial boundaries and under conditions that ensure the highest standards of product quality and uniformity. Coca-Cola Enterprises (CCE) manages most of the European bottlers. The Coca-Cola Company controls a 40 percent interest in CCE.

Coca-Cola Belgium. Belgium was introduced to Coca-Cola in 1927. Today Belgium is among the world's top 20 countries in terms of per capita consumption of Coca-Cola products. The Coca-Cola Company currently employs close to 2,000 people and serves up to 30,000 restaurants, supermarkets, and other customers in that country.

Coca-Cola France. Coca-Cola was introduced in France in 1933. Coke has been the number-one soft drink in France since 1966 with total sales doubling over the past eight years. Coca-Cola France employs more than 1,000 French citizens and has invested more than three billion francs in local economy since 1989. Today, French consumers drink an average of 88 servings of Coca-Cola products each year.

External Factors Involved

In May and June of 1999, it is fair to say that Coca-Cola executives vastly underestimated the sensitivity of European consumers to food contamination issues in light of the existing social and political environment. Contributing to the anxiety was the "mad-cow" crisis that had taken place three years earlier. Additionally, the Coke incident coincided with a recent governmental ban on the slaughter of pork and poultry in Belgium. Earlier in June, cancer-causing dioxin was found in a large shipment of meat, which was believed to have originated through contaminated animal feed. In the end, this scandal forced the resignation of Belgian Prime Minister Jean-Luc Dahaene as well as the country's health minister. With the Belgian government facing elections on June 13, all political platforms were under scrutiny.

In the wake of the Coke crisis, European government agencies were scrambling to protect their reputations as watchdogs, taking a high-profile role in contamination issues. Consumers had previously considered Coke invulnerable to contamination concerns due to the artificial, manufactured nature of the product.

In addition to its proximity to other food scares in Europe, the crisis also occurred at a time when Coke was looked upon unfavorably by the European Commission. Earlier in 1999, Coke had made plans to acquire Cadbury Schweppes brands around the world. The European Commission was opposed to this acquisition, viewing Coca-Cola as excessively dominant. The company was forced to scale back its acquisition plans.

Coca-Cola's Response

By the time the recall was completed, 249 cases of Coke-related sicknesses were reported throughout Europe, concentrated primarily in Belgium. A total of 15 million cases of product were recalled costing the bottler, Coca-Cola Enterprises (CCE), an estimated $103 million. When the outbreak began, Coca-Cola executives waited several days to take action. Viewing the issue as low-priority, an apology to consumers was not issued until more than a week after the first public reports of illness. Top company officials did not arrive in Belgium until June 18, ten days after the first incident was reported.

The company's casual and muted approach to the crisis was first made evident in its neglect to mention the May 12 incident – in which affected consumers suffered similar symptoms – once the other cases were reported, beginning in June. Ivester remained largely silent, at least publicly, throughout the crisis. He admitted that he happened to be in Coke's Paris office on June 11, shortly after the first wave of illness reports surfaced, and was briefed in person on the Belgian situation. Ivester and Belgian Coke executives attributed the problem to a bad batch of carbon dioxide and "hardly a health hazard." The next day Ivester boarded a plane back to Atlanta as planned.

On June 14, the Belgium government ordered all Coca-Cola products off the market and halted production at bottling plants in Antwerp and Ghent. The government took the lead to protect consumers from the health scare, rather than Coca-Cola management. Coca-Cola issued a statement on June 15 from Atlanta refuting the contamination claims. On June 16, Ivester released a statement under his name expressing regret for the problems, but he mostly left the public side of the damage-control campaign to company spokesmen and CCE.

On June 18, Ivester realized the magnitude and impact of the crisis and arrived in Belgium for the first time to manage the crisis. Ivester's mission to Europe was his most visible step during the crisis and came only after the number of reported cases had ballooned to more than 200. Coca-Cola officials avoided the media, however, stating afterward that this decision was in response to a request from the Belgian Minister of Health, Luc van den Brossche, asking that the crisis be handled out of the public eye.

Next Steps

Many have faulted Ivester's personality as "too rational" to initially consider the European contamination scare a "crisis." The media criticized Ivester's lack of responsiveness for allowing the health scare to spin out of control. Recognizing that the company has lost valuable time for action due to its lack of response until June 18, what should the company's strategy be to move forward? What audiences should Coca-Cola consider in the development of a communications strategy to address the crisis? What efforts can Coca-Cola employ to rebuild its reputation and restore consumer confidence in Europe?

Selected Reference Sources

Li, L.H., "Origin of Coke Crisis in Europe Is Termed Psychosomatic," *The Wall Street Journal*, April 2, 2000, p. A-21.

McKay, B. and Deogun, N., "After Short, Stormy Tenure, Coke's Ivester to Retire," *The Wall Street Journal*, December 7, 1999, pp. B-1, B-4.

"Coca-Cola Tests Find No Problem," *The New York Times*, October 26, 1999, p. C-1.

Hagerty, J. R. and Carreyrou, J., "Coke Drinks' Safety Arises Again as Children in Belgium Feel Ill," *The Wall Street Journal*, October 25, 2999, p. A-4.

"European Report Doubts Explanation by Coke," *The New York Times*, August 18, 2999, p. C-4.

Mitchener, B. and McKay, P. A., "EU Warns Coke Not to Use Rebates to Give Sales a Pop," *The Wall Street Journal*, July 23, 1999, p. A5.

Hayes, C. L., "Pepsi Acknowledges Role in Putting Coca-Cola Under Inquiry," *The New York Times*, July 23, 1999, p. C-4.

Hayes, C. L., "Coca-Cola Bottler Reports Surprisingly Big Slide in Sales," *The New York Times*, July 14, 1999, p. C-3.

Hayes, C. L., "Recall to Cost Coke Bottler $103 Million," *The New York Times*, July 13, 1999, p. C-7.

"Belgium Re-Opens Coca-Cola Vending Machines," *Reuters News Service*, July 8, 1999, http://famulus.msnbc.com.

Hayes, C. L., "Coca-Cola Recalls Water in Poland After Bacteria Are Found," July 3, 1999, p. B-2.

Sellers, P., "Crunch Time for Coke," *Fortune*, July 19, 1999, pp. 72-78.

Sewell, D., "A Tough Year for Coke," *The South Bend Tribune*, July 1, 1999, p. B9.

"Coke's Hard Lesson in Crisis Management," *Business Week*, July 5, 1999, p. 102.

Hayes, C. L., "Coke Expects Sales to Decline 1% to 2%, Mainly in Europe," *The New York Times*, July 1, 1999, p. C-8.

Hayes, C. L., Cowell, Al, and Whitney, C. R., "A Sputter in the Coke Machine," *The Wall Street Journal*, June 30, 1999, pp. C-1, C-6.

Deogun, N.; Hagerty, J. R.; Stecklow, S.; Johannes, L., "Anatomy of a Recall: How Coke's Controls Fizzed Out in Europe," *The Wall Street Journal*, June 29, 1999, pp. A-1, A-6.

"Coke Says It Investigated Early Report of Illness," *Reuters News Service*, June 29, 1999, http://famulus.msnbc.com.

"China Clears Coca-Cola After Contamination Tests," *Reuters News Service*, June 19, 1999, http://famulus.msnbc.com

"Coke to Reintroduce Products in Belgium on Wednesday," *Reuters News Service*, June 28, 1999, http://famulus.msnbc.com

"Coke Has No Plans to Sue as Probe Goes on," *Reuters News Service*, June 26, 1999, http://famulus.msnbc.com

Whitney, C., "Coke Bottling Site in France Is Given Clean Bill of Health," *The New York Times*, June 25, 1999, p. C-2.

Cowell, A., "The Coke Stomach Ache Heard Round the World," *The New York Times*, June 25, 1999, pp. C-1, C-2.

"Coke Says Phenol at Root of Scare," *Reuters News Service*, June 24, 1999, http://famulus.msnbc.com

"Coke Enterprises Apologizes for Tainted Drinks," *Reuters News Service*, June 24, 1999, http://famulus.msnbc.com

"Coke Says Found 800 Tainted Pallets from Dunkirk," *Reuters News Service*, June 24, 1999, http://famulus.msnbc.com

"Hysteria Made Coke Drinkers Ill: Belgian Expert," *Reuters News Service*, June 24, 1999, http://famulus.msnbc.com

"France Lifts Ban on Coke Drinks," *Reuters News Service*, June 24, 1999, http://famulus.msnbc.com

Jenkins, H. W., "The Customer Isn't Always Right," *The Wall Street Journal*, June 23, 1999, p. A-27.

"U. S., European Coke Analyses Find No Health Threat," *Reuters News Service*, June 22, 1999, http://famulus.msnbc.com

Hayes, C. L., "Coca-Cola Chairman Uses Ads to Apologize to Belgians," *The New York Times*, June 22, 1999, p. B-3.

"Coke Stumbles in European Contamination Crisis," *Inside PR*, June 21, 1999, pp. 1, 3.

"Coca-Cola Urged to Heed Consumers to Salvage Image," *Reuters News Service*, June 20, 1999, http://famulus.msnbc.com

"Coke Chief Ivester in Belgium to Head Crisis Control," *Reuters News Service*, June 20, 1999, http://famulus.msnbc.com

"Coca-Cola Learns a Health Scare Sometimes Is 'the Real Thing'," *Reuters News Service*, http://www.msnbc.com

Hayes, C. L., "Concern About Coke Products Spreads to Spain and Germany," *The New York Times*, June 19, 1999, pp. B-1, B-2.

Deogun, N., "Can Douglas Ivester End Coke's Crisis?" *The Wall Street Journal*, June 18, 1999, pp. B-1, B-4.

Hagerty, J. R.; Barrett, A., "France, Belgium Reject Pleas to Lift Ban," *The Wall Street Journal*, June 18, 1999, p. B-1.

Hagerty, J. R.; Deogun, N., "Coke Scrambles to Contain a Scare in Europe," *The Wall Street Journal*, June 17, 1999, pp. B-1, B-4.

Andrews, E. L., "Coke's Chief Apologizes for Response on Contamination," *The New York Times*, June 17, 1999, p. C-4.

Abelson, R., "In a Crisis, Coke Tries to Be Reassuring," *The New York Times*, June 16, 1999, p. C-2.

Hayes, C. L., "Coke Products Are Ordered Off the Shelves in Four Countries," *The New York Times*, June 16, 1999, pp. C-1, C-2.

Mitchener, B.; Richter, K., "Belgium Farmers Left Reeling as Fear of Dioxin Has Far-Reaching Results," *The Wall Street Journal*, June 7, 1999, p. A-19.

Hayes, C. L., "Worldwide, Things Are Not Going Better for Coke," *The New York Times*, March 2, 1999, pp. C-1, C-9.